Son of the Revolutic

Liang Heng met Judith Shapiro at Hunan
Teachers' College, and they were married in
China. They now live in New York, where he is
researching a doctorate in Chinese literature at
Columbia University and she is working as an
interpreter for the US State Department.

LIANG HENG
and JUDITH SHAPIRO

Son of the Revolution

FONTANA/COLLINS

First published in Great Britain
by Chatto & Windus (The Hogarth Press) 1983
First issued in Fontana Paperbacks 1984

Reproduced, printed and bound in Great Britain
by Hazell Watson and Viney Limited,
member of the BPCC Group,
Aylesbury, Bucks.

To the Chinese People

Contents

MAPS FOLLOW PAGE XIII.

Foreword
Jerome Alan Cohen

Seldom in modern times has a whole people suffered such a period of political stress as the Chinese during the past quarter of a century. From the campaign against "rightists" in 1957–58 through the huge— and disastrous—economic campaigns of 1958–59 to the ten-year-long "Great Proletarian Cultural Revolution," the life of virtually every Chinese citizen has been touched and changed in ways that Westerners find hard even to imagine.

How have the people of China reacted to this experience? What have the twists and turns of Party policy meant in the lives of many first-generation supporters of the new society and their children? After the downfall in 1976 of Chairman Mao's widow and other members of the "Gang of Four," their successors encouraged a veritable outpouring, via all the media, of stories of the personal tragedies that resulted from abuse of power and arbitrary rule during the decade of the Cultural Revolution, and sometimes as far back as the "antirightist" movement of the 1950s. In recent years the leadership has sought to stem this tide of woe, which had served the purpose of discrediting the "leftist" line, but which later threatened to get out of hand and undermine public confidence in the system itself.

Abroad, however, there have been few accurate personal accounts of life in the vortex of what has probably been the world's most profound revolution. Yet foreigners find that such accounts offer far more vivid insights into Chinese life than do either the limited impressions of the tourist or the generalized descriptions of the scholar. Fiction occasionally illuminates Chinese experience by humanizing it, but on such a controversial topic facts must be preferred; and surely the facts of China's modern history yield nothing in dramatic value to fiction. Thus Liang Heng's autobiography of growing up in central China, which ends in 1981 with his departure for study in the United States, fills a void. Indeed, like *Fan Shen*, William Hinton's classic description of village land reform in the late forties, it portrays the participants in the Chinese revolution not as stick figures in a political morality play but as flesh-and-blood people who share our common humanity.

Liang Heng's account, fascinating in itself, takes on larger significance when viewed against the background of recent Chinese history. Since the end of the nineteenth century, patriotic Chinese of many persuasions have sought to transform their motherland—for millennia a proud and legendary empire, but more recently, poor and downtrodden—into a strong, prosperous modern state. By creating and carrying through a Communist revolution, which culminated in the establishment of the People's Republic of China in 1949, Mao Ze-dong and his cohorts made impressive strides toward that goal. To be sure, they adopted many unattractive measures in the course of eliminating the influences of the Chiang Kai-shek regime, implanting their own political system, and achieving "socialist transformation" of the economy. Nevertheless, during the first eight years of the People's Republic the new leaders in Peking earned widespread popular support, including the enthusiasm of Liang's family, because they had unified the government, and improved social and economic conditions in a land that had been devastated by invasion, civil war, inflation, unemployment, famine and disease.

That support began to erode after unexpectedly severe criticisms by intellectuals during the campaign to "Let a Hundred Flowers Bloom" in 1956–57 and led the Communist Party to overreact by launching a mass movement to suppress "rightists" inside and outside the Party in 1957–58. This movement, which made Liang Heng's mother one of its many targets, was soon followed by the "Great Leap Forward" and the campaign to merge the country's agricultural cooperatives into large "people's communes." Those twin campaigns were supposed to enable China to catch up with the principal industrialized states, but instead plunged it into an economic depression that inflicted great hardship on both urban and rural residents, as Liang's account makes clear.

The more moderate policies adopted in the early 1960s under the leadership of Liu Shao-qi, Zhou En-lai, Deng Xiao-ping and others pulled the nation out of depression. Yet their very success sharpened what became known as "the struggle between two lines," because the somewhat discredited Chairman Mao and his "leftist" colleagues sought to regain the dominance they had enjoyed during the years of economic debacle. Their efforts produced the "Great Proletarian Cultural Revolution," which began in 1966 with a reign of terror by the Red Guards that divided the Party, overthrew Liu, Deng, and other "Capitalist Roaders," and brought China to the brink of another civil war. Liang Heng's adventures as a Red Guard give us a sense of what it meant for both the persecutors and the persecuted, as millions of teenagers wielded powers that were far beyond their understanding.

By 1969 restoration of public order by the People's Liberation Army set the stage for a prolonged power struggle among the Party leaders. That reached its climax in the fall of 1976, when Mao's death made possible the stunning arrest of his widow, Jiang Qing, and her three leftist comrades, thereafter vilified as the "Gang of Four." Although Hua Guo-feng emerged from this turmoil with an unprecedented monopoly of the highest positions within the Party, the government, and the military, Deng Xiao-ping gradually managed to gain control of the levers of power and installed trusted younger associates in place of Hua, who receded from the limelight.

Deng's ascension involved more, of course, than a colorful power struggle among long-standing antagonists. At the heart of the struggle was—and is—a continuing debate over how to modernize China, almost a quarter of humanity. By devising and implementing a successful modernization strategy, China's current leaders hope to rekindle the enthusiasm of their people for a political system that, by their own admission, has lost much of its earlier appeal. Deng and company recognize especially the need to enlist the energies of the country's intellectuals— people with the equivalent of a high school education, who, like Liang Heng's parents, suffered badly as part of the past generation. Moreover, their greatest challenge is to win the loyalty of the younger generation, that two-thirds of the nation's population who, like Liang himself, were born after the founding of the People's Republic and who cannot from personal experience compare the new society with the old. The demands of China's 650 million able and ambitious men and women under thirty—for higher education, satisfactory jobs, decent housing, protection against arbitrary exercise of authority, and at least a modicum of free expression—must be met if the country is not to become a tinderbox.

In many ways Liang, an articulate, straightforward, dynamic man in his late twenties, is a good representative of his generation, even though he took the unusual step of marrying a foreigner, his co-author, Judith Shapiro, whose writing skill and knowledge of what a foreign audience needs to know about China make this book a delight to read. Liang is not a product of the sophisticated coastal cities but of a provincial capital in the interior, the city of Changsha in which Mao Zedong went to high school. Liang also spent a good deal of time in the countryside, where 80 percent of China's population resides, and he gives us a rare good look at peasant life. He was neither a member of China's former bourgeois class nor from a landlord or rich peasant background that would have made him and his family special targets of "class struggle." Rather, his father served on the editorial staff of a provincial newspaper, his mother was a responsible official in the municipal police bureau, and both of them were ardent supporters, but not members, of the Communist Party.

The story of the Liang family, including Liang Heng's two sisters, grandparents and other relatives, seems to be quite typical of the lives of millions. As it unfolds, the reader will come to understand more fully the enormity of the task confronting Deng Xiao-ping and other leaders who seek to reform the present political and economic systems to achieve the long-awaited modernization of China.

Maps

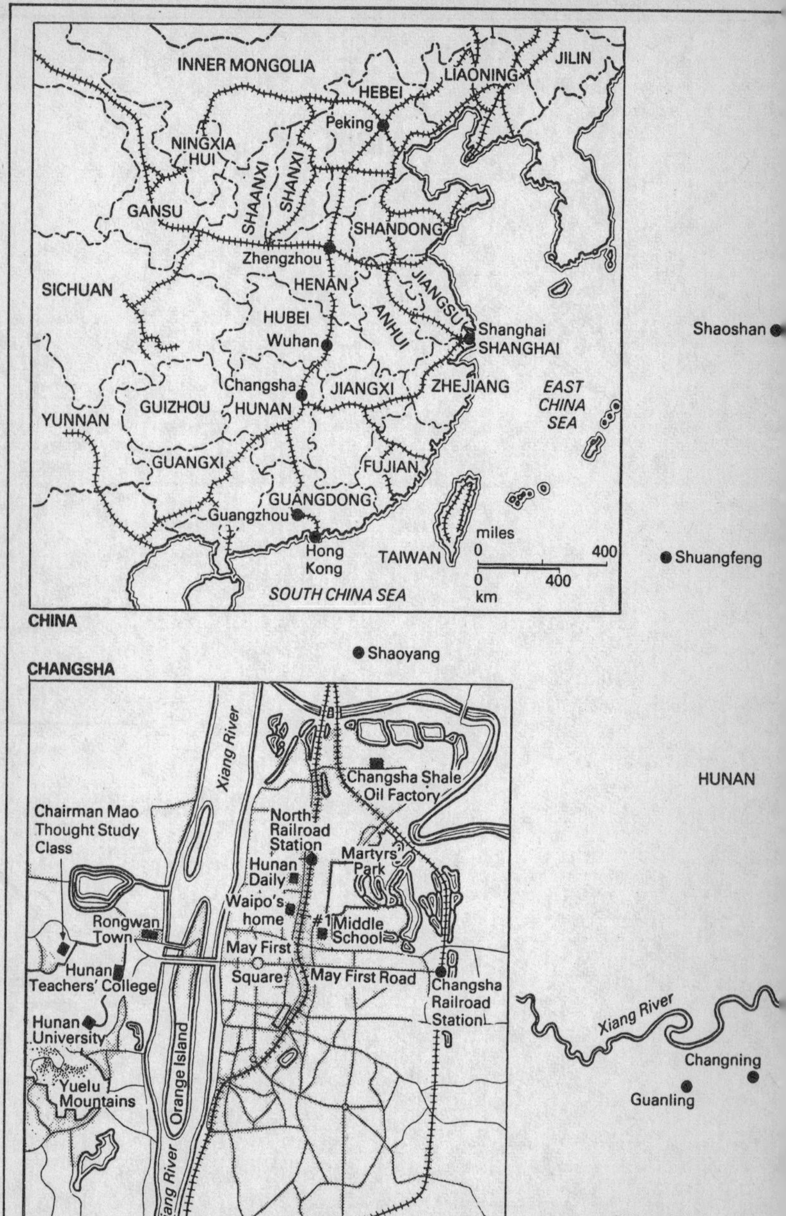
INNER MONGOLIA
JILIN
LIAONING
HEBEI
Peking
NINGXIA
HUI
SHANXI
SHAANXI
GANSU
SHANDONG
Zhengzhou
HENAN
JIANGSU
SICHUAN
HUBEI
ANHUI
Shanghai
SHANGHAI
Wuhan
Changsha
JIANGXI
ZHEJIANG
EAST
CHINA
SEA
GUIZHOU
HUNAN
YUNNAN
GUANGXI
FUJIAN
GUANGDONG
Guangzhou
Hong
Kong
TAIWAN
miles
0
400
0
400
km
SOUTH CHINA SEA
CHINA
Shaoshan
Shuangfeng
Shaoyang
CHANGSHA
HUNAN
Xiang River
Changsha Shale
Oil Factory
Chairman Mao
Thought Study
Class
North
Railroad
Station
Martyrs'
Park
Hunan
Daily
Waipo's
home
#1 Middle
School
Rongwan
Town
May First
Square
May First Road
Hunan
Teachers' College
Changsha
Railroad
Station
Hunan
University
Orange Island
Yuelu
Mountains
Xiang River
Xiang River
Changning
Guanling
Railroads

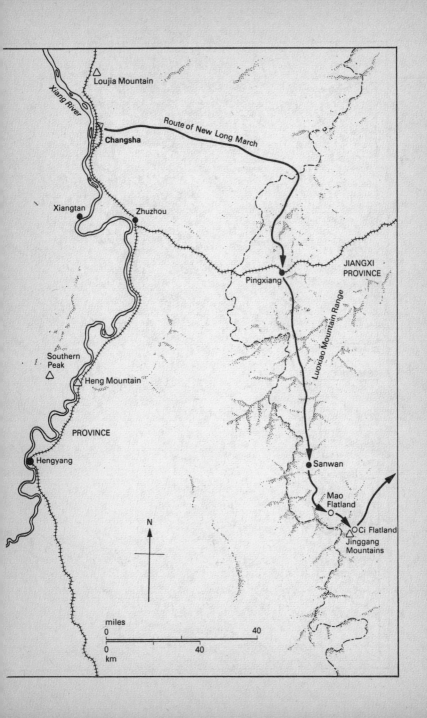

Loujia Mountain

Xiang River

Route of New Long March

Changsha

Xiangtan

Zhuzhou

JIANGXI PROVINCE

Pingxiang

Luoxiao Mountain Range

Southern Peak

Heng Mountain

PROVINCE

Hengyang

Sanwan

Mao Flatland

Ci Flatland

Jinggang Mountains

N

miles
0   40

0   40
km

Son of the Revolution

CHAPTER ONE

Chairman Mao's Good Little Boy

Once when I was nearly four, I decided to escape from the child-care center. The idea of waiting through another Saturday afternoon was unbearable. I would stand with the other children in the office doorway, yelling out the names of those whose relatives we spotted coming to rescue them. I would become frantic and miserable as the possibility that I had been forgotten seemed more and more real. Then at last the frail figure of my beloved Waipo, my maternal grandmother, would appear to take me away. But this week I wouldn't have to wait. I had just discovered a doorway leading from the kitchen directly onto the Changsha streets, left ajar, perhaps, by the cooks now that the bitter winter weather had passed. So, during after-lunch nap, I crawled over the green bars of my crib and stole softly out, past the sleeping rows of my fellow inmates, past Nurse Nie dozing in her chair. I crept into the coal-dark kitchen with its silent black woks. Then I exploded out the door into the dazzling light of freedom.

The child-care center was hateful. You couldn't eat sweets when you wanted to, and you had to fold your hands behind your back and sing a song before the nurses would let you eat your meals. Then, if you ate too fast, they hit you over the head with a flyswatter. The songs and dances—like "Sweeping the Floor," "Working in the Factory," and "Planting Trees in the Countryside"—were fun, but I was constantly in trouble for wanting to dance the army dance when it was time for the hoeing dance or for refusing to take the part of the landlord, the wolf, or the lazybones. I also had problems with the interminable rest periods.

We weren't allowed to get up even if we weren't tired, so I had nothing to do but stare at a small mole on my leg for hours at a time.

At the time, such early education was a privilege for which only the children of cadres were eligible. Although neither of my parents' ranks was high, my father's position as reporter, editor, and founding member of the Party newspaper the *Hunan Daily*, and my mother's as a promising cadre in the Changsha Public Security Bureau were enough to qualify me. My parents were deeply involved in all the excitement of working to transform China into a great Socialist country, eager to sacrifice themselves for others. They dreamed passionately of the day when they would be deemed pure and devoted enough to be accepted into the Party. It was only natural that the family come second; Father's duties at the newspaper often kept him away for several months at a time, and my mother came home only on Sundays, if at all, for she had a room in her own unit and stayed there to attend evening meetings. So at the age of three I was sent off to the child-care center for early training in Socialist thought through collective living, far from the potentially corrupting influence of family life. My departure may have been harder for my two grandmothers, of course. They had had the major responsibility for raising the three of us children; I was the last child to go and they would miss me very much.

I had lived first with my paternal grandmother, my Nai Nai, a tall, stern, bony woman who always wore traditional black. She lived in the apartment the *Hunan Daily* had allotted to Father, two rooms on the second floor of a cadres' dormitory, spacious enough but with a shared kitchen and an outhouse some distance away. She was a pious Buddhist and a vegetarian, strict with herself and everyone else but her own grandchildren.

At ten pounds, I had been the biggest baby ever recorded at Changsha's No. 1 Hospital, and Nai Nai had hired a series of seven wet-nurses before she found one who could satisfy my appetite. She was a nineteen-year-old peasant girl from a town beyond the city whose own baby had died. Nai Nai told me later that she was the only one who had enough milk so that I could suck her breasts dry without throwing a tantrum immediately afterwards; I have always given credit to her for my unusual height—I am 6'1". Then after she left because she had no Changsha city residence card, Nai Nai sent me to live with my maternal

grandmother, my Waipo, who lived off a winding little alleyway not far
away.

It was much more crowded there, since Waipo, my Uncle Yan,
and his wife and their small children made three generations in a single
dark room. But I liked the place for its liveliness and because I was
Waipo's favorite. She gave me candies and took me everywhere with
her, even to the free market to buy from the peasants who had carried
in their vegetables from the suburbs. Waipo was a tiny woman with big
twisted teeth and little wrinkled hands, talkative and lively and very
different from Nai Nai. Her husband had died when she was young,
after only two children, whereas Nai Nai's husband had given her nine
before he slipped and fell on the icy road in front of the old City Gate.
In the old society, a woman couldn't remarry and remain respectable,
so Waipo had supported herself and her children by making shoe soles
at home. She continued to do this even after Mother and Uncle Yan
were grown and had jobs, and the cloth patches she used were among
my first toys.

Another reason I liked living with Waipo was that Mother often
preferred to go there on Sundays rather than to our own home, where
Nai Nai was, because she didn't get along well with her mother-in-law.
Nai Nai sometimes carried her concern for others so far that she became
a busybody. She was always the first to sweep the public stairwell or
volunteer to lead neighborhood hygiene movements, and she was constantly scolding Mother for not dressing us warmly enough or not buying
us more milk to drink. She was so tall that she must have been imposing
for Mother to deal with, and tradition demanded that Mother obey her.
So although Mother was a feisty woman, she was supposed to look on
silently as Nai Nai spoiled us with candy and, in later years, did my
second sister's homework for her. Father was no help, because he was
bound by the same filial laws as she.

In any case, Mother's ties to her new home could not have been
strong ones, for she had hardly known Father before they married.
Someone had introduced them as prospective mates; they had exchanged
a few letters (Father was working in Guilin at the time) and decided
the question soon after on the basis of their common political enthusiasm. Father was far more intellectual than she, for he had been trained
by the Party as a reporter, had a wide range of literary interests,

and was an accomplished poet as well as an amateur composer and conductor. Mother was capable too, of course, a strong-willed person who liked to express her opinions, and a loving mother when she had the time. Still, as I thought back on it in later years, I realized my parents were so rarely together that it was almost a marriage of convenience.

So it was Waipo's home that was my early emotional center, and it was there that I went on the fresh spring day of my flight. I had to cross a large street, but fortunately I made it from one side to the other without mishap, and ran the remaining few hundred yards to the narrow room off the little gray alley.

To my utter dismay, Waipo didn't look at all glad to see me. "Little Fatso, what are you doing here?" she cried, and with scarcely a pause grabbed my hand and pulled me the few blocks to Nai Nai's home in the *Hunan Daily* compound. From there the two old ladies half lifted, half dragged me back to my confinement, ignoring my screams and tears.

The nurses had discovered my absence. Without any show of the politeness they usually maintained before their charges' relatives, they cursed and scolded me as if they would never stop. When my grandmothers had left, they locked me up in a room with two other offenders, saying, "You are not Chairman Mao's good little boy; you haven't upheld Revolutionary discipline. You can stay in there until you think things over."

My fellow captives were as miserable as I. One had stolen some candy, and the other, having graduated proudly from wearing slit pants, had promptly soiled his new ones. Although it was certainly convenient to be able to squat down anywhere and do one's business, among us children the slit was an embarrassing symbol of immaturity. It had another drawback too: Nai Nai's blows still stung on my bottom. I looked at the unlucky boy with pity. He would now be doomed to at least another year of babyhood and easy spankings.

The nurses' words had another kind of sting for me, since I had been taught Chairman Mao was like the sun itself. At home, "Mao" had been my first word after "Mama," "Baba," and "Nai Nai," for I had been held up to the large framed picture Father had hung over the doorway and instructed in the sound. Later I had learned how to say "I love Chairman Mao" and "Long Live Chairman Mao." But it wasn't until

I got to the child-care center that I really began to understand. He presided over our rest and play like a benevolent god, and I believed that apples, grapes, everything had been given to us because he loved us. When the nurses told me the next day that Chairman Mao had forgiven me, I was the happiest child in the world.

During the next year, my second at the child-care center, I learned how to write my first characters. The first word was made up of the four strokes in the Chairman's name. Next I learned to write the characters in my own name, and I discovered that I was not called "Little Fatso," as Waipo had proudly nicknamed me, but something quite different, with a political story behind it:

On the morning of May 2, 1954, the Vietnamese won a decisive victory over the French at Dienbienphu. That very afternoon my mother gave birth to me, a ten-pound baby boy, the distant sounds of drums and cymbals an accompaniment to her labors. My father, reporting the Vietnam story for the *Hunan Daily*, thought it only natural to name me Liang Dian-jie, "Liang Good News from Dienbienphu." He was flushed with a double victory, for at last he had a son to carry on the family line.

It wasn't the first time he had chosen a significant name for a child. My eldest sister was born in 1949, so she joined the ranks of thousands of children named for the birth of New China with the name Liang Fang, "Liang Liberation." My second sister, born in 1952 when the Chinese armies were marching across the Yalu River to defend Korea against the Americans, was called Liang Wei-ping, "Liang Defender of Peace." As we grew up we discovered that you could often guess someone's age by his name, and that at times, if someone had been named at the height of some movement that was later discredited, a name could become an embarrassment, a burden, or even a reason for being attacked. My parents' own names reflected an earlier, less politicized time; my mother Yan Zhi-de was "Yan the Moral," and my father Liang Ying-qiu was "Liang Whose Requests Will Be Answered," although he usually went by his literary name, Liang Shan.

I came gradually to recognize all of these characters and more, for during the third year and final fourth year at the child-care center we began our study properly, writing "Chairman Mao is our Great Saving Star," "We are all Chairman Mao's good little children," "The Communist Party is like the sun," "When I am big I will be a worker," (or peasant or soldier). We also learned simple arithmetic, paper folding and paper cutting, and were given small responsibilities like watering the plants or cleaning the classroom.

Meanwhile, whenever I went home to Waipo's, I hoped Mother would be there, for I loved her very much despite our limited time together. But when I was about four, I began to sense there was something wrong. She would come home looking worried and she never played with me, just talked on and on with Uncle Yan in a hushed Liuyang County dialect which I couldn't understand. Finally, one Saturday afternoon it was Nai Nai who came to get me, and I was told Mother had gone away and I shouldn't go to Waipo's house anymore.

Only years later was I old enough to understand what had happened, and more than twenty years passed before anyone, including Mother herself, got the full picture. In early 1957 the "Hundred Flowers Movement" had been launched. Its official purpose was to give the Party a chance to correct its shortcomings by listening to the masses' criticisms. Father was away in the countryside reporting on something, but in the Changsha Public Security Bureau, meetings were held and everyone was urged to express his or her opinions freely.

Mother didn't know what to do. She really loved the Party and didn't have any criticisms to make; the Party had given her a job and saved her from the most abject poverty. Still, her leaders said that everyone should participate actively in the movement, especially those who hoped someday to join the Party. Mother was already in favor; she had been given the important job of validating arrest warrants for the whole city. So, regarding it her duty to come up with something, she finally thought of three points she could make. She said that her Section Head sometimes used crude language and liked to criticize people, that he should give his housekeeper a bed to sleep on instead of making her sleep on the floor, and that sometimes when it came time to give raises, the leaders didn't listen to the masses' opinions.

But then, with utterly confusing rapidity, the "Hundred Flowers Movement" changed into the "Anti-Rightist Movement." Perhaps the Party was caught off guard by the amount of opposition and felt compelled to crack down. Or maybe, as I've heard said, the "Hundred Flowers Movement" had been a trap designed from the beginning to uncover Rightist elements. Anyway, every unit was given a quota of Rightists, and Mother's name was among those at the Public Security Bureau.

It was disastrous. When she was allowed to see her file in 1978, she found out that she had been given a Rightist's "cap" solely because of those three criticisms she had made. Perhaps her Section Head was angry at her; perhaps her unit was having trouble filling its quota. At the time she had no idea what the verdict was based on, she only knew that a terrible wrong had been done. But there was no court of appeal. Mother was sent away to the suburb of Yuan Jia Ling for labor reform. She lost her cadre's rank and her salary was cut from fifty-five to fifteen *yuan* a month. (A *yuan* is one hundred Chinese cents; see appendix, page 293.) My naïve and trusting mother went to work as a peasant.

Just as his wife was being declared an enemy of the Party, Father was actively participating in the Anti-Rightist Movement in his own unit. Father believed in the Party with his whole heart, believed that the Party could never make a mistake or hand down a wrong verdict. It was a tortuous dilemma; Father's traditional Confucian sense of family obligation told him to support Mother while his political allegiance told him to condemn her. In the end, his commitment to the Party won out, and he denounced her. He believed that was the only course that could save the family from ruin.

I still remember the first time Mother came home for a visit. It was a rainy Sunday in late autumn, and Father and Nai Nai were both out. There were footsteps on the stairs and in the corridor, but it was almost a minute before the knock came, timidly. Liang Fang opened the door.

Mother was almost unrecognizable. She was in patched blue peasant clothing, muddy up to the knees. The skin on her kind round face looked thick, leathery, and not too clean, and someone had chopped her hair off short and uneven. There was something both broader and thinner about her. "Mama!" cried Liang Fang.

Liang Wei-ping and I ran up to her too, and she was hugging us all at once, weeping, forgetting to put down her oilpaper umbrella. Then as my sisters rushed to pour tea and bring a basin of hot water for her to wash her face, she sat on the bed and held me tightly for a long time. After she had rested, she busied herself with all the housework Nai Nai couldn't do alone, sweeping, dusting, and sharpening our pencils for us, scrubbing our clothes, and cleaning the windows. She wouldn't speak of where she'd been, just asked us about our schoolwork, our health, Father's health. We were so happy. We thought Mother had come home.

She was tying bows on Liang Fang's braids when Father came back. He was astounded to see her, and not very warm. "What are you doing here?" he demanded. "Did you ask for leave?"

Mother lowered her head at his harshness. "Of course I asked for leave," she said defensively. "I can come home once a month."

This silenced Father for a few minutes, and he paced meditatively around the room, his tall thin frame overpowering hers as Nai Nai's used to do. Then he poured out a stream of words, political words—on the meaning of the Anti-Rightist Movement, on her obligation to recognize her faults and reform herself. It was as if he had turned into a propaganda machine. I suppose he thought it was his duty to help re-educate her.

For a while she listened in silence, her head bowed, but at last she protested. "All right, I'm a Rightist, it's all my fault. You don't have to say anything else, my head is bursting. I hear this kind of thing all day long, write self-criticisms every week, and now I come home and I have to hear it all over again."

"I don't think you recognize what you've done. You're just wasting your labor reform," he said.

"What makes you so sure?" Mother's face was white and defiant.

Father exploded: "Rightist element! Have some thought for your influence on the children."

It was Mother's turn to lose control. "What did I ever do wrong? The Party asked me to make suggestions, so I did. You give me one example—" But Mother stopped midsentence, for Father had struck her a ringing blow across the face.

She fell back on the bed, weeping; Father strode into the other room and slammed the door. Then slowly, painfully, she picked up her dirty jacket and umbrella as we sobbed miserably. When she was halfway out the door, Father emerged and shouted after her, "Don't come back until you've reformed yourself. The children in this house need a Revolutionary mother, not a Rightist mother." When she paused and turned her tear-streaked face to him, his voice became gentler. "It doesn't matter what you say here, I won't tell anyone. But please watch what you say at the labor camp."

Despite Father's cruelty, Mother came back every month to see us. She must have missed us very much to endure Father's lectures and the inevitable fights. Sometimes she slept in Father's bed and I slept with them; she never lay still and her pillow was always wet in the morning. On other occasions the quarrel was so fierce that she left again almost as soon as she arrived. Father often warned us against her, and if we defended her he became furious, calling us ignorant children who understood nothing.

We didn't know that Father had already raised the question of divorce. He must have reasoned that all of us were doomed unless he broke off with Mother completely, for the custom in such instances was that the whole family would be considered as guilty as the single member who had committed the crime. If there were no legal separation, Father would never be allowed to join the Party, and the files that would be opened on us when we came of age for middle school would say that we came from a Rightist background. We would be branded forever as people with "questions," and it would be difficult for us to go to middle school and college, get decent jobs, or find husbands and wives. Mother's misfortune might mean the end of all of Father's dreams for himself and for his children; he must have hated her for what she had done.

Mother was a proud woman. She believed so deeply she had been wrongly accused that she told him she would divorce him only after her Rightist label was removed. Her stubbornness enraged Father, particularly because there was a secondary movement to criticize those with Rightist tendencies, and with his Rightist wife, Father was a natural target. He had to criticize Mother publicly, write reports confessing his innermost thoughts. And the pressure became even greater after what happened to Uncle Yan.

When Mother first came under attack, her older brother had been as outraged as she. He went to the Public Security Bureau to argue in her defense, and spoke for her at his own unit, the No. 1 Hospital, where he worked with the Communist Youth League. He even came to our house to urge Father to try to help her, although Father thought he was crazy to stick out his neck like that. Sure enough, Uncle Yan was punished for his family loyalties and given a Rightist "cap" of his own to wear, bringing a second black cloud to rest over Waipo's home. His experience proved that Father's sad choice had been a practical one in view of the harsh political realities; when we were old enough to understand, we could hardly blame Father for what he had done.

Nai Nai was frightened to see how easily the Rightist label could spread from one member of the family to another. She had been an enthusiastic supporter of the "Get Rid of the Four Evils" hygiene movement, but where cartoons had once shown housewives sweeping away rats, flies, mosquitoes, and fleas, now they had added a fifth evil, Rightists. Nai Nai could no longer face lecturing lazy neighbors on the dangers of letting water stagnate; she could imagine what they might be saying behind her back about how she ought to get rid of that evil in her own house. When, with traditional filial deference, Father asked for her opinion on the divorce question, she agreed with relief. The family burden was too heavy for her.

Meanwhile, Mother was working hard to rid herself of her "cap." The calluses on her hands were thicker and sharper every time she came home, and her shoulders were rough where the shoulder pole rested. Her skin toasted to a rich yellow-brown. It was a hard life for a young woman who had lived between the protection of her mother's home and her Public Security Bureau office.

The Rightists at Yuan Jia Ling were all trying to prove to the political officials in charge that they had reformed themselves and were ready to leave. There were all types of people, intellectuals, high-ranking cadres, and ordinary workers, but friendships were impossible because the best strategy for gaining the officials' confidence was to report on others. Thus everyone was always watching everyone else, and a grain of rice dropped on the floor could mean an afternoon of criticism for disrespecting the labors of the peasants. Everything was fair game, even what people said in their sleep.

The second essential strategy was to write constant Thought Reports about oneself. Few of the people in the camp felt they were really Rightists, but the only thing to do was to confess one's crimes penitently, record one's lapses, and invent things to repent. Writing these reports eventually became a kind of habit, and Mother almost believed what she was saying about herself.

The last important route to freedom was hard work. One had to add deliberately to one's misery in small ways, like going without a hat under the hot summer sun or continuing to work in the rain after everyone else had quit. Generally the Rightists did ordinary peasants' work, like digging fish-breeding ponds and planting fruit trees, but sometimes they were taken in trucks to special laboring areas to break and carry stones. Then they were put together with ordinary thieves, hoodlums, and Kuomintang (KMT) spies. The people whose arrest warrants Mother had once been in charge of validating were now her equals; it was almost more than she could bear. Still, bear it she did, and all the rest of it, and after three long years, when she could carry more than a hundred pounds of rocks on her back with ease, a bored-looking official summoned her and told her she was no longer a Rightist. She could go home.

She came to the house late at night, looking like a beggar traveling with her ragged belongings. But when she spoke, her voice was clear and proud. "Old Liang," she announced to Father, "I'm a person again." She told us she had been assigned to the headlight-manufacturing plant on May First Road as an ordinary worker. Her salary would be much lower than it had been at the Public Security Bureau and the loss of her cadre status would be permanent, but she was free, a normal member of society. My sisters and I thought all the trouble was over, but that night as I lay in bed with them I heard talk not of the beginning of a new family life but of how to institute divorce proceedings.

The difficulty lay in what to do with us. We were fought over like basketballs that winter, for Mother insisted that she wanted at least one of us, preferably Liang Fang, who was already eleven and understood life better than Liang Wei-ping and I. Mother was staying at Waipo's, but she came every day to the house. When I got home from the *Hunan Daily*'s Attached Primary School, she was always there, waiting.

One bitterly cold Sunday she took the three of us out to the Martyrs' Park so we could talk alone. No one else was out in that weather; they were all at home huddled under their blankets or warming themselves by coal burners. We were bundled up in everything we had, and I felt as though I could have been rolled down a hill, but I was still cold. The park was desolate and beautiful, the huge monument to the dead martyrs a lonely pinnacle over the city, the pavilions gray and defenseless against the wind. We walked to the large man-made lake, the park's main attraction, and sat by the water, usually filled with rowboats but now covered with a thin layer of ice. I crawled between Mother's knees and Liang Fang and Liang Wei-ping pressed up on each side of her. She spoke to us with great emotion and tenderness.

"Your mother is an unlucky woman. When you're older, you'll understand how I've wept for all of us these three years. Now I won't be able to come see you anymore, but you can visit me at Waipo's house. Liang Fang will live with me, but I don't have enough money for all of you. . . ."

Liang Wei-ping and I were in tears, saying that we wanted to go with her too. Soon everyone was crying. Mother held us so tightly that I could hardly believe it was true that she would go away.

We stayed in the park for a long time, but when Mother noticed that my cheeks were chapped red, she took us home. She brought us to the stairwell and refused to come up. Her parting words were "Remember, Liang Fang, you'll come with me."

That evening Father called us into the inner room. "Children, you're still small and there are many things you don't understand," he said sadly. "If you went with your mother, your life with her would be unhappy. Look at the way your father has to criticize himself because of her. Stay here with me and Nai Nai and we'll take care of you."

Liang Fang wouldn't listen. "Mama isn't a Rightist anymore," she said. "What difference does it make who I go with? Isn't it glorious to be a worker?"

"Your mother's political life is over," said Father with annoyance. "Her file will always have a black mark, and the Party will never trust her again. Don't you know that if you want to go to middle school you'll be asked if your parents have made any political mistakes? If you stay with me, you won't even have to mention your mother, because there will be a legal separation. But if you go with her, you might not even get to go to middle school, to say nothing of joining the Communist Youth League or the Party. And you," he said angrily, turning to me and Liang Wei-ping. "Can't you guess why you haven't been allowed to join the Young Pioneers? Isn't it because of your mother?"

Nai Nai rushed into the room to urge him to control his temper, then she turned to us. "Children, your father is good to you, he understands the situation. Don't I wish I had a good daughter-in-law? Don't I know you need a good mother? But Fate is inevitable. Stay with us, children. It's the only way."

Ultimately, the question was decided in court. Father came home one afternoon looking exhausted and said, "It's settled, you'll all stay with me. Mother is coming in a little while to say good-bye."

We had dinner with her that night, and even Nai Nai's eyes were wet. No one said anything, and no one had any appetite for the fish or the tofu soup. As Nai Nai took the dishes away and washed up, Mother went through her possessions, leaving almost everything for us. Father sat smoking furiously, as he did whenever he was upset. Finally she stood up to leave.

Then the three of us broke out of our numbness and ran to her, begging her not to go, pulling her back, wrapping ourselves around her legs so she couldn't walk. Father didn't interfere; he just let her embrace us again and again and at last shake us off and close the door firmly behind herself. We ran to the balcony and called after her until her broad square figure turned the corner and she was gone.

In fact, Father had been much too optimistic, and the divorce did nothing to rid us of having a Rightist in the family. He even forbade our having the slightest contact with Mother, thinking that if we drew a clear line of separation, things might be better. But there wasn't the slightest change in our status: in the eyes of the Party, my sisters and I were the children of a Rightist and Father had a Rightist wife. Liang Fang still had to say she had a Rightist mother on her application to go to middle school, Liang Wei-ping still found "Rightist's child" written on her desk in chalk when she went to class, and I was still turned down when I asked to be allowed to join the Young Pioneers.

When I first went to the Attached Primary School in the *Hunan Daily* compound at age six, my classmates had often teased me about Mother. I had always shrugged off their taunts because I did well and achieved more than enough recognition to offset a few minor slights. I remember how pleased Father was when I started to take prizes for my paintings; my drawing of a morning glory was first in the whole primary school.

But as I got older, more and more stress was placed on the three stages of Revolutionary glory: the Young Pioneers, the Communist Youth League, and the Party itself. It became clear to me that success in the political arena was a prerequisite for success in anything else, and if I had the slightest ambitions for myself I had to achieve these basic signs of social recognition. Those students who had the right to wear the Pioneers' triangular red scarf received much more praise than those who didn't, no matter what their grades; and at home Father and Nai Nai were constantly asking me if my application had been approved. But it was no use. I was rejected year after year, until I found myself in a tiny minority of outsiders whose "political performances" were the very worst in the class.

One day I was given a clue to the trouble when our teacher gave us a lecture. "We all have to join forces to oppose Capitalist thought," Teacher Luo said. "Some students want to eat well and dress well from the time they are small. This is Capitalist thought. Some students are from good worker or Revolutionary cadre backgrounds; they should be careful not to be proud of themselves. And those students from families with questions—they must be more careful to draw a clear line of separation." He looked meaningfully at me and at the other boy with a Rightist in his family. And all the other students in the classroom turned to stare at us too.

In fact, after the divorce I had continued to go secretly to see my mother despite Father's warnings that doing so would harm my future. She was always overjoyed to see me, and, even during China's hard years, just after the breakup, she always found a way to give me a few *fen* (a *fen* is a Chinese cent; see appendix, page 293) or a roasted sweet potato. But after Teacher Luo's lecture, it really began to bother me when other students mocked me as a Rightist's son. And they became bolder in their mockery as well. They would slap me, or kick me when I wasn't looking, and then pretend not to have done anything. Sometimes I would get into real fights, and then there were reprimands from Father and the teachers. The other Rightist's son was as lonely as I, but we never spoke much, for that might have made things even worse.

So perhaps inevitably, over the years, I came to resent my mother for making my life so miserable. I began to believe that she really had done something wrong. My father and teachers said so, and my classmates hated me for her supposed crimes. At last I no longer wished to visit her despite my loneliness, and when I saw her at a distance I didn't even call out to her. I cut her out of my life just as I had been told to do, and became solitary and self-reliant. But that was when I was much older, and many things happened before then.

CHAPTER TWO

Hard Times

It was in 1960, just around the time of the divorce, that all China fell on hard times. I was almost seven. Rice, cooking oil, and soybean products were severely rationed, and meat, eggs, flour, and sugar gradually disappeared from the market completely. The cost of fresh vegetables went out of sight, and the *mantou* (steamed buns) we bought in the dining hall became rough and dark because the good flour was all gone. We were always hungry.

Father explained that the rivers and lakes had overflowed and the peasants couldn't grow anything for us to eat. "But you're lucky," he said. "You live in a big capital city, and the Party and Chairman Mao are giving you food from the storage bins. The peasants have to find a way out for themselves."

The situation dragged on and got worse, month after month, until a whole year had passed. I grew accustomed to going with my sisters to the Martyrs' Park to pull up a kind of edible wild grass that could be made into a paste with broken grains of rice and steamed and eaten as "bittercakes." Gradually even this became scarce and we had to walk miles to distant suburbs to find any.

Many of the old people and almost all the children I knew had the "water swelling disease," dropsy. Our bodies puffed up and wouldn't recede, and we walked listlessly to school and arrived exhausted. When acquaintances met, they squeezed each others' legs to see how swollen they were, and examined each others' skins to see if they were yellow.

It was a game for me to poke Nai Nai's cheek and leave a hole that would fill up again only very slowly, like dough.

One day Father came home unusually silent and depressed after he had been reporting on the situation in the countryside for a week. Finally he told us that in a commune in Hengyang District to the south, nearly an entire Production Team (see appendix, page 294) had died of hunger, and there was no one left with enough strength to bury the bodies. They were still lying scattered about in the fields from which they had been trying to pull enough to stay alive.

By the second year Nai Nai's condition was very bad, because she often gave away the small share that was hers. Father used his press card to buy a *jin* (just over a pound; see appendix, page 293) of sugar and a *jin* of candy for her every month at a special store for cadres, but she would pass it to us secretly, saying, "Eat it so you won't be sick. You still have a lot of growing to do." We were too ignorant and hungry to refuse.

Then one day, when my sisters got up, Nai Nai stayed in bed. She slept so long that at last they went to rouse her. Finally they called in Father. When he too failed to awaken her he threw himself on her body weeping, cursing himself for having been a bad son. I had never seen my father cry before, and found it strange and frightening. He was acting like a fellow child who had been beaten. I wished he would stop, but he cried for a long time.

The mourning took three days, according to custom. Many people came to pull the white cloth from Nai Nai's face, look silently at her, and bow three times. Incense was burned to cover the bad smell, and a big black coffin and a colorful wreath of paper flowers were purchased and placed below the stairwell in readiness for the burial. No one paid any attention to me except to pin a black armband to my left sleeve. Only one thing comforted me, which was that Waipo, whom I hadn't seen in many months, came to the house to pay her respects. When she uncovered Nai Nai's face, she wept for a long time. Then she embraced me tightly and called me "poor child."

Nai Nai was buried on Liberation Mountain in the suburbs, at what was said to be a favorable site, with good "wind and water," and a long view. A simple gravestone with the name Liang Shu-xiao (Liang "Devoted and Filial") buttressed the mound above her. After the funeral Father was silent for many days.

After Nai Nai died, there was no one to take care of us. Father brought rice and vegetable tickets at the newspaper compound dining hall, and we exchanged them for meals, staying there to eat when Father was away. My sisters mended our clothes and kept the house clean, especially Liang Wei-ping, who took on this role very early. But my father's colleagues knew that we needed a mother and urged him to remarry, and eventually he found himself a girlfriend, an old classmate of his whose husband had gone to Taiwan with the Kuomintang. She would have made an excellent match, since she was both a Party member and a high-ranking cadre in a factory.

Her name was Mrs. Yao, and she was very kind to us, even asking us to call her Mother. Sometimes she invited me to stay at her apartment and sleep in her fresh clean bed with her, as if making up for the early years of mothering she had missed. It was she who changed my name to Liang Heng, "Liang Constant," to show that I was beginning a new life of stability and perseverance. She was an interesting woman, plump, dark, and pretty, and the only woman I had ever met who smoked cigarettes. I used to stare at her in fascination whenever she lit one, and I got the distinct impression that Father didn't like her strange habit.

It seemed that the relationship was pretty much decided, except for that old trouble spot, my mother. Like everyone else, Mrs. Yao urged us to make a clean break with her, but in her case it was for the simple reason that she was jealous. My father must have explained that there was little feeling between his ex-wife and himself, but she probably believed that it had been a purely political divorce, like so many others at that time. Thus she was constantly accusing Father of maintaining relations with Mother's family, using my sisters' and my stealthy visits as evidence. Perhaps, too, Mrs. Yao had doubts about Father's relatively low salary and the fact that he was not a Party member. The relationship faltered and finally ended when an emergency necessitated Father's spending two entire days, including one night, with Mother.

It happened in April of 1962, when the government announced that Chiang Kai-shek was launching an attack against the mainland. Loudspeakers called at all hours for people to prepare for war: We were told that if the KMT made it to our shores they would shoot our cadres, steal our food, turn us all into slaves, and make us "suffer for the second time" by returning the country to its pre-Revolutionary feudal state.

Everyone not working or in middle schools or colleges—mostly young children and old folk, that is—was to be evacuated from urban areas for protection in the event of attack, and all the adults scurried about in alarm trying to make arrangements.

Of course, if you had relatives in the countryside, the question was settled, but if not, you had to find another solution. The government had no time to organize such things. Father had no one, but Mother had her aunt, Waipo's sister, so he was forced to bite back all his bitterness and bridge the gulf he had wedged apart so desperately. After an agonizing internal struggle between his loyalty to the Party and his loyalty to his family, he walked timidly to Waipo's house, and, speaking more politely to Mother than he had in years, he reopened commerce between the two families. Mother received him correctly and patiently, and agreed to write immediately to her aunt on Luojia Mountain outside Changsha. Liang Wei-ping, myself, my two younger cousins, and Waipo would go, leaving Liang Fang and my older cousin at home to continue attending middle school. Mother and Father would accompany us there, returning home the following day.

The railroad station was packed with refugees, most of them old grannies and children. All had brought, to the extent possible, their most precious belongings, hanging from shoulder poles in net bags, baskets, boxes, and parcels. They had brought furniture, woks, and bedding, clocks and lamps and fishing poles. Grandmothers clutched children, sisters carried siblings on their backs, and the sounds of babies crying filled the waiting room. Our family had brought less than most. I had my wooden gun and my books; my sister had her scissors and colored paper. Waipo clutched a little cloth purse tightly in her hand. She rarely left home, so she looked about nervously while Father went to buy tickets. Mother sat on the pile of bedding and fanned us gently, for the heat had already burned rashes onto our foreheads. She was overjoyed to be together with us again.

The stampede onto the platform was violent; fortunately, Father and Mother were able to find seats on the train for most of us. At every stop, simple country folk waited to meet city slickers; brown, coarse, barefoot peasants with economically shaved heads trying to identify pale, hysterical relatives and acquaintances whom they had not seen for years. It was a slow train, and it took us nearly an hour to get to Luojia Mountain. I had never met these relatives, but Liang Wei-ping had been there just a few years earlier to cure a scalp disease, so she immediately picked out Uncle Hou and his son in the crowd. He was Waipo's sister's son, and we called him "Uncle" for the sake of simplicity. Privately, we also called him "Uncle Big Ears," and said he would live to be one hundred.

It was ten *li* (a *li* is about a third of a mile; see appendix, page 293) through the fields and halfway up the mountain to his home. The countryside was lovely, with large lotus flowers growing in the ponds, and mud-brick houses with thatched roofs nestled in clusters of evergreen and palm trees. At last we arrived at what looked like a tiny village, for seven or eight families had built their homes onto one another to form a single courtyard. Waipo's sister and the rest of the relatives and neighbors were waiting by the entranceway to meet us. Our greataunt was even shorter and thinner than Waipo, but with the same big twisted teeth. She stood up with a little cry and received her sister with tears in her eyes.

"It seems it takes a terrible thing to happen for me to have the chance to see you," she said in a thick country accent, tears of joy in her eyes. "Maybe I've done something to offend the Heavens."

My first view of the inside of a peasant home left me both more curious and a little repelled. It was much dirtier than our tiny apartment, with an earthen floor pounded hard by many feet, and a layer of ash over everything from the open fire in the kitchen stove. The mosquito netting had been patched so often it was hard to tell if it was made of newspaper or cloth, and there were spiderwebs in every corner. But the rooms were big, with a large threshing room in the center, and piglets and chickens ran freely from the courtyard into the house, delighting me.

The peasants were very courteous, bringing out a special tea I had never tasted before, brewed with soya beans, sesame seeds, salt, and ginger. Then they served dinner, explaining with embarrassment that there had been some very lean years, and that usually there wasn't much rice. There was no meat, but they brought out a small dish of smoked fish. Uncle Hou had caught it months earlier and had been saving it for a special occasion. The rest was squash, gourds, and cabbage, dishes that were to become our staple foods for nearly a month.

After dinner, Uncle Hou showed us our room. It was large and dark, empty except for two beds and a variety of farming tools, grass capes, and conical peasant hats, which hung on the wall. After some discussion, a rather strange sleeping arrangement was worked out. Waipo would sleep on one bed with Liang Wei-ping and the two cousins; I would sleep on the other with Mother and Father.

I was still a child so I didn't pay much attention to what certainly must have been a peculiar situation for my parents emotionally. They had barely spoken to one another during the trip or during dinner, but did nothing to correct our peasant relatives' impression that they were still happily married. Perhaps they didn't want to mention their shame or spoil the festive atmosphere of family reunion. In any case, they put their pillows at opposite ends, placed me in the middle, and got into bed on each side of me. I don't know if they slept well or not; there had been a lot of excitement in one day for a small boy, and I fell asleep almost immediately. I'm sure I would not have thought about it one way or the other had I not later been called upon to bear witness to the position of the pillows.

My parents left early the next day, not walking beside each other as they had on our arrival, but far apart, as if they were strangers who happened to be traveling the same road. I watched them go with an aching pain. My mother was a good person and her kindness toward us had never wavered. Why did she have to be a Rightist? Why couldn't they be together like they were yesterday? My overwhelming loneliness suddenly became mixed with anger, and with tears of confusion, abandonment, and fury, I turned back into the house.

I found my way to the rear of the main room, where there was a niche for the ancestral tablet, a wooden placard on which were written the names of all the Hou family ancestors. It was carved on top with a golden dragon with a long tail and sharp talons. At the foot of the tablet were some wooden figures and a blue-and-white porcelain incense burner. With sorrow I realized that if we had been from the countryside we wouldn't have known how to write down our parents' names because Mother wasn't allowed to be our ancestor anymore.

Then I discovered Waipo at my side. "Little Fatso," she said, "do you know what those little figures are?"

I found comfort in her voice and answered, "Aren't those supposed to be Uncle Hou's ancestors?"

"No, those are spirits. That big one there is in charge of keeping mountains steady. And that one keeps away drought, he's the water

Buddha. The others protect us from fire, disease, and ghosts. And there's another Buddha near the stove in the kitchen, and one hidden up near the roof to bring wealth to the family."

"Why don't we have any Buddhas in Changsha?" I asked, happy to be distracted.

"We used to, but just after Liberation the army asked the people to stop believing in superstitions. We all brought our Buddhas to be burned. But every time somebody goes to the temples on the Southern Peak of Heng Mountain, I ask him to burn incense in our names."

I looked at Waipo with a new curiosity. "Does Mama do that too?"

She smiled. "No, such foolishness is only for us old people. And the peasants like to keep the old traditions too, because they have many things to worry about. But you shouldn't trouble yourself, because you're going to grow up to be big and strong. Now let's go out to the well and wash our faces for breakfast."

Our life in the countryside was harsh and primitive, but we children liked it very much, for we ran about freely with the peasant children and had no schoolwork to trouble us. Even the work was a kind of game. Every morning we had to get up when the sky was as pale as the belly of a fish and search the wet grass for droppings left by the dogs during the night, for use as fertilizer. We had to hurry through the mist, or the children from the other households would pick it all up first, and we would have to go home to Uncle Hou emptyhanded. Then, after a breakfast of squash or pumpkin, Uncle Hou's son took us up a nearby mountain to collect brush.

Firewood had been a big problem in the countryside since the Great Leap Forward of 1958 to 1960. Chairman Mao had ordered the peasants to stop tilling the fields and cut down the big trees to run iron and steel smelting furnaces, and now there was little fuel left except for the brushwood and grass on the mountainsides and the rice grass in the fields left over after threshing. It was always difficult to keep the kitchen fire going under the stove, and usually one of the girls had to feed it constantly while an older woman cooked. The kindling burned fast, and the rice grass often went to feed the Production Team's water buffalo, make a mattress, or repair a roof, so we had to go out nearly every day for more. Even leaves were welcome, and we put everything into two big bamboo baskets for Uncle Hou's son to carry on his shoulder pole.

While Uncle Hou's son, buried under the huge collections of vegetation, was making his trips down the mountain, we children played games. Most of them were about Chiang Kai-shek. The peasants knew nothing about him, so we city kids gave full rein to our imaginations, painting for them a picture of a true monster who killed and burned everywhere he went, just as we had seen his armies do in the movies. We'd draw a picture of his head in the earth with a stick, round and bald, and have contests to see who could come closest to hitting him with a stone; we boys had a second version as well: long-distance peeing and spitting competitions in which he was always the target. The peasant children loved us for introducing these new games and for telling them about the outside world. When we were all tired out from our play we would talk about things like trucks and buses and airplanes, and they listened in openmouthed wonder, confusing the *ji* in *feiji* (airplane) with the *ji* that meant chicken, and wondered how a flying chicken could get up above the clouds.

We learned from them, too, wonders we could never have imagined on our own, such as how to make fishing poles out of bamboo to use in the pond, and how to catch fish with our bare hands in the rice paddies. We also learned how to capture wild birds in baskets overturned and baited underneath with a little food: You propped up the side with a stick tied to a long string, and when the bird was underneath, you pulled the stick away, the basket dropped down, and the bird was yours.

The peasants' eating schedule we found very strange, for after the nine o'clock breakfast, lunch wasn't until three, and then there was the long nap and the long wait until dinner at nine. There never was anything to eat but beans, pumpkin, squash, and wax gourds, and I was frequently hungry even though Waipo often gave me part of her portion, telling me to grow up big and strong and fight Chiang Kai-shek.

The peasants never read books, nor did they seem to think much about anything but the weather and their planting, transplanting, and harvesting. The only time there was any conversation was right after dinner, when Uncle Hou would light his brass water pipe and tell a story about the hard life before Liberation, pointing to the carved table that had belonged to the local landlord and saying, "Chairman Mao is truly our Great Saving Star. If Chiang Kai-shek comes back, he will take my table away again."

It was during that brief period after dinner that they told us about the ghost who lived in the pond just outside their door. A bad little boy had been pulled into the water, never to be seen again. "You can hear him at night," Uncle Hou's wife said, "calling to his mama from the bottom of the pond."

At first we didn't believe it, because we were city children and our father had told us there were no such things as ghosts. But then Uncle Hou inhaled deeply and said with real nervousness, "I saw him one night myself, a little white water ghost, deep in the middle of the pond. He was very pale, not like a person, but you could see his little arms and legs, and he was moving toward the bank as if he had seen me and was going to pull me in."

At these words, we four city children trembled, for Uncle Hou was a grownup, and he knew everything about the land and what it could do. Hadn't he cured Liang Wei-ping's scalp disease by putting buffalo manure on her head and binding it up in a turban? But his wife burst into laughter and said, "Anyway, you have nothing to worry about. Your ears are so big you'll live forever. I'm sure it wasn't you he wanted to eat."

So we all laughed, and went to bed, but in the darkness beneath the mosquito netting, with nothing but the bedbugs and fleas and the whine of the mosquitoes to keep us company, I clutched my cousin tightly and imagined I could hear the soft squish of wet footsteps just beyond the window.

The peasant children loved nothing better than to imitate the ghost to frighten people. They usually caught us city kids on dark nights when we were walking outdoors, and because of the political situation, they had plenty of opportunities. It was August, when one crop was being harvested as the new one was being planted, the busiest time of any year, and this year there were also many meetings aimed at mobilizing against the threatened invasion. The slogan TO GROW A SINGLE ADDI-TIONAL GRAIN OF RICE IS TO PRODUCE ONE MORE BULLET AND KILL ONE MORE ENEMY was written on all the walls. People scarcely had time to eat, for the fields were nearly one *li* away from home. Thus, we children often had the job of carrying food to the men in the fields at dusk, and on our way back home again it would be dark, with black trees on either side of the path. It was then that the little ghosts came out to play.

The first time it happened, my cousin and I were with our neighbors Little Fellow Lan and his little brother, Buck Teeth Lan. The moon was low and bright, and it cast our shadows long and trembling on the ground. The brothers had gone slightly ahead, and when we came to a twist in the path two ghostly white figures leaped from behind a rock, groaning and wheezing and calling our names. Weeping with fear, we ran stumbling all the way home, dark footsteps in pursuit, until we fell gasping into Waipo's arms.

When the adults heard what had happened, they seemed strangely unconcerned. I suppose that they were accustomed to the children's pranks, and had evoked ghosts themselves commonly enough as a threat when they wanted to keep discipline. So they told us it was only a game and that we should just go to sleep and forget about it. But I couldn't forget about it. When I awoke the next day I was still furious.

It was about a week later that Little Fellow Lan's grandmother died. The coffin was placed in the central room, between our families, with the ancestral tablet and the Buddhas. As in the city, the three days of mourning began. In the countryside they couldn't afford a beautiful wreath of paper flowers like the one we had bought when Nai Nai died, so instead the peasants made what looked like little white flags with strips of cloth, bamboo wheels, and poles, and placed them on the coffin. A blind man came and sang songs all night long for three nights to accompany the mourning. He sang very sadly and very beautifully, sometimes about the old woman's hard life and how kind and honest she had been; sometimes ancient and moving songs about history, like "Mrs. Meng Jiang Weeping at the Great Wall," about a woman who traveled to the North to look for her missing husband, conscripted to work in construction by the emperor, only to find her husband dead and the completed Great Wall in his place. The peasants came from miles around to hear the singer, many of them strangers to the family, and even they wept bitterly.

I felt extremely ill-at-ease among all these mourning adults. Liang Wei-ping and my cousins were of no help, for they were staring at the singer with glazed eyes, so I decided to go to the storeroom and get a sweet potato to eat. I soon emerged with my booty, and my cousin saw me and went in and got one for himself. Little Fellow Lan soon followed. By that time I was ready for seconds, and made my way back under the dark lintel.

And then my heart stopped and my stomach contracted to the size of a pea, for I was attacked by a real ghost, grabbed under the armpits from behind and tossed to the ground with what seemed like superhuman ease. In the blackness, all I knew was that I was to die, to spend the rest of my existence under the water as a white shade calling out to unsuspecting little boys. Now I would never be able to go back to the city to tell my playmates all about my new experiences; now I would never be able to fight against Chiang Kai-shek.

The next moment I heard the familiar laugh of Little Fellow Lan, well pleased with his success at ghostliness and ready to share it with me. But my rage was beyond all control. I seized him blindly and bit him as hard as I could in the shoulder, then threw him back against the sweet potatoes. He kicked back instinctively, and I ran out of the storage room, my fury at him expanding into fury at his entire family. Like a little mad bull, I attacked it at what I must unconsciously have known was its most sacred spot.

I ran to the coffin where the flaglike offerings were arrayed and seized a large one on a good-sized bamboo pole and swung it in an arc, knocking the whole display into the group of mourners and reducing the blind singer and the whole funeral to horrified silence. I was bawling incoherently, and when the peasants rushed to restrain me, I began to howl, kicking myself out of their hands. No one could control the hysterical guest from the city except Waipo herself, who spoke to me sharply and threatened to tell Father if I didn't quiet down.

As the peasants restored the paper offerings to their places and the "night songs" resumed, Waipo lectured me severely on paying respect to the dead. Then she made me kneel down before the ancestral tablet and the Buddhas, with everybody watching, and place my forehead on the ground and recite, "I am wrong I should die, I am wrong I should die, I am wrong I should die." And I felt it was true, for I was so wretched and ashamed that I really wished my life were over and I could travel on the road to Heaven too. But then Waipo helped me up and dried my tears and held me while we listened together to the songs for the dead lady. The next day, Waipo's sister brought me a large thick silver circlet borrowed from a neighbor. "You should wear this around your neck, and then no ghost will dare to harm you," she said. I had seen other children wear this charm, large, awkward, and shining against their skinny naked chests. I had thought it laughable and superstitious, but, when I considered that Little Fellow Lan might believe its power, I consented to put it on, and wore it for the duration of our time in the countryside. My great-aunt also found a blunt-tipped iron ghost-repelling sword, which she placed in my bed, and after that I had no more trouble with squishy footsteps or ambushes in the night.

As the summer wore on, I began to long to go back to school, and I missed Liang Fang and my parents. Then one early September evening Mother's brother, Uncle Yan, showed up with the news that there would be no invasion and he had come to take us home.

The whole village turned out to see us off. I gave Little Fellow Lan the wooden gun he had always coveted, and he gave me a live magpie on a string that he had caught for me in an overturned basket baited underneath with rice. I felt sad and promised to write, but I knew it was useless because he couldn't read anyway. At the train station, Uncle Yan let my magpie go because he said I would have nowhere to keep it, and it flew crookedly up into the air with its long string trailing behind it. I worried all the way home about how it could live with a string tied to its foot.

While we were away, Father's temper had gotten worse, for now he never offered to read us stories and became furious if we quarreled. Liang Fang told us that maybe it was because Mrs. Yao and he weren't getting along; she came less frequently and when she did, they argued.

Then one evening after we had been home several weeks, Father asked me not to go out and play. "Auntie Yao is coming to our house, and she wants to ask you something. Just answer whatever she asks."

When Mrs. Yao arrived, she looked as plump and strong as ever but seemed a bit worried, and she lit a cigarette as soon as she sat down. Father looked unhappy. "You can ask Liang Heng now if you want to," he said.

But she seemed unwilling to say anything, and finally Father asked, "Do you still remember that day your mother and I took you to the countryside? Tell Auntie Yao if you slept on the same pillow as Father or on the same pillow as Mother."

I thought this was a very peculiar question indeed, but I answered immediately, "I slept in the middle, and I wasn't on anyone's pillow. My head was near Father's back and my feet were near Mama's." I felt as if they were questioning me about something I had done wrong, but I couldn't figure out what it was.

Apparently my answer was not good enough; after that, Mrs. Yao never came to the house for dinner again.

When Father lost Mrs. Yao, his wish that we cut all ties with Mother became an obsession. He did everything he could to separate himself from her, even requesting a reduction in his already low salary to prove his ideological purity. It was all useless. The culmination of his efforts came when he asked Liang Fang to write a report exposing Mother, which he planned to send to her factory on May First Road. He hoped in this way to prove that his loyalty to the Party superseded all ties to his ex-wife, and to help Liang Fang in her struggles to join the Communist Youth League.

Of course Liang Fang didn't want to write the report, for she still missed Mother desperately, and had continued to go see her long after I had stopped. Father was furious whenever he found out, and she was always afraid that Liang Wei-ping and I might tell on her, as we did more than once. There was greater temptation for her since Uncle Yan's oldest daughter was in her class, always willing to carry gifts of food and clothing and messages arranging meetings. Liang Fang often went all the way to Mother's factory to see her, afraid to go to Waipo's because it was too near the *Hunan Daily* and someone might tell Father. Years later she told me that until she was more than thirty years old she had a recurring nightmare that Father found her out, beat her, and informed her school and the Communist Youth League branch. When she gave in to Father's angry pressure it was the first in an agonizing series of concessions to the demands of society; according to his instructions she accused Mother of Capitalist thought, saying she had always told us we should try to go to college rather than do manual labor, and that she had tried to gain influence over us by giving us gifts of clothing and food.

This sort of thing made me unusually thoughtful for a young boy. I was finding out how life worked. As Chairman Mao said, everyone had his own class position, and human relationships were class relationships that could not be transcended. There was no room for a personal life outside the one assigned to you by the Party, and the Party's values had to govern your private life or you would be punished like Uncle Yan and Mother. The Party had made us strangers to the woman who loved us more than anyone else in the whole world. It didn't make sense, but it was reality.

CHAPTER THREE

Our New Mother

Two years after the divorce, when I was nine, a mathematics teacher who had always been relatively kind to me came up while I was waiting for my turn to play ping-pong. "Tonight we're all going to your house to eat sweets," she said, smiling.

I didn't understand, and stood there not knowing what to reply. It was true that something had been afoot the last few days. Father had asked my sisters to help him clean the apartment from top to bottom, and he had borrowed a lot of chairs and placed them along the walls of the larger room in a square. Then the day before, he had told us that an "Auntie" was coming, and she would take care of us from now on. What he hadn't told us was that that "Auntie" was to be our mother.

Father had brought her back with him from the bus station, a short plump woman with a red face. She had a bag with her, and she put it down on the table and took something out. "Come here, children," she said. "I've brought you something delicious, fried sweet potato chips." She poured them into my outstretched hands, and I thought that I liked this Auntie very much.

Father had met her when he was out reporting on conditions in Shuangfeng County to the west of Changsha. A colleague in the local propaganda department, concerned about Father's "personal problem" (as finding a mate is called), introduced him to a recently divorced primary-school teacher named Zhu Zhi-dao. They had seen each other only a few times, but the decision was made because the match seemed objectively suitable for both of them and would save them the trouble of continuing to look. This was a major attraction for my career-oriented father.

That day of the wedding even Teacher Luo was kind to me, telling me not to stay to clean the classroom but to go along home right after class. Climbing up the stairs to our apartment, I found my two sisters in the smaller outer room, sitting awkwardly among all the furniture. Apparently they felt uneasy about what was happening in the inner room. I peeked inside, and discovered the house had never looked so clean and beautiful.

The tables in the center were covered with a red cloth and laden with packs of red-wrapped cigarettes and large bowls of peanuts and sweets. A red paper lantern covered our usually bare hanging lightbulb, and a huge red "Double Happiness" pattern was pinned squarely in the center of the wall, framed on both sides by paper butterflies, birds, and lanterns. Father and Auntie were seated by the far wall talking to three early guests and admiring their gift of a piece of Hunan's famous Xiang embroidery, sewn by hand with silk thread as fine as chick's fuzz and showing a pair of peacocks, one male and one female. Four or five more people arrived just behind me, bringing a porcelain tea set from Liling County. Since Father and Auntie were too busy to notice me, I went and sat down in the outer room with my sisters.

After a while we heard the martial music signaling dinnertime crackle over the loudspeaker just outside our window. Since no one invited us to do differently, we took our rice and vegetable tickets and went to the dining hall as we did on ordinary days. It was a very cold winter day, with a rare hint of snow in the air, so we lingered in the dark by the coal stove in the dining-hall kitchen, and went back only reluctantly after we had finished eating. All the neighbor children were crowded in front of our stairwell waiting for the end of the wedding, when all the remaining candy would be tossed in a big ring, and they could scramble for it like dogs for morsels of meat. It all seemed unreal. I could hardly believe that this ritual I had taken part in so often was this time connected with my own family.

Inside, a neighbor was performing a song from Chairman Mao's favorite kind of opera, Hunan's piercing and humorous *huaguxi*. His quavering falsetto was greeted with considerable applause and cries of "Let's have another one," but our neighbor demurred modestly and the spotlight shifted to one of my father's fellow-reporters, who stood up and recited a Tang dynasty poem, not in the strict rhythmical manner of our teachers, but in the ancient style, as if he were singing it. Father, sitting with our Auntie at the head of the room, seemed to enjoy this very much, for he applauded loudly. Then Teacher Zeng did bird and animal imitations, and a typesetter from the newspaper sang a folk song.

At this point the fat editor, who seemed to be in charge of the proceedings, initiated a game. He hung a piece of soft candy from a chopstick by a string, and the rule was that Father and Auntie had to take a bite from the candy at the same time. Father protested and Auntie blushed a bright red, but the crowd demanded its price with a unanimous voice and they had to give in.

I had never seen adults so wildly amused. The editor played with his victims as if he were teasing fish with a line, always pulling it away when they were about to close on the bait. They tried and failed and tried and failed until at last they bumped noses and Auntie turned an even deeper shade of scarlet. The guests were in tears of laughter by the time their torturer relented and held the candy in one place long enough to get a nibble at both ends. Then there was a thunderous applause, and cries of "Well done!" "Again, again!"

But they were rescued, because Senior Assistant Editor Meng and some other high leaders pushed their way into the room. They were all in formal suits with high collars, and Senior Assistant Editor Meng, who usually had a heavy beard, was freshly shaved. Under his right arm were bright red copies of the four volumes of *Chairman Mao's Selected Works*, and in his left hand was a set of scrolls. The guests clapped politely and the fat editor held up both hands for silence. Senior Assistant Editor Meng cleared his throat and began to speak in the ponderous manner typical of high-ranking cadres.

"Today, ahem, Comrade Liang, ahem, is getting married. I represent the Party organization in presenting him with the precious gift of the *Works* of Chairman Mao. I hope that the new couple will study them seriously, and work hard to remold their world views, develop their Revolutionary thought, and establish a happy, ahem, Revolutionary family."

There was general applause. While Auntie got a cup of tea and some sweets for the officials, someone else unrolled the scrolls and hung them up. They were on red paper in black ink, two to face each other and one over the top, like a doorway. The lefthand one said, *zhitong daohe xieshou qianjin,* YOUR THOUGHTS AGREE, YOUR WAY THE SAME, ARM IN ARM ADVANCE TOGETHER. The righthand one said, *enai huzhu baitou daolao,* YOUR LOVE IS TENDER, YOUR AID MUTUAL, WHEN YOUR HAIR IS WHITE YOU WILL STILL BE TOGETHER. The top line read, *geming daodi,* REVOLUTION UNTIL THE END. Again the guests applauded, and discussed the good calligraphy and the appositeness of the sentiment.

Then Senior Assistant Editor Meng spoke again. "You, Liang Shan and Zhu Zhi-dao. Let's have a song."

According to custom, the bride and groom had to sing something with a dialogue, and they spent a long time deciding what it should be. Meanwhile, someone brought out an *erhu,* a two-stringed Chinese violin, and had it tuned up and ready when my father started to sing:

> Liuyang River, how many bends have you turned?
> How many *li* is the water road to the Xiang River?
> Which county lies beside the river?
> Did it produce a man known by all the world?

Zhu Zhi-dao answered in an unsteady voice:

> The Liuyang River has turned nine bends,
> It arrives at the Xiang River after fifty *li*.
> Xiangtan County lies beside the river,
> It produced our Chairman Mao, known by all the
>   world.

This was the climactic performance of the evening. When all the guests were gone, my sisters swept the peanut shells, cigarette butts, and candy wrappers into a small mountain, while Father sat by the little coal burner with his arm around our new mother.

"How did I sing tonight?" he asked Liang Fang. He prided himself on his voice, and often sang to us in the evenings.

"Maybe it was just a bit hoarse, Father. I think you were a little nervous."

Liang Wei-ping said, "You should have sung that song you like, 'Why Is the Flower So Red?'"

"Well, maybe I'll sing it now," he said. And as the last of the debris disappeared out the door, he sang softly to our new mother,

> Why is the flower so red?
> It's red like a burning fire,
> And it shows my love for you . . .

As I fell asleep that night, two thoughts were uppermost in my mind. One was that now we wouldn't have to eat in the dining hall anymore, and the other was that at last people wouldn't look down on me for having a mother who was a Rightist.

Before a week was out, I had discovered I was wrong on both counts. On the second day after the marriage Father explained that Auntie had to go home now but after a while she would come back and live with us. So we waited and waited, but she was never there except on festivals and holidays, and then all she and Father ever talked about was the question of her transfer.

Her file and residence card were located at her primary school in Shuangfeng, and getting them moved to the *Hunan Daily*'s Attached Primary School would have been a long and complicated procedure. My father simply did not have the time to see it carried through. First, a report had to be written to the Changsha school to find out whether or not another teacher was needed. If there was a place, then the Shuangfeng school had to be persuaded to release Auntie and send her file with all her background information and political black marks and gold stars to the Changsha school for review. If the Changsha school decided then that they wanted her, reports had to be submitted to the Shuangfeng County and Changsha City Education Sections, which in turn had to be approved by the District, and then by the Provincial Bureau of Education. If the transfer passed all of these barriers, then the Changsha Public Security Bureau had to give permission for the removal of her residence card from Shuangfeng to Changsha. Such permission was unlikely, because though it was always easy to leave a large city for a smaller one, and a smaller one for the countryside, it was enormously difficult to reverse the process. There was no way around all this, either, since even if my father's salary had been enough for both of them, without a city residence card there would have been no rice coupons, and without rice coupons Auntie could not eat. So even though Auntie wanted very much to come to the capital where so many more goods were available and life was more comfortable (in fact, I suspected that was one reason she had married Father), they gradually resigned themselves to living apart.

So for us it was as if there had been no change in our lives. The house remained lonely as ever, with Father away sometimes for months at a time, Liang Fang returning so late that her food was usually cold, and Liang Wei-ping and I rattling around a place that seemed like an empty shell, with no voices and no smells of cooking and no laughter.

Nor was there any relief from my life as a Rightist's son. I was still mocked and ill-treated on the slightest provocation. This amazed me and made me furious. Why did they still curse me when I had a new mother? I had long since stopped going to Mother's house, but she dogged my footsteps like a black shadow. I came to dread going to school, and sometimes pretended to be ill to avoid it.

To make things even worse, having a new mother left me open to a new kind of teasing. The neighbors used to ask me, "What do you call her? She's not your real mother and she's not your real auntie!" They seemed to find this hilarious, and I grew so sensitive to the issue that I never brought her name up in conversation except with my own sisters.

Fortunately, at around this time I was transferred to the Three Mile Primary School, because the *Hunan Daily*'s Attached Primary School had only four grades. There things were better for me, since my new teacher's husband was himself a Rightist, and her own son had been victimized like me. Furthermore, she had great praise for my paintings and compositions, and she understood how it felt to be the only student who was not a Young Pioneer. So she asked the other students to train me in preparation for joining.

I did not feel confident, though, and I was eager to forestall trouble before they found out too much about me. So all by myself, before it became a national phenomenon, I figured out a way of "going through the back door," or buying influence. I told the student officers that my father would soon be giving me a lot of money, which I would use to buy them a soccer ball. On the strength of this they agreed to let me become a Young Pioneer, and within two weeks I was initiated. Months passed and no soccer ball appeared, but they could do nothing. I wore my triangular red scarf defiantly everywhere.

My grades at the new school were much better than they had been, because I had received superior training at the Attached Primary School and because my situation was happier. I was soon asked to edit the school's blackboard newspaper, and I began to reread the stories Father had once read aloud to me, searching for materials. I became so voracious a reader that the few *fen* Father gave me as pocket money were not nearly enough to sustain my habit. I couldn't afford to buy books, of course, but there were outdoor "libraries" where, for a small sum, you had the right to sit on a curb and read a book. Unfortunately one *fen* got only two books, which were hardly enough. I decided to go to work pushing carts.

At about two *li* from the *Hunan Daily* compound was the Changsha North Railroad Station for freight trains. Nearly all the cargo was distributed to stores and units by carts pulled by men, and every day more than a thousand of these carts left the station to draw a web over the whole city. The pullers were salaried workers, but they often needed a pusher behind them, especially up the steep hill just beyond the station, and it was there that I hoped to pick up my book money.

The station was probably the filthiest place in the city, with mud, bricks, soot, and garbage everywhere. It was a haven for anyone out of work and hoping to pick up a penny. There were plenty of beggars, gamblers, crazy people, and other bad types, and also a lot of children, dirty and snot-nosed and in rags, speaking nothing but the filthy Changsha street language. These children clustered outside the high bamboo fence around the cargo area, waiting for a puller to come out so they could descend upon him begging for ten minutes of work.

The standard rate for pushing a cart up the hill was two *fen* (two Chinese cents), but I discovered a clever way to make quicker money. Whenever a puller came out, I shouted that I was willing to push for only one *fen*. In this way I rapidly took a lot of business for myself, and after only a few hours had nearly a whole *jiao* (ten Chinese cents). As I walked home at twilight, I was enormously pleased with myself. I had enough money to read almost twenty books, and I wore my aching back and legs and shoulders like badges of merit to take home to show my father. I decided that this was so profitable that I would go every day after school, and I would soon save up enough money to actually buy some books instead of forever reading on street corners.

The next day I couldn't walk without pain, but I forced my body back to the railroad station. However, no sooner had I arrived than I was encircled by a group of the street urchins I had priced out the day before. The biggest one seemed to be their leader, and he spoke to me roughly. "Where are you from, wild dog? You think you can steal our rice bowls?"

I didn't know what to say, and just mumbled something. Then the big one shoved me and someone else pushed me back again, and I was really afraid. "If you want money, I can give it to you. Just don't hit me," I begged, and to prove my words I emptied my pockets of their seven or eight *fen.*

But they didn't take my money, they just wanted to frighten me. Still, it was absolutely clear that if I tried to compete again they would beat me up. With that, my career as a cart pusher came to a precipitous end, and I had to turn to collecting empty toothpaste tubes for the recycling station to make my book money.

My new school was nearer to Liang Fang's No. 1 Middle School than my old one had been. This pleased me. I had always admired her more than Liang Wei-ping, because she was brilliantly intelligent whereas Liang Wei-ping was only average in school and seemed most competent in the house. Liang Fang's friends discussed important things; Liang Wei-ping's friends liked to gossip and idle their time away. So I would go and wait for Liang Fang at school like a faithful little dog, hoping to be included in some interesting conversation or to be allowed to tag along to some new place. However, my sister was at the age when boys and girls dislike being together, and a little brother's attention was a great burden and embarrassment to her. Furthermore, she was doing everything possible to join the Communist Youth League, the only route to glory, a good job, and public respect, and she was sensitive about any public contact with her Rightist family. She would make me wait outside the gate of the school, and then I had to follow behind her at a safe distance. I was too young to understand her feelings and went to meet her anyway, waiting patiently to be thrown scraps of love.

In this way I came to understand, more than Liang Wei-ping or my father, her suffering at not being allowed to join the League. She truly turned herself inside out to meet the requirements, and could answer Father's angry questions only with the unhappy excuse that the No. 1 Middle School had too many progressive students and the competition was too fierce.

I knew she kept her grades above ninety and often stayed after school because she had volunteered for some unpleasant task. She even went every Sunday with other students from "bad" backgrounds or who "sought to be progressive" to help workers collect feces from the out-houses and bring it to the docks to be shipped out to the countryside. Once I followed her on her rounds but was unable to control my nausea when I saw her wielding her huge ladle, scooping out wet masses of stench and white worms and pouring them into her cart. And she always came home depressed or weeping, all her efforts to no avail.

One day when she was out, I was leafing through her notebook and discovered page after page of Thought Reports to the Communist Youth League. She wrote about how she was collecting excrement in order to struggle against her Capitalist vanity and Capitalist fear of filth, hoping to cultivate a true proletarian humility and understanding of the glory of labor, remembering, when she felt she would vomit, the great proletarian hero Lei Feng and his sacrifices for the people. She confessed her weakness in going to see her Capitalist mother, and her determi-nation to overcome such tendencies, saying she hated herself for their past contact. She even said she wanted to renounce all family ties and let the Party be her true father and mother, because only then could she become a true Revolutionary and work for the glory of Socialism.

I felt sad when I read these things. I could understand why she hated our mother, since sometimes I felt that way too. But I wondered whether she hadn't gone too far. How could the Party be her parents? No matter what I felt during the day, I still dreamed at night of our lives when we were all together before the divorce. Could anything change that? I was afraid that I too might be led to cut off the last of my feelings to try to achieve an impossible goal; soon I too would be of age to join the League.

My teachers and father had always taught me about the importance of the Young Pioneers, the Communist Youth League, and the Party. I had joined the first only through guile, and that only after most of my classmates. And I knew about Liang Fang, how month after month and year after year, she had been turned down by the League at the No.1 Middle School. I resolved that I would never go through the same thing she had. There must be an easier way. Liang Wei-ping, at the No.13 Middle School across the street from the newspaper, only had to go wash public buses on Sundays.

So when I finally finished primary school, my chances for getting ahead were a major consideration in my selection of a middle school. According to the system in effect at that time, we were all to have an opportunity to go, but the assignment to the particular school was to be on the basis of our grades and our own requests. Although my grades were good enough to qualify me for the No.1 Middle School, I wanted one where there would be less political competition. The No.3 Middle School met this criterion, and it was also so near the Xiang River that I would be able to go swimming after school. So I completed the request forms and went cheerfully home to wait for the notification. But in fact it would be years before I would see the inside of another classroom.

CHAPTER FOUR

"Are You a Bloodsucker?"

By the time I graduated from primary school—in May of 1966 when I was just twelve—the Cultural Revolution was already approaching. The newspapers were full of criticism of the "Three-family Village," a group of writers whose works they called "poisonous weeds." After I had been at home only two weeks, I was summoned back to school for a meeting, just like a real grownup. This was the first time my classmates and I participated in what came to be known as "political study," an activity now as integral to urban Chinese life as lining up at the dining hall for a breakfast of rice gruel and *mantou*.

Our teacher read to us from the newspapers about how our class enemies were working from within to deliberately attack and smash the Party and Socialism. These "enemies" had derided the Great Leap Forward of the late fifties as "just a lot of boasting." They had slandered the dictatorship of the proletariat, and even told our great Party to "take a rest." Our teacher explained that workers, peasants, and soldiers must join together to fight against these insidious "black" intellectuals, and not be taken in by their devious and subtle methods. Even though we were still small, he said, we too had a part to play. We should begin by writing compositions denouncing our enemies. We should take out our notebooks and "open fire."

I didn't really know what to write, but I found several phrases that sounded right to me and set them down carefully:

> The Three-family Village is evil. They attack the Party and Socialism.
> Down with the Capitalist elements! Down with Wu Han! Down with
> Deng Tuo! Down with Liao Mo-sha!

I felt extremely busy and important, and after the meeting I hurried
home to tell my sisters everything. But they were just as excited as I
was, having been through the same things in their own schools. Liang
Fang put me in my place. "Everyone is denouncing those people. What
makes you think you're so special?"

On the next two days we learned songs and dances with simple
lyrics like "Down with the Three-family Village! Workers, peasants,
and soldiers unite! Angrily open fire on the Black Gang!" There was
also a pageant in which three students imitated the writers. One, bent
over and gnarled, pointed upward and said, "The sun is black," while
a second chortled evilly and agreed. "Not all flowers are red!" The rest
of us were workers, peasants, and soldiers, and wielded huge cardboard
pencils like bayonets, shouting, "Angrily open fire!"

Such activities were a lot of fun, and a welcome break from the
aimless life at home in the newspaper compound. I was sorry when our
meetings were over. In Changsha city, though, the wave of criticism
was still mounting, and we heard more and more about a "Great Proletarian Cultural Revolution" that was to expose the Reactionary Capitalist stand of the academic authorities who opposed the Party and
Socialism. It was all extremely confusing, so one rare evening when
Father was at home reading his newspaper under the hanging lightbulb,
I asked him what he thought.

He sighed pensively and began to reminisce, as he often did when
he wanted to teach me something. "You know, before Liberation I
suffered terribly. After your grandfather died, my mother couldn't feed
my brother and sisters and me, so she put us in an orphanage. The rest
had already died. Then after the orphanage was bombed by the Japanese,
I was lucky if I could get even one bowl of rice to eat every day.
Fortunately some relatives helped me go to a school, and while I was
there I joined the KMT's Youth League, thinking they had the way to
save China. Then in Kunming I met some Party members working
underground. They taught me about Revolution and gave me books to
read. I gradually understood how important Socialism was for our people,

and began to participate in Party activities. I wrote poems and articles for them, and eventually they trained me to become a reporter. I was lucky enough to help found the *Hunan Daily* when Changsha was liberated. Did you know I helped to edit the very first issue ever printed? We took over the old KMT *Central Daily* and called it the *New Hunan News*. And the calligraphy for our masthead was written by Chairman Mao himself. Those were exciting days!"

I had heard these things many times before, but I loved hearing them again. It was just like the old days when Father used to tell us stories. I sat very still hoping he would continue.

"The Party saved me, and I have always believed that the Party understands far more than we ordinary people ever can what is right for our country. My greatest dream is that someday I'll fulfill the conditions and be accepted as a Party member, for there could be no greater honor for a writer on this earth. But meeting the requirements is no easy matter. Sometimes we have to struggle with ourselves. The Anti-Rightist Movement was a terrible test for me, but I conquered myself and supported the Party. It makes me very sad to see that some people have Capitalist ideas and want to oppose the only system that can build China. They're not bad men, but we should help them see their errors. You should help them, too, and at the same time you can learn for yourself about how important it is always to support the Party. You can learn about principles of Revolution so you will never make political mistakes the way they have."

My father's words filled me with pride, because he was talking to me about his own thoughts almost like a grownup. I felt I understood better why he had been so strict with Liang Fang on the question of breaking with our mother, and why she had tried so hard to reform her thought and join the League. Now I knew why Father was always asking us to study the works of Chairman Mao and write self-examinations when we had done something wrong. Although I had heard many of the same words from my teachers, coming from him they had much more impact, and I was filled with a sense of great responsibility to the Party. I resolved that I would always try to make Father proud of me, and actively help the Party to fight against Capitalism.

But it seemed I was to have no chance because the criticism movement appeared to be over. Liang Fang told me it was because Work Teams had been sent to all the schools to supervise the Cultural Revolution, but instead of helping to carry out the movement, they were upholding the leaders' conservative views and holding back the eager students. They were even collecting information about the more radical students, and labeling them counterrevolutionaries and "small Rightists" because they had gone to present petitions at the Municipal and Provincial Party Committees. Liang Fang had been an activist, and was furious. "We thought the Work Teams would support us," she said. "But instead they organized student spies to gather 'black materials' about us, and they claim *we're* obstructing the Cultural Revolution! They call us 'monsters and demons' and want to 'sweep us away,' when they're the ones who are counterrevolutionary. Everything's backwards. Well, we'll see who's right. We'll see who's doing the obstructing!"

For a while it seemed that Liang Fang was wrong. The Work Teams had control. The situation was quiet the way hot water is when the fire is down low, merely simmering. But when, on July 16, 1966, Chairman Mao swam for an hour in the Yangtze River, it boiled.

I will always remember that event, partly because it was the first occasion on which the newspaper was printed in red ink. (Later, it happened often; in fact, the printing color became an issue of unusual Revolutionary sensitivity. Once, when black ink was used when it should have been red, there were demonstrations for days.) The issue was also distributed free of charge, so the lines of people waiting for their copies stretched way down the street.

The whole nation rejoiced because our beloved leader had battled the waves for so long at the age of more than seventy, turning his feat inevitably into a metaphor. "The current of the Yangtze is strong and there are many waves, but if a person is not afraid to struggle he will overcome all difficulties," he said. His swim celebrated his strength and the strength of his policies; it was another spur in the side of Revolution.

Great congratulatory festivities were held in every unit, and the streets shook with drums and firecrackers. Changsha looked just like it did on National Day, with red flags in a row over the gateway to every unit and special red lanterns glowing at night. I felt close to this great leader who had always been a little mysterious to me. I understood swimming. I knew what it was like to feel tired after being in the water for a long time. I was twelve years old and very strong, but I doubted that I could swim for as long as Chairman Mao had. At last I knew that

Chairman Mao was made of human flesh and blood, and at the same time I was moved with an even greater respect. I resolved once again to serve him with all my heart.

A little more than a week after the swim, Liang Fang came home flushed and ecstatic. "We've won," she announced. "The Work Teams are being withdrawn. The 'black materials' that they collected will be burned, the students' 'caps' will be taken off, and everybody will go home and write self-criticisms!"

Father arrived soon after, and he knew more; through the newspaper he often heard things before everyone else. He told us how while Chairman Mao had been away from Peking in recent months, the Central Committee had taken a Revisionist line, stifling the Cultural Revolution while pretending to support it. As soon as Chairman Mao returned to the capital after his swim in the Yangtze, he held a lot of meetings, and the Cultural Revolution Directorate ordered the withdrawal of the Work Teams. Suddenly Father lowered his voice, as if he couldn't quite believe his own words. "Even Chairman Liu was criticized, and will have to write a self-examination. It's amazing." He shook his head and paused. "You'd better not tell anyone, because it's still 'internal' information."

I felt a thrill of pride that my father knew so much, and was bursting with the desire to tell my friends. But my excitement was tempered by the fact that Father was obviously troubled by the news, as if he couldn't quite accept the idea that there was conflict within the Party. I realize now that his faith was being challenged for the first time.

The secret was out soon enough, for on August 5 Chairman Mao put up his famous BOMBARD THE HEADQUARTERS poster. He criticized leaders "from the Central down to the local levels," accusing them of "supressing Revolutionaries" and "juggling black and white." His major targets were obviously Liu Shao-qi, Chief of State and Vice-Chairman of the Communist Party; Deng Xiao-ping, General Secretary of the Central Committee Secretariat; and Tao Zhu, Secretary of the Central South Party Committee. Soon the whole city was transformed into a circus of posters. New Work Teams appeared at the *Hunan Daily*, and within a day posters went up on the modern Soviet-style office building. Unlike the general denunciations of the past, they were now pointed attacks against specific individuals. One of the first to go was Senior Assistant Editor Meng.

I read about him with amazement. First of all, the posters said, he had willfully obstructed the Cultural Revolution. Second, he had pretended great Revolutionary purity in order to hide his landlord background. Third, his personal life was immoral and suspicious, for when his wife died, he took her older sister as his second wife. The death had been far too convenient, and the posters demanded to know who was really responsible. I felt a thrill of fear. That familiar, pompous official who had given my father the *Chairman Mao's Selected Works* as a wedding gift was a secret criminal!

Another victim was a typesetter in his fifties, a man on good terms with my family who had invited Father to his home several times. He had been a cavalry officer for the KMT, and photographs of him on his horse in all his military splendor were taken from his file and prominently displayed on the office building wall. He had of course discussed his past with the Party before, and given them everything they asked for, including the pictures. I was fascinated to discover this grizzled neighbor transformed into a grand military officer with a gleaming sword, and wondered which of my other neighbors would prove to have extraordinary alter egos.

All this was an exciting process which none of us dared to question. It seemed that every day good people were exposed as evil ones lurking behind Revolutionary masks. Friendly people were hidden serpents, Revolutionaries became counterrevolutionaries, and officials who usually rode cars to meetings might actually be murderers. It was confusing because the changes came so fast, and we used to joke with each other saying, "They dug somebody else up today," meaning that, as the newspapers liked to put it, "The telescope of Chairman Mao Thought has been used to enlarge our enemies and reveal them in their original states." Still, most people felt that the Cultural Revolution was a wonderful thing, because when our enemies were uncovered China would be much more secure. So I felt excited and happy, and wished I could do something to help.

Then one morning when I was sitting at home with nothing special to do, Little Li walked in. He was the smartest of my playmates and my good friend, and I was pleased to see him. He sat down with his customary seriousness on the edge of the bed and said, "You know, everyone has been quoting Chairman Mao, saying, 'There is no wrong in Revolution; it is right to rebel.' We should do something too. There are a lot of Capitalist tendencies in our old primary school. Remember how Teacher Luo was always quoting the Russians? We should organize the other students and launch a Cultural Revolution there, too."

I thought this was a great idea. We would be following Chairman Mao just like the grownups, and Father would be proud of me. I suppose too I resented the teachers who had controlled and criticized me for so long, and I looked forward to a little revenge.

As it turned out, so did many of the other students, and they were delighted to be able to use Chairman Mao's stamp of approval to do what before they could only do under the cover of darkness with a slingshot and a window. Our unity was instantaneous, and we met at Little Li's apartment that evening. We had the place to ourselves because his mother lived at her own unit and his father was a proofreader who worked the night shift.

Little Li went to the newspaper to get some paper and ink and returned with his arms full.

"They support us!" he told us excitedly. "They say we can have all the supplies we need, and maybe later even an office!"

This was more than we had dared to dream of. We divided up the paper happily, one sheet for each person and a pile for me since I was to draw satirical cartoons. But then, faced with the vast open spaces before us, we suddenly discovered we didn't know what Capitalism and Revisionism really were. Little Li was the only one able to come up with anything, and he painted with a flourish ANGRILY OPEN FIRE ON THE *HUNAN DAILY*'S ATTACHED PRIMARY SCHOOL'S CAPITALIST REVISIONIST LINE!!! We all thought this was just fine, but it was obviously not enough, and we sat in worried silence until my friend Gang Di's older brother, Gang Xian, made a good suggestion. "Why don't we go out to the street and see what other people have written?"

That was the first time in my life I didn't go home to bed. We spent half the night wandering around writing down the words on the big character posters. The low gray buildings along Changsha's main streets were literally white with paper, shining in the dull yellow lamplight. The glass shop windows were unrecognizable, and posters even hung from between the parasol trees, rustling like ghosts in the night. Even at that hour people were rushing about shouting and putting up new posters, as if all the grievances that had been suppressed for so many years were coming out at once, shaking the city.

I suppose the workers felt somewhat the way we did, and were using the Cultural Revolution to get back at their superiors for everything from tiny insults to major abuses of policy. The posters on the Sun Yat-sen Road Department Store attacked the leaders for allowing the workers no freedom of discussion and willfully speaking for all. They accused the leaders of taking home government property and using influence to get scarce goods and special privileges. They denounced one leader for insulting women by touching their shoulders when he spoke to them, and another for wearing slippers to work and taking off his shirt in the office.

The leaders of the Grass Pavilion Street Residence Committee were attacked for sitting around in their offices reading newspapers and playing mah-jongg instead of resolving the people's problems, those at the car repair factory for caring more for dancing than administration and for delivering reports while dressed in their shorts. Leaders at the North District Party Committee were guilty of all of these abuses and more, including taking up the Revisionist ways of the departed Soviet experts by living in their abandoned guest houses. The lists of crimes went on and on, and it was clear to us that everything was fair game. It was hard to sort it all out, but by the time we returned to Little Li's house at 1 a.m., we knew what to write.

Gang Di denounced the music teacher for her high heels and coquettish voice. Little Monkey said Teacher Chen used a Capitalist teaching method by always telling us stories for ten minutes before class to calm us down. The son of a press photographer wrote about how the math teacher wore perfume in the summertime. Gang Xian had once been harshly punished for farting in class; he criticized the hygiene teacher for making us sit with our arms behind us and our hands on our elbows, a criticism that we all applauded heartily. But best of all was Little Li's criticism of Teacher Luo, in which his boasts of using advanced Soviet teaching methods were used as proof of his surrender to the USSR. I illustrated this with a picture of a man with a shiny bald head standing before a blackboard with a piece of chalk in one hand and a Soviet flag in the other.

I also drew Teacher Chen holding a baby with twenty heads in her arms, and the math teacher with a bottle of perfume held to her armpit and a swarm of flies buzzing around her head. ("Why does it stink?" the caption read. "It is the stink of Capitalism!") Everybody liked my cartoons very much, and we decided our work was so good that we should post it in a prominent place where everyone in the newspaper could see it.

It was near dawn when we went to put up our masterpieces on the old brick dining hall. As we scooped the messy paste out of our basin with our hands, we imagined how everyone would praise us as Revolutionary Pathbreakers. At last we put up a blank sheet and all of us signed our names. Then we separated. I went home with Little Li and didn't wake up until noon the next day.

My friend was very excited, for he had already been to the dining hall. Many grownups were crowded around our posters, praising us and saying we were very brave. I imagined the great respect we would now enjoy, so I hurried eagerly home to listen to Father's compliments.

He was there waiting for me, but he didn't look happy. "Well," he said sarcastically. "So the Revolutionary Pathbreaker is home. Did you break a path to anything to eat?"

His words stung me and I didn't answer, going to the table and picking up a cold *mantou* left over from breakfast.

"Put that down." He was very fierce. "Sit down, I want to talk to you."

Suddenly I wanted to rebel at home, too. I was tired of being controlled so tightly. Between home and school I felt I could barely move. I yelled, "It's right to rebel, it's right to rebel, it's right to rebel." I found myself stamping my feet and flailing my arms in rhythm.

"You should see how stupid you look," commented my father dryly.

"Cursing a Revolutionary Pathbreaker is what's stupid," I returned. I grabbed a piece of paper and my father's writing brush. "We'll see who needs posters," I said.

"Put down that brush," he commanded. "You never touch my brush, understand?"

I shrugged and picked up a pen and wrote in big characters, IT'S RIGHT TO REBEL! LIANG SHAN SAYS A REVOLUTIONARY PATHBREAKER IS STUPID. IF HE DOESN'T ADMIT HIS WRONGS, LIANG HENG WILL OPEN FIRE ON HIM!! I marched into his bedroom and stuck my poster on the foot of his bed with a thumbtack.

But Father was only amused. "If Chairman Mao knew, I wonder what he'd think of you?" he asked.

"Chairman Mao wants us to rebel," I answered immediately.

"Calm down now, why don't you. Sit down," he said gently. "Let's talk together."

Unfortunately, my experiences as a Rebel were only an evening long, so in the end I sat down, my self-righteous passion transformed into the apprehension of a small boy.

Father said, "Last night you did an unglorious thing. You thought you were really something, didn't you, with so many people looking at your cartoons? But why did you want to be so disrespectful to your teachers? Don't you understand how disgraceful your behavior is?"

It was unbearable to be lectured after I had expected so much glory. I answered bravely, "Doesn't Chairman Mao want us to criticize Capitalist thought? If teachers have Capitalist thought shouldn't they be criticized? Didn't you tell me yourself that we must obey the Party and carry out the Cultural Revolution?"

"Capitalist thought?" he exclaimed. "Do you think the things you drew pictures of were Capitalist thought? Your teachers were so good to you, giving you knowledge when you were still so small, training you, caring for you. And then not only don't you thank them, you insult and humiliate them. Of course it's right to heed Chairman Mao's call, but the purpose of this movement is to ferret out our enemies, not to attack our friends. Now I want you to take a book of quotations from Chairman Mao and study it carefully. Find out what he really wrote." Father went into his bedroom and study, where there were bookcases with several hundred volumes, and returned thumbing through a precious copy of the *Quotations of Chairman Mao*, the "Little Red Book" that as yet had been distributed only to high-ranking cadres and newspapermen. "Look here," he said. "Chairman Mao may have said, 'It's right to rebel,' but he also said, 'Among Revolutionary comrades, one should not use a rough manner.'"

I took the book and looked at the place Father had marked, and my heart hesitated because he was right. Chairman Mao *had* said those words. "Eat now," Father said, "and think about it. This afternoon you can study the *Quotations*, and when you have finished you can write a self-examination for me."

It was 2 p.m., and my father went to work. I was miserable. I knew I had been wrong. "Although the teachers have Capitalist tendencies," I wrote, "they are still Revolutionary comrades. We should help them, not insult them. I think I was wrong . . ."

When Father returned after five he held out his hand for my paper. I gave it to him and he read it carefully. "Good," he said finally. "But I think you need to do one more thing, because what you did was very wrong. You should go to your teachers' houses and apologize."

My heart sank. What would my classmates say? That I was a coward? A traitor? But Father stood there smoking, and his eyes bored through his glasses and deep into me as if they saw everything. I moved reluctantly through the door.

It must have taken me a full half hour to walk to the Attached Primary School, which was really just ten minutes from our house. I found new alleyways among the brick buildings and lingered at the basketball court, always imagining how angry the teachers must be, and wondering whether they would ignore me or yell at me. When I finally came to Teacher Luo's dormitory I was in such a state that I would have run home if a cat had darted out of the bushes.

Teacher Luo's wife was taking the laundry in from the balcony. "Liang Heng!" she cried, and it was too late to escape. Then she called inside. "Luo Qing-guang! Liang Heng is here!"

Teacher Luo came out immediately, and to my utter shock, he was smiling and nodding as if he hadn't seen me for a long time. "Liang Heng! Come right upstairs and have some tea. We'll have a talk."

When I was uncomfortably seated with a dish of candy before me and a cup of tea at my elbow, Teacher Luo said, "Your father came to see me this afternoon." He continued gently, "It doesn't matter, it all belongs to the past."

I said, "Teacher Luo, please pardon me. I'm very sorry."

He said, "Forget about it. If you ever have any question about your schoolwork, you're always welcome here."

A very special feeling choked me, and I got up in confusion and nodded and ran out the door so he wouldn't see me crying, nearly knocking over the dish of candy as I went. How could he be so kind to me after what I had done to him? Didn't he remember that I had painted him with the Soviet flag in his hand?

Father had been to see all the other teachers, too, and they all treated me kindly and accepted my apologies. But as I walked home, I was in a panic for fear one of my classmates would see me and ask where I'd been. I would never tell them what I had done. From then on I would choose my methods more carefully, so that I would never again be placed in such an ignoble position.

Of course, I had no intention of giving up rebellion, not when the whole country was involved in the Cultural Revolution. The next step was to give our Rebel group a more formal status. Little Li organized us, about thirty young teenage boys from the newspaper, and after much discussion we chose the name Criticize Revisionism Struggle Team. I did not speak so loudly as before my apology to the teachers, but I certainly was an active member. We announced ourselves on red paper one sunny afternoon, all thirty of our names painted in black ink. The *Hunan Daily* Cultural Revolution Committee gave us an unbelievably big two-room office, a printing press and paper, blankets, and a red flag. No one could have been prouder than Little Li and I as we surveyed our new domain.

But the next morning, as Little Li, Gang Di, Gang Xian, and I were writing our blackboard newspaper, the photographer's son ran up gasping, "Something terrible, something terrible. They don't want to be in our organization anymore."

Little Li's eyebrows were as straight as a sword across his square face as he demanded, "Who doesn't want to be in our organization?"

"All of them. They've taken their names away."

We ran over to the dining hall and were dumbfounded. Twenty-three names had been inked out, and our red poster now looked like a slice of watermelon full of black pits. The seven remaining names were all those of the sons of intellectuals: editors, reporters, the photographer, and the art editor.

We stood looking at each other. Finally Little Li spoke what was in our minds. "Well, we'll keep going anyway. We'll protect Chairman Mao's struggle to the death." His words were the same as those we heard on broadcasts, but braver and more inspiring. We nodded our heads resolutely.

But before we'd recovered from our shock, something even worse happened. One of our ex-comrades walked by and sneered at us and then spat on the cement at our feet. "You sons of Reactionary Capitalist stinking intellectuals. Run and look at your fathers' big character posters. Then hurry home and criticize *them*, why don't you."

I was simply unable to comprehend his words. My father wasn't a powerful official, had never accepted bribes or used public furniture, had never used power to criticize a worker unfairly. He was just a low-ranking cadre working for a Party newspaper, and no one in the whole world loved Chairman Mao better than he. How could there be posters about him? How could anyone say he had Capitalist thought?

As in a dream, we hurried to the office building. There had been a lot of new activity. Now the posters stretched all the way up to the fourth floor, and ropes hung with still more had been strung from one wing of the L to the other. To get through, you had to push posters aside like hanging curtains. We began the painful search for our fathers' names. What would have been a game the day before was now a nightmare.

We found Little Li's father first. PUBLICLY EXPOSE THE KMT SPY LI XIAO-XIONG!!! the poster cried.

Although Li Xiao-xiong is an old Party member, he wears his Party cloth to disguise his true mission. Before Liberation, he was an active reporter for the KMT's *Central Daily*, and he volunteered to stay behind as a spy when we routed Chiang Kai-shek's dogs and they fled to Taiwan. Every day he gathers information for them, and works against us from within. As a proofreader, he has had many opportunities to show his hatred of the Party, as on the occasion when he deliberately turned the character "ten thousand" upside down. But our Great Leader Chairman Mao will live ten thousand and ten thousand years despite such pernicious spies. Down with Li Xiao-xiong!!!!!

I couldn't believe it. Little Li had told me so many times about his father's glorious career as an underground Party member before Liberation. At times I had even been envious, wishing I could be as proud of my own father. This was like seeing him in a distorting mirror. Could Little Li have been lying to me? I turned to look at my friend. He was staring like a statue and biting his lower lip, while two tears rolled down his motionless face.

Then Gang Di pulled me by the sleeve. He had found my father's posters. I followed him numbly through the gaily painted paper, still believing there had been a mistake. But then I saw the terrible words, burning characters on brilliant yellow paper. EXPOSE THE PLOT OF THE REACTIONARY SCHOLAR LIANG SHAN TO THE LIGHT OF DAY!!!!!

There were too many sheets, maybe ten or more, each as tall as a man. And every word engraved itself on my heart with a blazing knife, every phrase struck me with a blow that was even greater than terror. I would never believe the ground was steady again.

Liang Shan is a thoroughly Capitalist newsman, our newspaper's Three-family Village. He has used the knowledge given to him by the Party to attack the Party, writing many Reactionary articles. In one of them, an essay about the growth of a sunflower, he dared to fart that the flower relies on its own lust for life. How evil, how poisonous! The Three-family Village said the sun had dark shadows, meaning the Party has made errors. But Liang Shan says the sunflower doesn't need the sun at all! His insidious idea is that China can be strong without the Communist Party. Isn't this singing the same tune as Capitalist KMT Reactionary Revisionism? Liang Shan is worse than Capitalism, fiercer than the KMT, more dangerous than Revisionism. Down with Liang Shan!!!!!

The poster went on to a second topic, STRIP AWAY LIANG SHAN'S SKIN!!!!!

That Liang Shan opposes the Party and Socialism is only natural. Let's investigate his history. His father was a doctor who came from Zhejiang to Hunan through tricking his "private patients" out of their money. So Liang Shan learned this skill from his family. When he was young, he eagerly entered the KMT's Youth League. His ex-wife is a Rightist, and she certainly became a Rightist under his influence. Then he saw by what happened to her that it won't do to oppose the Party openly, and he used articles and poetry to try to undermine it secretly. So his injury to the Revolution is even greater than his wife's. Chairman Mao teaches us, "Sham is sham, and the mask must be stripped off." Now the Great Proletarian Cultural Revolution is stripping off Liang Shan's skin to reveal his true appearance!!!!!

The third section went:

LIANG SHAN IS A BLOODSUCKER!!!!!
Liang Shan has not only failed to make a contribution to the Revolution, but has stolen a lot away. Although in the past he gave up a level of his salary, that was his pretense of progressiveness. In fact, he earned a lot of extra money for his articles. Every penny he earned was the

blood of the people. He used the blood he sucked away to fatten himself up, and what did he give the people? Not artwork, but shit, garbage, poisonous weeds!!!!!

The fourth section:

WHAT DID LIANG SHAN ACTUALLY DO?

For many years Liang Shan edited a magazine called *Correspondent* for our young newspapermen, and his sole purpose was to propagandize the Capitalist news viewpoint and to instruct our young reporters in Western news techniques. He said news should be "true," and to him this meant it should attack the Party's faults, and even slander our Party. He said, "A reporter should have power, and when he needs information he should use his courage and ingenuity to get it by any means possible." Isn't his meaning clear? He wants intellectuals to lead the country! Moreover, he used the magazine to gild Western writers. In all those years, he used only one quotation from Chairman Mao, but hundreds from Tolstoy, Balzac, Shakespeare, Mark Twain. . . . Liang Shan! Your eyes are blind. Go for a walk on Wall Street, why don't you? Here, you will bump into things until your head is bloody. Are you Chinese or a foreigner's dog? You have given our young reporters too many poisonous ideas. We now order Liang Shan to confess his crimes, or else we will break his dog's head!!!!!

There was more, but the words wouldn't stay still. I was trembling all over. The bright paper posters floating about me had become walls of iron, the unknown sandaled feet glimpsed beyond them those of enemies. Everything was backwards, distorted, corrupted, insane. I didn't know if I was dreaming or if my life at home was a dream. I hugged myself, pinching my arms, but I didn't wake up. I closed my eyes and opened them but the words were still there. My Revolutionary father was an enemy. My father whose dream it was to join the Party was a Capitalist. How had things been ruined? Why had he ruined things? I didn't know where to put my misery and my hatred. I would never trust my perception of reality again.

Then I discovered the press photographer's son standing a few feet away from me crying softly. Dazed, we turned back toward our headquarters, equally silent, equally miserable, equally afraid to see anyone, equally afraid to go home. Little Li and the Gang brothers were already there, ashen and waiting. It was almost as if an instinct bred in us through our short careers in Chairman Mao Thought told us to return to our Revolutionary base, to turn automatically toward the Revolution for security when our homes fell away beneath us. We had no words for each other, but we felt tremendously close. And we knew that even though our fathers were now Capitalists and spies, we must go on rebelling. What we did not yet understand was that from that day forth we had lost the right to express our love and our loyalty; Revolutionary fervor would no longer be permitted to us. But we did have some kind of premonition that our office would be taken away.

Sure enough, near dinnertime a worker in glasses named Zhou Sa-wu arrived with about ten of our classmates at his heels. He didn't have much to say. "This is no place for you, stinking intellectuals' sons. Get out."

Then the other children grabbed our writing materials and pushed us out. Someone kicked me hard in the back of the leg. The door slammed sharply behind us.

We stood for a long time in the courtyard hugging trees and looking up at our old headquarters. At last we began to cry.

When the signal for dinner sounded, there was nothing to do but walk slowly home. We set off in our various directions, hating ourselves and the world, envying our Revolutionary classmates, afraid of the knowledge that something terrible had begun, not yet comprehending its magnitude. I barely registered the loudspeaker's announcement that there would be an important radio broadcast that evening, and I passed the basketball court without really seeing the people preparing drums, flags, blank red posters, and fresh white paint for the parade. I was no longer part of that world. I had been kicked off the team. I was an outcast.

Someone had taken the lock off our door, but it was shut tight. Our home presented a peculiar, sad, unfriendly appearance, which only deepened my misery. I pushed my way in and discovered Father sitting in a dense cloud of cigarette smoke, which he was concentrating on making thicker, the butts lying on the wooden floor like wreckage after some disaster. He barely moved when I came in. It hurt me to look at him, so I headed toward the drawer where the meal tickets were kept. My hand shook on the handle.

Then it was as if something swept over me, and I found myself swinging around, screaming out the question in my heart. "Father, is it true that you're a bloodsucker?" Suspicion, love, anger, sympathy, and hatred struggled against one another. I felt as if I would explode.

Father was silent, signaling that he had heard me only by crushing out his cigarette and lighting a new one. I stared at the stub on the floor, long, white, and barely smoked.

"Tell me," I demanded. "Tell me, you should tell me. I have to know."

He remained silent, not meeting my eyes.

I wanted to shake him. "Why won't you say anything?"

He finally spoke, in what was close to a whisper. "You should always believe the Party and Chairman Mao."

He hadn't answered my question, and I stood staring and waiting.

He made another effort. "The Cultural Revolution is a mass movement. The people who criticized me have deep proletarian feelings and a great love for Chairman Mao." I could hardly believe my ears. It was all true, then. Father continued, "I've made a lot of mistakes. I should examine myself thoroughly. But as long as I'm faithful to the Party and Chairman Mao, it won't be long before I mend my errors."

I was scarcely listening. I could only repeat his crimes numbly, as if reciting a lesson. "Is it true you said China can be strong without the Party? Is it true you used articles and poems to undermine it secretly? What about how you tried to teach Capitalist news reporting? How do you explain those things?"

My father's hand trembled as he struck another match. Then in the silence we heard a great clattering on the stairs, and Liang Fang and Liang Wei-ping burst into the room. They were both crying, and they ran directly to their bed and threw themselves onto it, hugging the pillows. Their sobs were terrible in the silence.

Soon Liang Fang started accusing Father. "I'm so miserable being born into a family like this. First I had a mother who prevented me from joining the League. Now that I'm finally accepted as a Revolutionary, you have to ruin everything. Look," she cried, taking out a piece of paper. "Tonight I was supposed to be a marshal at the parades. This was the plan for the march. Do you think I can possibly face anyone now?" With a wail, she ripped her map into little pieces.

Father sat by the table with his head in his hands, passively accepting Liang Fang's fury as if he deserved it. He reached automatically for his pack of cigarettes, but it was empty. Liang Wei-ping, always the gentlest of us, nudged Liang Fang as if asking her to control herself and went into the other room and got another pack. As she handed it to Father I asked him, "Do you know what they called us today? 'Sons of Capitalist Reactionary stinking intellectuals.' They've cut us out of all their activities, kicked us out of the office. They won't let us do anything anymore."

Father raised his head and repeated, "You should believe the Party. Believe Chairman Mao." His words sounded like a prayer, a principle kept in his heart to invoke in times of trouble. They had been the key to his spirit for the past twenty years.

But Liang Fang raged. "Others don't believe *you!* They say you're a Capitalist, a bloodsucker, a foreigner's dog!"

Then my father stood up, his face white, his words tumbling out in one breath. "It's because I'm none of those things that I believe the Party and Chairman Mao. I've done nothing to wrong you. You can continue to participate in the Revolution. If you want to, you can break off with me. Go live at school if you like. But I'll tell you one thing. No matter how you hate me, I've always been loyal to Chairman Mao. And I've always supported the Party and Socialism."

"If I have to go, I'll go!" she shouted, grabbing at her bedding and clothing. "I don't want this counterrevolutionary family. I don't need this counterrevolutionary father and mother!"

Liang Wei-ping followed her older sister's lead. "I'm going too," she said with resignation. "Maybe it's better that way." She stood up and started gathering her things.

Father's eyes were red. "Go, go, all of you go. I won't blame you. I don't want to hold you back."

I don't know how the evening would have ended if the loudspeaker hadn't sounded outside our window. "The Red radio waves have happy news. Everyone please tune in and listen carefully. Everyone please tune in."

From force of habit cultivated only over the last few months, we rushed to the tiny transistor on the table. We arranged ourselves around it and laid our heads down so we could concentrate. Crackling from the radio came, "The August 8th Decision of the Central Committee of the Chinese Communist Party Concerning the Great Proletarian Cultural Revolution."

It seemed that one of the purposes of the statement was to clarify the targets of the Cultural Revolution. And as we listened the heavy stone that we bore on our backs became lighter and lighter, especially when we heard the Fifth Article.

> Who are our enemies and who are our friends? . . . The main target of the present movement is those within the Party who are in authority and are taking the Capitalist road. The strictest care should be taken to distinguish between the anti-Party, anti-Socialist Rightists and those who support the Party and Socialism but have said or done something wrong or have written bad articles or other works. . . .

When all "Sixteen Articles" were finished, there were tears of joy in Father's eyes and he said triumphantly, "See, your father is no counterrevolutionary. I'm the third type of cadre, someone who has made serious mistakes but is not an anti-Party anti-Socialist Rightist."

My sisters smiled and looked embarrassed at having been so upset; I felt ashamed that I had thought so harshly of Father. We began to discuss the posters calmly and decided that since he had already talked with the Party about his membership in the KMT Youth League and about our mother, those problems wouldn't be regarded as serious crimes. His failure to quote Chairman Mao frequently in his writings would be considered a matter for education. The foul language and abuse in the posters merely showed the passion of the people and were not to be taken seriously.

Just as we were enjoying our renewed intimacy, we heard a blast of firecrackers and drums like an earthquake under our feet. Liang Fang jumped up as if she had forgotten something. "The parade!" she cried. "Oh Father, I *do* want to go live at school, but that's just for convenience in the Revolution, not because I want to move away from home."

So Father helped her to pack her bag, and tucked some cakes and sugar in the side to show he had forgiven her. She left in a great hurry because she was late, and we stood on the balcony and watched her go. From then on, she was always off making Revolution somewhere, and never really lived at home again.

Liang Wei-ping went into the kitchen to cook noodles because we had been so upset we had missed going to the dining hall. I sat and talked with Father. I was still in shock because of what had happened to me that afternoon.

Father comforted me. "Don't be discouraged. Even if you don't participate in their group, your thought can follow the Cultural Revolution and you can still learn from it. Every day you can read the newspapers, and you and I will have our own study class, and make a plan for reading the whole of Chairman Mao's works. We'll sit together in the evenings and discuss them." I felt a lot better, because I loved reading with my father. Still, nothing could make up for being excluded by my classmates.

After dinner, Father suddenly said, as if just struck by the idea, "Maybe we should look through our things and see if we have anything that's not so good. If we get rid of it now, it might save us a lot of trouble later on. Remember how when China and Russia broke relations I had to get rid of all my books about the Soviet Union?"

So we went into the large inner room and looked through his books. He selected only a few, pulling them out with regret; they included Liu Shao-qi's famous *Discussion on the Training of a Communist Party Member*. I knew the earnest way my father always read everything, underlining and annotating; every book represented hours of labor and thought. We went through the magazines, too, where I came on a picture of Liu Shao-qi standing with Chairman Mao. "What about this one?" I asked. "Should we throw away the part with Chairman Liu on it?"

"Oh no, better not do that. We'd better turn it in to the Work Team," my father answered. (At the time, I thought he was being overcautious, but as it turned out, his political experience saved us from disaster. Our downstairs neighbors cut Liu Shao-qi out of the picture, and they were denounced for deliberately ruining a photograph of Chairman Mao. This kind of thing happened so often that eventually a rule was established that whenever someone wanted to replace an old picture of Chairman Mao with a new one, he had to notify the leaders of his unit and get their permission.)

The books and pictures made a small pile on the table, and

with them as reminders of his crimes, Father sat down with his brush and ink to criticize himself. When I woke up in the middle of the night to go to the bathroom he was still writing, his normally well-groomed hair in disorder, concentrating so hard that he didn't even hear me get up.

CHAPTER FIVE

The Smashed Temples

I noticed the prettiness of the morning as the gentle strains of "The East Is Red" sounded through the loudspeaker at dawn the next day. The early light had soothed away the unhappiness of the day before, and Liang Wei-ping was singing as she got dressed. Father also seemed much calmer when he returned from the dining hall with our rice gruel and *mantou*; he had run into a fellow reporter who was similarly optimistic after hearing the broadcast. He left for work carrying the pile of books and his thick self-criticism, and Liang Wei-ping went off for meetings at her school. In fact Father would never receive a shred of the protection spoken of in the "Sixteen Articles," any more than any of the other intellectuals would. But for a few hours ignorance was bliss, and I settled down happily with my father's copy of the *Quotations*, ready once again to enter the ranks of the Revolution.

At about 9 a.m., two men in huge straw hats came to the house. They smiled in a very friendly way and asked if this was the Liang family home, so I invited them to come in and sit down. The older one, a short man without much hair, made the introductions. He called me "Little Liang" as an older adult to a younger one, and not "child" the way most people still did, so I felt very proud. "My name is Jiang and I'm from the Rural Department of the Provincial Party Committee. This is Comrade Du from the Forestry Bureau. We've been sent 'from the five lakes and four seas for a common Revolutionary purpose': We're on the Party's Work Team."

I recognized the quotation from Chairman Mao and smiled and

nodded as I poured water for their tea. Du had picked up my notebook from the table and was leafing quickly through it. "I see you've been studying your Chairman Mao. You're quite a fine young fellow, aren't you? Your notes are wonderful."

I knew he hadn't looked at them carefully, so I suddenly felt suspicious, but his next words warmed me up again.

"Do you know what Chairman Mao calls people of your age? He calls you the morning sunlight." He pointed to the ray of light illuminating my father's brush and ink. "Just like that. The hope of the Revolution. You have a bright future as a Revolutionary Pathbreaker. Your cartoons aren't so bad either, eh?"

His words gave me great comfort, as if he were restoring the power of the Revolution to me after all. They were treating me so differently than the worker Zhou Sa-wu had the day before. Maybe they knew about how we'd been kicked out of our group and had criticized Zhou and my classmates. Now they had come to tell me I could join again. I felt wonderful, like a soldier waiting for his assignment.

Jiang spoke this time, fanning himself with his hat, his voice soft. "Little Liang, it takes great courage to rebel. You need to take concrete action according to the practical situation." He looked at me intently to see if I had understood his meaning, but I felt confused and shifted uneasily in my seat.

Du said, "Let's get everything out in the open. Little Liang, what do you think of the posters about your father?"

His question was too abrupt, and it caught me off guard. I didn't know how to answer. Instinctively, I found Father's own words. "We should believe the Party and believe Chairman Mao."

My guests broke into smiles, and Du patted me on the shoulder. "Right, right. And in specific terms you should believe us, because Chairman Mao sent us here as a Work Team. If you have anything to say, you can tell us freely, and if Chairman Mao wants to communicate something to the people, he can do it through us. So you should trust us, we should work together."

Jiang took over. "The most important thing you can do now is help your father. Help him recognize his faults. Be courageous, criticize him so he can change himself."

I was stunned. I hadn't realized that returning to the Revolutionary ranks would mean this! I said, "I wouldn't know how."

"First go look at the posters again to get an idea of what to say. Then you can write your material and bring it to us in the office this afternoon when you're finished. We'll be waiting for you."

"But I don't know how to write anything like that," I protested feebly.

Jiang thought for a moment, and then smiled. "Just call it 'Expose and Criticize My Father Liang Shan.' That will be a good title. You're a fine young man, really devoted to Chairman Mao. We're proud of you."

They stood up, putting on their big hats. "We'll go then, we're very busy. See you this afternoon." They shook my hand warmly and disappeared out the door.

I felt very sad. How could I criticize my father when I knew how loyal he was? I knew without having to think about it that I could never write anything. Suddenly I had lost all interest in the Revolution, and when Father came home at noon, I didn't tell him about the Work Team's visit. I figured that maybe because I was only twelve they would just forget about me and let the matter drop. I envied my sisters for being away at school and avoiding the whole problem.

But things were not so easy as I had hoped. At noon the next day the loudspeaker announced that at 2 p.m. all members of families of people employed at the newspaper were to meet in the auditorium with the Work Team. One person was to remain on duty for every seven or eight buildings; everyone else was to show up without exception.

Nearly everyone who could be classified as a "family member" was retired or a schoolchild. That hot afternoon the old ladies appeared with their canes and little bamboo stools, babies strapped to their backs; old gentlemen with no teeth limped slowly under the shade of black umbrellas; young boys and girls hurried through the poster maze and clattered up the stairs to the auditorium, holding, if they were lucky, copies of the *Quotations of Chairman Mao* in their sweaty little hands. Those who never had reason to leave their own courtyards had to pass through the debris of political struggle, and even those who couldn't read were forced to confront a *Hunan Daily* transformed.

The auditorium was on the top floor of the office building, a rather elegant modern room reserved for meetings in which none of us had ever been important enough to participate. Now we squeezed into the seats and spilled into the aisles, fanning ourselves uselessly against the August heat.

A short fat man carrying a black fan came to the podium and almost lost his audience when he ordered the ceiling fans turned on; everyone instantly stared upward in awe and admiration. "Keep order, keep order. Pay attention," he cried, and gradually managed to attract attention. "We need to be as well trained as the People's Liberation Army. To participate in this meeting everyone must have a deep proletarian feeling for Chairman Mao and the Party. There is to be no talking, moving around, or leaving early. If children cry, they may be taken from the meeting room but they must be brought back again as soon as they are quiet. There is to be no reading or embroidery. Those of you with education must take notes. Now this meeting has two main subjects. First, we will study the 'Sixteen Articles.' Then we will talk about what contribution you can make to the Cultural Revolution."

Someone else came up and read the document from beginning to end, as we had heard it over the radio. A baby cried and was removed. Children normally mischievous sat silent, and only the electric hum of the fans accompanied the drone of the man at the podium. This was the first such meeting we had ever attended, and we weren't quite sure what to make of it.

Then the short fat man came back and spoke. "The Great Proletarian Cultural Revolution has made a good start in our unit, but for it to be the mass movement it should be, everyone must participate, and family members mustn't lag behind. We must launch a great Revolutionary competition to see who can have the deepest feeling for Chairman Mao, who can have the greatest political awareness, who can be most active in the movement, who can hold the firmest political position.

"You must be clear about certain questions. If someone in your family is criticized, this is a good thing, because those comrades are being saved from falling into the quicksand of Capitalism. Unfortunately, some people don't fully understand the Cultural Revolution, so they don't welcome such criticism. While this is understandable, it is wrong. The thought of such people has not kept pace with recent events. So today we must mobilize each other to enter the ranks of the Revolution.

"Our Work Teams have already spoken with certain family members, and many have written materials and deserve great praise. But others have dragged their feet. Today we give them another chance. For now, we won't shame them publicly by mentioning their names. But if they don't join us soon, we will have no other choice but to criticize them openly for obstructing the Great Proletarian Cultural Revolution."

He paused and scanned the room as if seeking out the laggards. I sank into my chair and tried to look inconspicuous. "All right," he said finally. "This part of the meeting is over. The Work Team asks all family members to go out and read the big character posters. The students should read them aloud to the old people who can't read, so everyone will know their meaning. Next time you'll come to look at them on your own, to further your own Revolutionary educations. That's all."

It was too hot, and there were too many posters. I avoided the section where Father's were hung. A lot of babies were crying, and when the old ladies got tired they sat down on their little hand stools and fanned themselves. The crowd was a lively one, not yet soured, but I felt exhausted. At last Work Team members told us over their megaphones that we could go home.

Father returned for dinner. He had been reading big character posters and writing self-criticisms all day. He took his bowl of rice, fatty pork, and sweet potato noodles and brought it to his lips with a sigh. I had already devoured most of my food when Liang Wei-ping announced, "Well, it looks like we'll be putting up our own big character posters now."

Father lowered his bowl. "What do you mean?"

"The Work Team wants Liang Heng to write posters about you."

"No, no," I interrupted. "Not posters, they just want me to turn in some materials."

"What's this all about?" Father demanded.

"I don't want to talk about it," I said.

Father smiled bitterly. "You don't trust me, do you? You think I'll try to keep you from writing anything."

Actually, it was I who didn't want to write anything. I told him about the visit and the meeting, and how the Work Team had threatened to criticize anyone who didn't cooperate.

"How can you be so foolish?" Father asked in alarm. "Write something quickly. Turn something in right away."

I didn't understand his meaning but Liang Wei-ping was quicker than I. "Yes, you have to write something or they'll think Father wouldn't let you and things will be even worse for him."

"I don't know what to write," I protested.

"Just write that you don't know, then. But you have to hand in something." Liang Wei-ping had taken the bowls into the kitchen and her voice was shrill over the sound of running water. Then she came out and picked up her schoolbag. "I have to go back to school for another meeting," she said. "You'd better write something."

I sat at the table staring out the window at the sunset. Criticizing my father wouldn't be easy the way criticizing my teachers had been. I lived with him and knew his thoughts. I felt a hand on my shoulder and Father sighed. "There are too many things in this world that are hard to make sense out of."

"What?" I looked up.

He retracted his words hastily. "Nothing, nothing. I was thinking about the sunset." He took some mosquito incense out of a drawer for me and lit it, and then disappeared into the next room to write his nightly self-criticism. I traced out the words "Expose and Criticize My Father Liang Shan," then stared at the tidy black characters and felt myself close to tears. But by the end of the evening I had managed to fill the page, drawing on the family's discussion the night we listened to the "Sixteen Articles" on the radio together. I went to bed miserable.

Early the next morning I took my material to the Work Team. Du was at the desk and looked at me ironically. All the warmth of our earlier meeting was gone. He held out his hand for the paper. "So you had to bow to the situation, didn't you? Next time judge it earlier and more accurately and you'll save yourself a lot of trouble."

That was my first lesson in self-protection in modern society.

While the criticism movement was getting started, college and middle-school students were forming the first Red Guard units. They were relatively conservative, protecting most of the Party leaders if only because those leaders were also the Red Guards' fathers and mothers. Fiercely proud of their "good" backgrounds—so much so that they would allow only students descended from the "Five Red Types" (Revolutionary cadres, Revolutionary martyrs, Revolutionary soldiers, workers, and poor and lower-middle peasants) to join them—these first Red Guards focused their attack on the so-called Five Black Types: landlords, rich peasants, counterrevolutionaries, "bad elements," and Rightists. Their slogan was, "If the father is a hero, the son is a brave man; if the father is a reactionary, the son is a bastard," thus settling the question of class standing for all eternity. The irony of the situation was that these sons and daughters of high-ranking cadres were creating a movement that would soon double back to attack their parents; they themselves would become the victims of their own Revolutionary fervor.

In Changsha, the initial group was called the "Red Defense Guards," and by an incredible fluke Liang Fang managed to become a member. Because there were so many cadres' children at the No. 1 Middle School, that school was among the first to become organized, and because Liang Fang took part in the organizing work, the issue of her Rightist parent was temporarily overlooked. She had finally achieved her long-coveted Revolutionary glory. She must have renounced our mother with extraordinary enthusiasm in order to pass muster.

Liang Fang rarely came home, of course. We got most of our news of her through Liang Wei-ping, who moved about a good deal and saw her through school activities. One day Liang Wei-ping returned in a state of great excitement. Liang Fang had told her that the Party Secretary of the No. 1 Middle School had denounced himself for betraying the Communists to the KMT before Liberation, and then had hanged himself in the cellar where he was being kept a prisoner. A real class enemy exposed! The other news was that a lot of students were preparing to go to Peking to report to Mao's wife, Jiang Qing, and the other members of the Cultural Revolution Directorate. There was an off-chance that they might be able to see Chairman Mao himself.

The August 18 *Hunan Daily* was a red-ink issue. It told of thousands of Red Guards gathering in Tian An Men Square, and Chairman Mao making an appearance and allowing a student to pin the Red Guard armband on his sleeve. Great numbers of middle-school and college students had been permitted to mount the tower and shake hands with him, and it was plain that a broad new movement had been launched.

We felt the first echoes in Changsha soon after. The representatives of the first Peking Red Guard group, the "United Action Committee," arrived from the capital bringing with them a first taste of the violence that would spread throughout China. They were staying at the luxurious government hotel near the Martyrs' Park when they got into a fight with one of the hotel workers, a boy whose grandfather had been a landlord before Liberation. I don't know the details of the argument but they nearly beat him to death with their wide leather belts.

What amazed me was the reaction of the Party Committees to this episode. There was a glass propaganda case by the front gate of the newspaper, which usually held exhibits on factory production, "little friends" dancing in nursery school, or instructive displays on the life of the model soldier Lei Feng. Now appeared photographs of the violence, hailed as "Revolutionary heroism." Changsha wasn't the first practice ground for this new breed of terrorism, of course, but the incident was the first most of us had heard of. Later, such events would become all too familiar.

After their visit, the local movement spread beyond the "Red Defense Guards," although membership was still restricted to the "Five Red Types." The groups usually chose their names from some poem or quotation from Chairman Mao, so we had the "Jinggang Mountain" group, the "East Is Red" group, the "Chase the Exhausted Enemy" group, the "Struggle with the Waves in the Middle of the Current" group, and many more. We got used to seeing the Red Guard costume— People's Liberation Army green pants and jacket, a wide leather belt, and the prized bright red armband. Liang Wei-ping wanted to join, but because of our mother she was told she could only work at school, which had been converted into a Red Guard hospitality station, a kind of inn for Red Guards from other provinces. She was crushed, but glad to be allowed to help at all. They kept her very busy boiling water and pushing desks around to make beds for all the guests.

The "Sixteen Articles" had stressed the need to criticize the "Four Olds"—old thought, old customs, old culture, and old morals—and this was the thrust of the Red Guards' first campaign. The immediate and most visible result was that the names of everything familiar changed overnight. Suddenly "Heaven and Heart Park" became "People's Park." "Cai E Road," named for a hero of the Revolution of 1911, became "Red Guard Road." The Northern Station where I had pushed carts for a day was now to be found on "Combat Revisionism Street," and a shop named after its pre-Liberation Capitalist proprietor became "The East Is Red Food Store." Changsha quickly acquired a "Red Guard Theater," a "Shaoshan Road," a "People's Road," and an "Oppose Imperialism Road."

All this was extremely confusing, especially for the old people, and everybody was always getting off at the wrong bus stop and getting lost. To make matters even worse, the ticket-sellers on the buses were too busy giving instructive readings from the *Quotations of Chairman Mao* between stops to have much time to help straighten out the mess. Of course, there were some people who never did get used to it, and to this day they live on the ghosts of streets whose names today's young people have never heard of. (Ten years later an old man asked me where Education Road was, but I had no idea there was such a street. Then he asked a nearby policeman, but he didn't know either. More and more people got involved, forming a circle around him and telling him that he was mistaken, that there was no such street. Finally he protested, "How could I be wrong? Changsha already had that street by the thirty-seventh year of the Republic of China!" Everybody burst out laughing; he was using the obsolete pre-Liberation system of counting years dating from the 1911 Revolution.)

People changed their own names, too. One of my classmates rejected his old name, Wen Jian-ping ("Wen Establish Peace"), in favor of Wen Zao-fan ("Wen Rebel"). My neighbor Li Lin ("Li Forest") called herself Li Zi-hong ("Li Red from Birth") to advertise her good background. Zao Cai-fa ("Zao Make Money") became Zao Wei-dong ("Zao Protect the East"). Another friend got rid of the "Chiang" in his name because it was the same as Chiang Kai-shek's.

So, there was a lot of excitement in the city, but at home it was very quiet. Father spent every evening at his writing, and Liang Wei-ping and I never felt much like talking. We were sitting silently like this, reading and writing, on the hot night that Liang Fang came home. I hadn't seen her in more than three weeks. She was a changed person.

She looked splendid, never better, strong and slim where her leather belt cinched in her waist. Her green army-style uniform with its cap of authority over her short braids gave her an air of fashion and confidence I had never seen in her before. She looked a real soldier, and I sat up straight and stared with big eyes, unsure whether or not she was really my sister. My desire for my own Red Guard uniform dated from that instant.

Father emerged when he heard voices and looked glad to see Liang Fang. "How have things been going?" he asked. "We haven't seen you in a long time."

"The situation is excellent," she answered in the language of Revolution. "We're washing away all the dirty water. But I never sleep. Every night we're out making search raids."

"What's a search raid?" I asked.

"You know, before you've been on a search raid you have no idea what's really going on in this society. People have been hiding all sorts of things. Counterrevolutionary materials, pre-Liberation Reactionary artworks, gold, jade, silver, jewelry—the trappings of Feudalism-Capitalism-Revisionism are everywhere."

My father looked surprised. "What do you care about those kinds of things?"

But Liang Fang was too involved in her story to answer. "We have a schedule to follow. Every night we go to a series of homes and go through every book, every page to see if there's any anti-Party material. It's an incredible amount of work. We have to check all the boxes and suitcases for false bottoms and sometimes pull up the floors to see if anything's been hidden underneath."

Liang Wei-ping brought her a basin of hot water and a towel to clean her face, and when she stood up to wash, her eye fell on a traditional painting of a horse by Xu Bei-hong. "What are you doing with *that?* Xu Bei-hong was denounced ages ago. You people are too careless." She went over to take it down, but Father's voice stopped her.

"What's wrong with it? That has nothing to do with any Capitalist-Revisionist line. Leave it be."

She said, "But you don't know what's been happening. It's not just a question of paintings, but of all the old things. Where do you think I've been all day? I was up on Yuelu Mountain with the Hunan University students trying to get rid of those old monuments and pavilions. And it wasn't an easy job, either. Half the stuff's made of stone. We had to use knives and axes to dig out the inscriptions. Stinking poetry of the Feudal Society! But it's all gone now, or boarded shut."

"Can we still go play there?" I asked.

"Well . . . ," she hesitated. "Maybe for now you'd better not; people might think you were there for the wrong reasons."

Father had found his voice. "How could you destroy the old poetry carved in the temples and pavilions? What kind of behavior is that?"

"What kind of behavior? Revolutionary action, that's what. The Hengyang District Red Guards have already destroyed all the temples on the Southern Peak of Heng Mountain. So much for the 'sacred mountain'!"

When I heard the words "Southern Peak" I remembered that Waipo had told me how people went to burn incense, setting out from their doorsteps and kneeling every few paces all the way to the mountaintop. If Waipo knew the temples were gone, what would she do? Who would light incense for her now?

"Who asked you to do those things?" Father demanded.

"Father," she answered with exaggerated patience. "You really don't understand the Cultural Revolution at all, do you? We have to get rid of the Four Olds. That includes *everything* old. Don't you even read your own newspaper? You'd better keep up with things or you'll be in trouble."

Father protested, "It's one thing to get rid of old customs and ideas, and another to go around smashing ancient temples."

"What good are they? They just trick people, make them superstitious. They're a bad influence on the young people."

"Who ever influenced you?" Father demanded. "No one in your whole life ever asked you to believe in any Buddhas."

Liang Fang didn't have an answer, which irritated her. "Well, anyway, they're all old things. Why aren't there Revolutionary poems, Chairman Mao's poems, statues of people's heroes, workers, peasants, and soldiers?"

Father despaired. "It's all over! China's old culture is being destroyed." He hit the table with his finger for emphasis. "Such precious historical treasures. All those symbols of China's ancient culture gone in only a few days. You've wronged your ancestors."

Liang Fang lost her temper. "No wonder people criticize you. You just keep following the Revisionist line and refuse to change, don't you?"

Father said angrily, "All right! I don't care, then. But I forbid you to touch that picture."

The quarrel ended on that note, as Father went into his inner room and closed the door. I couldn't figure out who was right, but I knew that Chairman Mao supported the Red Guards. So I said to Liang Fang, "Forget it, why don't you? It's hard for him to give up his ideas. Why don't we talk about something more pleasant?"

But Liang Fang was angry and didn't want to talk.

"I just came home to get a good night's sleep, anyway," she said. "What a family." She walked over, lay down on the larger bed, and was asleep almost immediately.

CHAPTER SIX

"Traveling Struggle"

The search raids soon spread to the newspaper. It was a terrifying time, because every night we heard the sounds of loud knocks, things breaking, and children crying. Like every family with a member attacked in the posters, we knew the Red Guards would eventually come to our house, and we were constantly on edge. During the day we went to see the exhibits of confiscated goods; at night we lay dressed, sleeplessly waiting for our turn.

At eleven one night the knocks finally came, loud, sharp, and impatient. We sat up in bed automatically. Father emerged from the inside room and turned on the light. He motioned with his head for Liang Wei-ping to get the door.

There were seven or eight of them, all men or boys, and the small room seemed very crowded. Despite the heat they were all wearing white cloths over their mouths and noses, and dark clothes. The one who seemed to be the leader carried a long metal spring with a rubber tip. He struck it against the table top with a loud crack.

"Liang Shan!" he said. "Is there anything Feudalist-Capitalist-Revisionist in your house?"

Father stammered, "No, no. I had pictures of Liu Shao-qi but I turned them in to the Work Team. Nothing else."

"Farter!" The man sliced at the table again.

Liang Wei-ping started to cry.

"What are you blubbering about? Cut it out. You and the boy, get over there in the corner."

We cowered there, trying to keep our sobs silent.

"What you must understand is that this is a Revolutionary action," the man announced. "Right?"

"Yes, yes, a Revolutionary action." I had never seen my father plead with anyone before. I had never seen him without his dignity.

"You welcome it, don't you! Say it!"

Something stuck in my father's throat.

"Shit. You've always been a liar!" Two Red Guards took him by each arm and grabbed his head, pushing it down so he was forced to kneel on the floor. They shook him by the hair so his glasses fell off, and when he groped for them they kicked his hands away. "Liar!"

The others were already starting to go through our things, some going into the other rooms for the books, others to the boxes. For several minutes there was silence except for the rustling of paper and the opening of boxes and drawers. Then one of them cried out.

"Quite a fox, isn't he? We said he was a liar!" The Red Guard had two Western ties and a Western-style jacket. "What's the meaning of this?"

"Ties," my father mumbled.

They kicked him. "Ties! Do you think we're children? Everyone knows these are ties. Capitalist ties. Or hadn't you heard?"

Father was pointing excitedly. "They were ordered through the newspaper. For some jobs. It wasn't my idea. For receptions and—" The spring slammed down on his hand and he cringed in pain.

"Who told you to point your finger? Think you can order people around still, don't you? Stinking intellectual!"

Liang Wei-ping cried, "How can you go hitting people that way? He can't even see properly."

"Shut up, little crossbreed, or we'll be hitting you next," snapped the Red Guard standing by the bureau. "Look at this! Fancy pants and sleeves with three buttons!"

From the other room came two Red Guards with armfuls of books. They dumped them unceremoniously on the floor near where Father was kneeling and went back for more. Tang poetry fell on top of histories, foreign novels on the Chinese Classics. Our house had always looked very neat and spare; I had never realized we had so many books.

After an hour they had finished going through everything. My comic books of the Classics had been added to the pile; the Xu Bei-hong horse had been crumpled and tossed on top. Everything we owned was in disorder on the floor, and even our pillows had been slit open with a knife. Father had been on his knees for a long time, and was trembling all over. The Red Guards were stuffing things into a large cloth bag when one of them got an idea for another game.

He put our large metal washbasin on the floor and built a little mound in it out of some of the finest books. He lit a match underneath and fanned it until the whole thing was aflame. Then he fed the fire, ripping the books in two one at a time and tossing them on. Father turned his head away. He didn't need his glasses to know what was on the pyre.

"What's the matter, Liang Shan? Light hurt your eyes?" The leading Red Guard held the metal spring out in front of him like a snake. "'A Revolutionary action.' Say it. 'It's a good fire.'"

Father was silent. I prayed he would speak.

"You shitting liar. Say it!" The man grabbed Father by the hair and twisted his head to make him look at the flames. "'It's a good fire!'"

My father's face looked very naked without his glasses, and the light from the fire shone on it and glistened in the tear lines on his cheeks. I could hardly hear him.

"A Revolutionary action," he whispered. "It's a good fire!"

They let him go; it was over. They shouldered the bag and filed out, the last putting our transistor radio into his pocket as he passed the table. We three couldn't find a word of comfort for each other; we just put things back in order in silence. The next day we discovered they had also helped themselves to Father's salary for that month.

The feeling of terror remained in our hearts for many days without fading. Then one evening when we were eating dinner, Liang Fang came home again. Somehow I didn't feel as glad to see her as usual.

Liang Wei-ping seemed to feel the same way. "Oh, you're back," she said, and continued eating. Maybe it was that Liang Fang was participating in the things that had hurt us so much. She must have sensed something, for she just got herself a bowl and sat down with us.

Then she noticed that the house was not the same. "What's wrong?" she demanded. "Has there been a search raid here or something?"

"There certainly has," Liang Wei-ping said. In great anger she told her what had happened that night, emphasizing the way the Red Guards had treated Father.

Finally Father interrupted coldly, "What's the point of talking about it? It's all 'Revolutionary action.'"

Father's sarcasm stung Liang Fang and she said defensively, "Father, I swear I would never do that type of thing. Whenever any of the boys in our group hit anyone, we girls always criticize them afterwards. And I would never take advantage of a search raid to fatten my own purse."

Even though she must have been terribly angry at Father because of the posters about him, it seemed she needed his understanding. And in spite of how hurt he had been, he still felt concerned for his daughter. "How have things been going lately?" he asked finally. "I'm always worried about you."

"Since the end of August there have been two Red Guard factions, and I'm in the real Rebel group now," she answered. "I quit the Red Defense Guards because they refused to attack the real seats of power, the Party leaders, and just wanted to denounce intellectuals. Also, they were getting more and more elitist. Finally the snobs asked everyone to get proof from their units that they had good backgrounds. So one day I came here to the newspaper . . . ," she paused and looked awkwardly at Father, embarrassed at not having stopped by the house. "At first the people in the office wouldn't give me anything because they said there was no precedent, and then I finally persuaded them. Well, it turned out that they wrote about Mother being a Rightist. I ended up throwing the paper into the outhouse, and I had to quit the group.

"But now I'm very happy, because there are even more people in our new Rebel group. Now I'm on my way to a cotton mill to drive out people with Conservative 'Protect the Emperor' viewpoints. We're going to organize the workers to seize power from the leadership. There'll be people going to all the units. I've heard it'll be mostly students from Hunan Teachers' College coming here to the newspaper."

Father interrupted. "But which faction is right? It would be terrible if it turned out you were on the wrong side."

She laughed. "The Cultural Revolution Directorate in Peking supports us. The Conservative Red Guards are done for and some of their leaders are being arrested. They were wrong to try to make Revolution into a private club. Madame Jiang Qing criticized them for their elitism ages ago. The issue is the Party leaders themselves now. No one is immune anymore." She paused and picked up her bowl and started shoveling food in with her chopsticks.

When the meal was over, Father asked her whether she needed anything. "I don't need money," she answered. "I get eight *jiao* a day, plus four *liang* [one *liang* equals fifty grams] worth of rice coupons. All the Rebel groups get stipends now." She hesitated. "But I could really use a mosquito net."

This wasn't such a simple request. There were three beds, my father's in one room, one for me, and one for my sisters in the other. Each bed had a net, but this was no ordinary luxury. To get one you not only needed 40 *yuan*, nearly a month's salary, and scarce cotton coupons, but also a special mosquito net coupon. Father got the coupon for the new net on his bed only because of his marriage. But he was very generous. "Take mine," he said. "I'll use mosquito incense."

Liang Fang refused at first. "How can I take yours? I thought Liang Heng could sleep with you and I could take his."

"Take it, take it. If the Revolution needs it, I'll give it up gladly." This was the first joke Father had made in months. We all laughed together.

But after Liang Fang had left, he seemed worried again. This Cultural Revolution was getting more complicated. It was hard to keep track of who was right and who wrong. "One day you're black and then you're red and then you're black again," he said. "Children, whatever you do please remember to be careful what you say. Never give your opinion on anything, even if you're asked directly. Just believe Chairman Mao's words, they're the only thing that seems to be reliable anymore."

I remembered his words for many years. They were another lesson in self-protection in modern society. And events showed that a lot of other people had learned the same lessons as I.

The next day, students from the colleges on the West Bank of the Xiang River gathered in front of the *Hunan Daily* gateway. They had come to organize the Rebel group. Young reporters and workers from the printing and repair shops put up posters welcoming them, and the students lined up in formation, waving copies of the *Quotations of Chairman Mao* and shouting, "Learn from the *Hunan Daily*'s Rebel group!" Then they marched in to the sounds of drums, red armbands reading "Chase the Exhausted Enemy" on every sleeve. All the old newspapermen left their desks, and it would be a full ten years before most of them returned. My father was among them. That day marked the end of his newspaper career.

But as Liang Fang had predicted, the arrival of the student Rebels coincided with a change in the focus of the attack, away from intellectuals like my father and toward the Party powerholders. Our old primary school was turned into a makeshift prison for about ten of the top political leaders, while their families were moved to a broken-down building near the newspaper compound's wall. Once I went to Gang Di's home and could hardly believe how the eight of them were living crammed into one tiny room. His mother and sister slept on a bed, but everyone else was sleeping on benches and chairs pushed together. And all thirteen-odd families shared one kitchen with a huge hole in its crumbling wall.

The family meetings held by the Work Team yielded to criticism meetings with attendance obligatory. There were all kinds, every day, big and small, but the one that made the deepest impression on me was the sort called "traveling struggle." It was a lot like the way the People's Liberation Army had dealt with the landlords after Liberation (I'd seen that in movies), but even more cruel.

The loudspeaker called us all outside, and in a few minutes I saw it coming. A group of Rebels were in the lead shouting "Down with the Capitalist Roaders" and "Long Live Chairman Mao Thought." Following them were about ten of the old "leading comrades" tied together on a long rope like beads on a string, their hands bound. They were wearing tall square-topped paper hats inscribed with phrases like I AM A BASTARD or I AM A FOOL, and around their necks were wooden signs with their names and crimes like FU KAI-XUN, CAPITALIST ROADER POWER USURPER or MENG SHU-DE, FILIAL GRANDSON OF THE LANDLORD CLASS. Those on the Editorial Committee had milder labels, such as DEVOTED ASSISTANT TO THE CAPITALIST ROADERS. Behind them, unbound, walked my father and some of the other intellectuals; they were less important, so their placards were light and made of paper, and they wore no hats. Still, they saddened me. They walked with their heads bowed low, carrying brass gongs, which they beat in time to the chanted slogans. As Father passed our doorway he bowed his head down even lower; he must have known I was watching him.

The Team walked very slowly, picking up more people with each building it passed. I followed at a distance, not wanting Father to see me, and I was astonished to hear a few low voices speaking in a very different spirit from that of the slogan shouters in front.

"Those placards must be terribly heavy," a woman's voice said.

"Some of those Rebels aren't such models of purity themselves," a man muttered. "Someone ought to investigate *their* backgrounds." The words comforted me even though I didn't know who had said them. Probably a family member like myself.

In a crowd, we passed the dining hall, the basketball court, the clinic, and all the dormitories, and went back past the primary school, finally reaching the auditorium on the fourth floor of the modern office building where we had had our Family Member meetings. There was a huge picture of Chairman Mao on the wall directly behind the platform, and the words BIG CRITICISM MEETING were written in huge characters on a hanging banner. On the side walls were more banners, with quotations from Chairman Mao and Rebel slogans. The Capitalist Roaders were already kneeling on the platform, their hands tied behind their backs with long ropes; the intellectuals "assisting" at the meeting were standing on each side with their heads bowed, facing inwards. Father was on the right toward the back, so I chose a seat on the far right beyond his line of vision.

First came a test for the intellectuals. Each in turn was ordered to recite one of the "Three Essays" by Chairman Mao, either "On Serving the People," "In Memory of Norman Bethune," or "The Foolish Old Man Who Moved the Mountain." If anyone made a mistake, he would have to kneel in apology before the picture of Chairman Mao until the end of the meeting. The test applied to the intellectuals alone; as a Rebel leader declared, "Capitalist Roaders don't have the right to recite the works of Chairman Mao."

Several people had their heads on the floor in humiliation when it came Father's turn, and my heart was in my mouth. They ordered him to recite "On Serving the People," and when he had said only two sentences, he abruptly stopped. I was nearly in tears. Suddenly all around me, I heard the next line whispered, as if people were reciting along with him, prompting him. Father adjusted his glasses for a moment. Then, in a strong clear voice, he recited the whole thing without stopping, supported by what I knew was his confident love for Chairman Mao.

When the Capitalist Roaders' turn came, they had to recite the big character posters attacking them. The meeting went on and on, and whenever someone stumbled there were cries of "Give him an airplane ride, give him an airplane ride!" At this the Rebels tossed the rope binding the man's arms behind him over a pipe at the top of the auditorium and hoisted him up in the air, letting him squirm in agony like a dragonfly with pinched wings.

Some of the family members couldn't bear it and left the auditorium in tears. Gang Di's older sister ran out with a loud sob, pulling Gang Di behind her, when their father was hauled aloft. It wasn't my father who was being tortured, but I couldn't bear it either, and followed them out. Luckily no one noticed, and we got away.

I had hardly reached home when Liang Wei-ping came in, panting for breath. I didn't want to talk, but she insisted on telling me about a big demonstration she'd seen on May First Road. Fifty or sixty open trucks had passed on their way to the execution ground in the eastern suburbs. "The woman who was going to be shot was in the first truck, standing there tied up with a handkerchief stuffed into her mouth and a huge bamboo sign on her back, which reached way over her head," my sister said, pacing excitedly. "There was a big red X on it, and below it said she was a KMT spy about to be executed! And on each side of her there were two Red Guards holding her by the back of the neck and pushing her head down." The same truck carried Reactionaries who had already confessed—some wore heavy iron placards that made them bend under the weight; others, less serious offenders, had wooden ones. And they all had gongs and were shouting things like "I am a counterrevolutionary, I am wrong" or "Thank you, Chairman Mao, for not making me die."

I couldn't bear to listen. It made me miserable. But she rattled on. "My classmates said they were probably all teachers, movie actors, old cadres, writers, and people like that. There were Rebels with bayonets in all the trucks. I never saw so many Red Guards before." Liang Wei-ping hadn't noticed that Father had come slowly up the stairs and was standing quietly in the doorway, listening. "Everybody was shouting slogans and the children were throwing rocks and sticks. One of them hit the KMT spy right in the head."

"Stop it," I finally broke in. "Don't talk about it anymore. Can't you see that Father's tired?"

Liang Wei-ping turned in embarrassed surprise and said, "Father, I didn't know you were home. I'll get some hot water for you."

While she was busy with the thermos and basin and towel, I led Father into his bedroom and fluffed up his pillow for him. Soon she came in with the steaming towel, and he rubbed his face and neck as if to wash away weeks of dirt. When he was finished he looked up wearily. "Well, Liang Wei-ping. It's a good thing you watched other people's 'traveling struggle' and not mine. You might not have found it so entertaining." He lay slowly back against the pillow and closed his eyes.

We shut the door softly behind us. As if she hated herself, Liang Wei-ping said, "I feel terrible, talking about those things in front of Father." She sat down on her bed and stared out the window for a long, long time.

CHAPTER SEVEN

A Counterrevolutionary Incident

One day not long after the "traveling struggle," my friend Little Monkey and I were playing with marbles on the cement in front of one of the dormitories. Suddenly a group of people came running around the corner right through our game and disappeared into the alleyway between two houses. We thought it must be another public criticism meeting or a search raid, so we pocketed our marbles and ran after them to see whose family was in trouble this time.

There was a big crowd in front of the old dormitory opposite the medical clinic, then being converted into another temporary prison. I pushed my way through. There on the wall somebody had scratched DOWN WITH CHAIRMAN MAO deeply into the fresh plaster. The characters glistened wetly under the autumn sun. Men from the Public Security Bureau were taking photographs from all angles and yelling at people to stay behind the chalk line they had drawn to hold back the crowd.

I knew it was serious, but I thought it was exciting all the same. As Little Monkey and I walked back, we tried to imagine who had done it. He said it must have been a KMT spy who hadn't been caught yet, but I was sure it was a big landlord. It never occurred to us that anyone but spies and landlords could possibly oppose Chairman Mao.

Father was horrified when he came back that evening and heard the news. "Counterrevolutionaries like that are really evil. Whoever opposes Chairman Mao must be punished severely," he said. Liang Wei-ping and I were confident that the culprit would be caught in no time. No one would be willing to help such a criminal hide for long.

That evening at around nine, there came the loud knocking at our door that we had learned meant trouble. We were afraid, of course, but in some strange way we were already fairly used to such things. So we opened the door, and three men wearing dark clothes with red armbands came in. Their eyes were bloodshot and they looked tired. I recognized one of them as a typesetter named Zheng, another as a young maintenance worker named Liu. Before the Cultural Revolution they had been friendly acquaintances of ours; now they were "Revolutionary Workers," busy putting up posters about intellectuals and Party leaders. To me, Zheng was one of the most frightening of the Rebel group, for his hairy face gave him a particularly intimidating expression and his Shaoyang accent made it difficult even for Changshanese to understand him. I had often watched him beating the Capitalist Roaders. I didn't know the third man, but later I learned he was a Red Guard from the Hunan Teachers' College across the river, on hand to help the *Hunan Daily*'s Rebels write the newspaper. This time, instead of seizing my father or opening drawers and boxes, they walked up to me and said, "Let's go."

Father was trembling, but Liang Wei-ping grabbed my hand and said, "No. Where do you want to take him?"

Liu said, "This question is very serious."

"What is it?"

"Don't you know that there was a counterrevolutionary incident here this afternoon?"

At these words, my family fell silent. There was no way out. I had to go with them.

They took me down the stairs of the office building, past a print shop reeking with paper and ink, and into a dirty basement room. It was empty save for three wooden chairs lined up in a row and another one facing them, a bench with a thermos and three teacups, a bare lightbulb hanging in the center of the room, and a fan in the corner, which Zheng turned on when he walked in. The small ventilating window below the ceiling was shut tight, and the fan did little to relieve the dank stuffiness.

Zheng took a rope from behind the door and tied me tight to the chair with my arms behind my back. The man I didn't know took out a pen and notebook and waited expectantly. Liu was the first to speak. "Did you see the big demonstration go by the gate of the newspaper today?"

The demonstration he meant had been one like that which Liang Wei-ping described to me on the day of Father's "traveling struggle," a pre-execution parade. They had become common in Changsha. When it passed the *Hunan Daily* that morning, I had gone out to watch with everyone else. So I said warily, "Yes, I saw it."

"Raise your head and look at the slogan on the wall. What does it say?"

It was a quotation from Chairman Mao, a big red billboard-sized sign with eight yellow characters: *tanbai congkuang, kangju congyan*— LENIENCY TO THOSE WHO CONFESS THEIR CRIMES; SEVERITY TO THOSE WHO REFUSE.

"Read it."

I read it.

Then Zheng asked me, "Do you know why that counterrevolutionary was executed today?"

"He was treated with severity because he didn't confess," I replied.

"And why were some people on the trucks saying, 'Thank you, Chairman Mao?'"

"Because they got leniency for confessing their crimes."

Zheng smiled, and said sarcastically, "Not bad. You know the policy very well."

Liu spoke up. "So now you can begin to confess your crime of writing the counterrevolutionary slogan."

I was very surprised. I could hardly believe they could suspect me. I had thought they wanted me to expose Father again. So I answered eagerly. "I didn't do it. I don't know anything about it."

Zheng began to interrogate me. "What were you doing at noontime today?"

"I was playing."

"Where were you playing?"

"In the grape arbor in front of the hospital."

"What were you doing there?"

I remembered that I had been shooting down grapes with a sling-shot, but I didn't want to admit it. "Nothing," I said.

He slammed his hand down on the table. "Nothing?" I was frightened. "What was in your hand?"

It seemed they knew everything. "I had a slingshot," I said. "I was using it to knock down some grapes."

Zheng became even fiercer. The teacups shook. "You're full of shit. That slingshot was what you used to write that counterrevolutionary slogan with! Your little playmates have already exposed you. A boy playing with a slingshot was seen writing that slogan, and you're the only child in this unit who has one."

I trembled. "Yes, I do have a slingshot. It's to hit birds with. I was using it to knock down grapes. I would never do something like that. I didn't do it."

"You won't admit it?" he shouted. "You'll be sorry! Listen." He pointed up at the ceiling. I could hear thuds and a man's anguished cries. The sounds were always changing; perhaps several people were being beaten. I heard someone protesting, and then the crash of a chair falling. The whole building became very silent. I was sweating all over.

Zheng said, "Raise your head. This thing is also your father's crime. Your father must have told you to do it, because he hates the Cultural Revolution."

From then on, they tried to force me to admit I had done it because of Father. My back ached and my wrists were itching and raw where the rope bound them. I squirmed in my seat but it didn't do any good.

The third man, keeping notes, said nastily, "So the rope feels uncomfortable, does it? If you don't like it, why don't you hurry up and confess?"

I was exhausted. Many hours had passed. Upstairs, there were the sounds of renewed argument, and Zheng and Liu decided to go see what was going on, leaving me alone with the note-taker. He smoked and didn't ask me anything. Finally, somehow, I nodded off.

I awoke to the pain of Zheng shaking me by the hair and laughing, "Oh, so you want to sleep, do you?"

Fortunately, the note-taker looked at his watch. "It's getting late." He looked at me. "You're not allowed to tell a single soul what happened tonight. Go home. When we come get you tomorrow, you'd better be there."

I ran home with my remaining strength. As soon as I opened the door, my father and sister hugged me as if they would squeeze the life out of me.

"Don't cry," I said. I was a little surprised they were so upset. After all, it hadn't been as bad as all that.

Father asked, "Where did they hit you?"

"They didn't hit me."

"You probably just don't want to admit it," my sister said. "But I saw you being beaten with my own eyes." I thought this was very strange.

Father explained that after the men took me away he and Liang Wei-ping were so worried that she went to the office building to find out what was happening. She heard people being beaten upstairs, so she went up and looked through the keyhole of the room the noise was coming from. She saw a man beat someone with a stick as thick as a fist, and thought it was me. Running back home, she told Father. They had both been waiting for me, frantically worried, ever since.

I explained that it must have been someone else, because I was downstairs in the basement.

"Why did they take you away?" asked Father.

"They said I wrote the counterrevolutionary slogan." I had hardly finished my sentence when Father grabbed me by both shoulders with all his strength and cried, "What? What? You wrote it? How could you do a counterrevolutionary thing like that? You've harmed not only yourself but our whole family. You . . . Why did you want to go and do a thing like that?"

I was crying for the first time that night. "No, no, I didn't do it."

Father's expression changed in a flash, as if he had been waiting for just these words. He embraced me like a madman. "I believe you, I believe you. I believe you because you are my son. You will never oppose our beloved Chairman Mao. You will never do that kind of evil thing." He looked around nervously. "Good. You must never say you wrote it no matter what they tell you."

At dawn the next day, the note-taker came again to our house. "Let's go," he said. I followed him back to the same building, where he brought me upstairs to a big meeting room. Sitting inside were the other teenage sons of the newspapermen who were being criticized— sons of cadres, editors, and reporters. The Gang brothers were there, and the son of the press photographer. Most of them were older than I, but one boy was only nine. It was to be a familiar group. In months to come, whenever anything happened in the unit we were always the suspects.

A man from the Public Security Bureau came in carrying a big bag, and Zhou Sa-wu, the worker who had kicked us out of our office. He gave each of us a piece of paper and a pencil, and ordered us to write down two sentences: "Long Live Our Beloved and Great Leader Chairman Mao" and "Down with the Capitalist Roaders." Then he collected our papers and gave them to the policeman. We whispered to each other, "They're comparing the handwriting."

After a long, whispered discussion they ordered most of us to go, but five or six of the older boys had to stay behind. They were locked up in the nursery school near our old primary school where their fathers were being held; later we heard that they were supposed to expose their parents. They didn't come out for nearly a month. Once I passed by and, through the barred window, saw two teenage boys handcuffed together, leaning against the wall and turning their rice straw bedding idly with their feet. One of them was the son of the cadre in charge of the printing house, the other the son of Senior Assistant Editor Meng. On the wall was a huge sign: LENIENCY TO THOSE WHO CONFESS THEIR CRIMES; SEVERITY TO THOSE WHO REFUSE.

No one ever found out who wrote the slogan, but among us children it was rumored that it was the young son of one of the editors, a boy of only eight or nine. The strange thing was that it was he who told the Rebels that a boy with a slingshot had been playing near the dormitory wall.

CHAPTER EIGHT

Flight to the Countryside

So, although we hadn't been driven out of our home like the Capitalist Roaders' families, and I had escaped being locked up in the nursery school, my family certainly had its share of troubles. I was harassed when I went out, and even at home we were not immune. So many stones were thrown at our windows that soon we had only two or three that were intact. My life became an automatic, colorless routine. I had less and less to say to Father, and Liang Wei-ping stayed away longer and longer at the hospitality station. The only books left after the search raid were the works of Chairman Mao, Marx, and Lenin, so I had no stories or picture books to help me while away the time. I no longer dared to go out and play with Gang Di and Little Monkey for fear of running into the Rebels' children. How I envied Little Li for being able to go live at his mother's unit! Since she was new there and little known, things were much better for him.

One of the things I dreaded most was going to the dining hall to get food. The Rebels' children could cut in front of me or order me to the back of the line, and I had to obey, since the adults either encouraged them or paid no attention. I was lucky if I escaped without being kicked or spat upon, and the best food was always gone by the time I got to the window. But even worse than going to the dining hall was emptying the garbage, for that was the special province of children, and the Rebels' children were despots in that little world.

A worker pulling a large wooden cart collected the garbage daily, usually in the late afternoon when I was alone in the house. When we children heard his bell ringing, we knew it was time to take down the big metal dustpans with the long wooden handles and upend their contents with a dusty "whoom" into the never-never land of coal ashes, watermelon rinds, vegetable leaves, and chicken innards. Before the Cultural Revolution, the arrival of the garbage cart had been a great social event heralding games and gossip, but now taking down the garbage was just another occasion for humiliation. I never knew when I was going to get an apple core in the head. It was at the garbage cart one day that I received one of the worst beatings of my life.

The Rebels' children had it in for me because of what happened the day before. When my father was taking his nap after lunch, I had heard the sound of a huge crash coming from his room. Running in, I saw Father sitting up dazed, holding his leg, shards of broken glass all over his bed and a large rock at the foot of it. "They nearly killed me that time, the fools," he said. "They have some nerve."

Looking out of the window, I saw four or five Rebels' children, two of whom had once been friends of mine. I was furious. "If you were worth anything you wouldn't do this kind of thing when you think everyone's asleep," I yelled. "Cowards!"

Father pulled me back urgently. "It doesn't matter, forget it. How can a forearm fight with a thigh? We'll patch it up with cardboard like the rest." I knew he was right and left the window, already regretting my fury because I was only one and there were so many of them.

So I was very nervous when I brought down the dustpan the next day, and my worst fears were confirmed when I saw seven Rebels' children waiting calmly with their dustpans, among them Wu Dong, the oldest of their group and a notorious bully. He had been hitting back at the world for his ugliness ever since he was a small boy.

He smiled broadly when he saw me. "It's brave Liang the garbage man, just in time to help us with our heavy dustpans."

I bit back my fear and anger, and dumped the contents of all seven dustpans into the cart as they watched, showering myself with dust with each load until I was coughing and my eyes were running. Then I took the handle of my own dustpan, praying they would let me empty it and go back up the stairs.

"Wait a second," said Wu Dong, his fleshy lips twitching. "What do you think you're doing? Didn't you ask us yesterday to do things out in the open? Well, here we are." He took a step toward me, and several others moved around behind. "Now when I slap you, I want you to turn your face in the direction of the slap. Then don't move until I slap it back the other way." He hit me with all his strength before I had had a chance to register the meaning of his words, and I looked at him in shock and surprise, my cheek exploding with pain. "Stinking intellectual's son. So you dare to disobey us?" He slapped me back and forth four or five times, and I reeled and almost fell. Then they were all on top of me, pummeling me with all their strength.

Through my agony I could hear the garbage collector's voice, "Stop fighting, what are you doing?" and their answer, "His father stinks more than your garbage. Keep out of this."

While the man was saying, "Go somewhere else and fight, then. You're knocking over my cart," I saw my chance. I crawled out of their knot and ran. A metal dustpan struck me sharply in the back but I made it to the stairwell. They let me go.

I managed to climb the stairs and get into the apartment, locking the door behind me. I was weeping with fear and pain. My shirt was torn, I was covered with cuts and bruises, and I was shaking so that I could hardly pick up the thermos and pour hot water into the basin. When I had washed, I looked in the mirror and saw that the side of my face had swollen to the size of a small eggplant. I crawled into bed and closed the mosquito net, turning my face to the wall and nesting my bruise in the pillow. I was so exhausted that I was soon asleep.

Soon I heard my father come home, and his worried voice. "What's the matter? What are you doing in bed?"

I knew he would be upset if he found out. "My stomach hurts," I said.

"Does it hurt a lot? Shall I call a doctor?" he asked.

"No, no," I said hastily. "I'll be all right in a while."

"You should eat something, though," he said, and I heard the sound of a drawer opening. "I'll go to the dining hall."

The door opened and closed and everything was silent. Then after a while it opened again and I heard a rattle of dishes as my father put the basket roughly down on the table. "What's this? You got into a fight? The neighbors told me you got into a fight! Turn over," he ordered. I resisted, but he pulled my shoulder back. "Good heavens," he gasped. "Look at your eye." He helped me to a sitting position and brought a cold washcloth, mopping my face gently and folding the cloth where the blood stained it. He rinsed it out and told me to hold it in place, looking at me anxiously for a long time, his forehead creased and his eyebrows knitted.

Suddenly he let out a loud sob and fell to his knees before me, embracing my legs. "My son, I'm so sorry. It's all my fault. It's all because of your damned father. I've hurt you so, you must hate me."

I put my arms around his shoulders, holding him. His coarse blue jacket felt strong and reassuring, but the man inside was shaking. We both wept for a long time. It was as if we were weeping out all the sorrow and pain accumulated since he had first been attacked. At one point, he looked up and said, "My son, you must believe me. Your father is not a bad man. Someday all of this will be straightened out and we can have normal lives again."

I answered, "Father, I don't blame you. You are still my good father, my kind father." I didn't care about my problems anymore. I saw for the first time that what we were going through must be a thousand times worse for him than it was for me.

Father was terribly worried about me because he knew I couldn't avoid my tormentors; I couldn't very well stop going out entirely. The upshot was that I would go to stay with my Auntie in Shuangfeng County. Nobody there knew anything about Father.

I packed a change of clothing, a letter from Father to Auntie, and a copy of the now readily available *Quotations of Chairman Mao*. Liang Wei-ping took me to the long-distance bus station. It was raining hard. I found my window seat by a peasant wearing a cloth turban, and realized it was going to be an unusually wet journey: the window in front of me was broken, the woman sitting next to it had opened an umbrella, and all the run-off was spilling into my lap. I wrapped my "Little Red Book" protectively under my shirt and prepared to get soaked; since she was older than I, I had no choice but to bear the rain for the duration of the four hours to Shuangfeng.

It wasn't a bad trip at all, though. I was in a good mood because I was leaving my troubles behind and going to a new place, a place that might be just as wonderful as Uncle Hou's had been four years before. There were a lot of Shuangfeng Red Guards on the bus who got the passengers singing Revolutionary songs, playing Revolutionary games, and studying Revolutionary texts. I felt happy that at last I was allowed to be a member of society again, and in competition shouted, "Long Live Chairman Mao," louder than anyone else, thus winning Revolutionary glory for the entire back of the bus.

The rain stopped a few hours into the trip and although the fields were yellow and dead, the autumn scenery was very pretty, with stark black trees along the road and clear blue mountains in the distance. At noon we came to the town of Xiangxiang, where the roofs were all black tile, with eaves upturned in the ancient style. We stopped at the bus station for lunch, and when I got out I saw a beautiful red-walled temple, huge, with dragons and phoenixes carved on the roof.

Remembering what Liang Fang said about how I'd better not go to the temple in the Yuelu Mountain, I found it odd that the temple gateway seemed full of people. So while the rest of the passengers went to buy spicy rice noodles, peanuts, and roasted sweet potatoes, I went over to take a look.

The people were criticizing an old monk, and I was very curious because I had never seen a monk before. He had a little wrinkled face and his head was shaved bald. His clothes were faded black, with little black slippers of a style I didn't recognize. He was kneeling and beating a gong before a broken stone tablet on which I guessed was inscribed the history of the temple or some Buddhist scripture—I couldn't read it as the words were all in the old-style script. As he beat the gong, he chanted, "I have tricked the people, I should be punished," and "Buddhism is a lie, only Marxism-Leninism–Chairman Mao Thought is the truth." I thought he looked old and tired, especially in contrast with the excited young people shouting at him, and I wondered what he would do now that his temple was a forbidden place. I would have liked to have stayed to look at him longer, but the stop was only for fifteen minutes.

After another hour of riding, we finally came to my destination, Green Tree Town, just beyond the Shuangfeng county seat. There was only one street, long and cobblestoned, and muddy because of the rain. When I asked someone where the primary school was, he pointed down along the two long rows of red slogans and said that the school was at the very end.

Aside from its narrowness and the occasional glimpses of broad yellow fields when there was a break between the dark wooden houses, the street was rather similar to some of the older lanes in Changsha. I was particularly happy to find that every doorway was large and open so I could look inside to see what the inhabitants were doing. I saw young women spinning thread, old women rocking babies; there were the sounds of iron being pounded and the rushing breathing of a wooden hand-bellows. The people looked brown and poor, although a lot more of the old ladies were wearing traditional jade bracelets and gold earrings than did in Changsha; most of them also wore soft old-style black velvet hats with jade figures sewn to the brim, and black shirts with cloth buttons at the side and shoulder rather than modern button-down shirts. Some of the men were barefoot and they wore their pants rolled up, and I noticed their bandy legs and broad peasant toes open in the fresh wet mud. I remembered Luojia Mountain once again, and my feet itched inside my cloth shoes, already wet and heavy with earth. The children seemed small and thin, their clothing patched, but like us city children they lined up before the man cranking his black iron puffing-machine. Like us they held their bowls of uncooked rice and soybeans, waiting for the big "boom" that would tell them it was another child's turn to have his ordinary fare turned into a special treat. Everyone looked at me curiously when I passed, probably because strangers were rare and my clothing and haircut identified me as being from the city. I didn't mind, though, since I was just as curious about them. Anyway, they didn't seem unfriendly.

I soon arrived at what was obviously a primary school, a compound with a sportsground on which some children were playing ping-pong. Before going in, I stopped at the gateway to read what seemed to be big character posters, although written on old newspaper as if paper were too expensive. Then, to my utter shock, I discovered one which read, DOWN WITH ZHU ZHI-DAO, CORRUPT DAUGHTER OF THE LANDLORD CLASS!!! In a flash I realized that my visit might not be as much of an escape as I had hoped. I hurried inside lest I draw attention to myself, and found out that Zhu Zhi-dao lived at the last doorway of the long teachers' dormitory. As I walked quickly along, I heard the sounds of familiar Revolutionary songs as if a rehearsal were going on, and the piercing wail of a strange country horn.

Auntie opened her door with a cry of utter astonishment. "What are you doing here?" she asked. "Come in." I had a funny feeling my presence might not be altogether welcome, so I took out my father's letter and gave it to her.

Then before either of us had a chance to say anything more, there came a male voice from outside. "Zhu Zhi-dao, who is your visitor?"

"It's Old Liang's son," she answered, blushing at having to mention something about her personal life. Soon there were a lot of voices, and children crowded at the windows, looking in.

"People here like to gossip," she said. "You aren't my real son, so they'll be talking about it. Don't let it worry you."

Her words were so direct that I felt even less welcome than before, as if somehow I had no right to call on her for protection. I smiled awkwardly.

Then she said, "I'll go to the dining hall and get some hot water for tea," and went out. I looked around the room and found it long, narrow, and extremely humble, with only wooden slats in the windows and a little iron container for coal briquets. The walls were covered with yellow newspaper. The outhouse, water tap, and dining hall would be outside. No wonder she had wanted to transfer out of there and move to Changsha.

When she came back with the thermos, she closed the door tightly and listened for a moment before she said in a low, worried voice, "Liang Heng, it's not too good for you to be here right now, because I have to take part in criticism meetings every day. It's worse here than in the city. People with bad backgrounds are watched all the time." Her eyes filled with tears. "Heavens knows what I've done. Even my letters are checked, so I've stopped writing." I knew this was true, because we hadn't had a letter from her in a long time. "Your Cousin Bing will take you to his older brother's house in the countryside. It's about eight *li* from here. It should be all right if you stay there for a week or so. I'll give you money and food coupons to cover your living expenses. I'm sure they'll welcome you."

Cousin Bing arrived in a few minutes, and I studied him while my stepmother was explaining the situation. He looked about three years older than I, very strong, barefoot like the men I had seen on the street. He had a strange bowllike haircut that shaved the lower half of his head to mid-ear and left an untamed growth on top. But what drew my attention most of all was a beautiful Chairman Mao button, of a size that in the city was extremely rare. I was dying to ask him where he'd gotten it.

We set out. Cousin Bing immediately picked a narrow path between the rice fields, walking very quickly as the peasants do, so I had to trot a bit to keep up. I was very happy to be going back to the countryside; the air smelled sweet and clean and even the earth beneath our feet looked warm and inviting.

"Wait a minute," I called out, and stepped out of my muddy shoes so I could walk barefoot too.

"Let me carry them for you," said Cousin Bing, and I took advantage of his kindness to ask my burning question.

"Where did you get that beautiful Chairman Mao button?" I asked. "I've never seen one so big."

"Oh, our school organized us to go to Shaoshan," he said proudly. "When we visited the house where Chairman Mao was born, they gave one to each of us. Shaoshan's only one hundred *li* from here." That explained it. I resolved that someday I would go too, even if I had to walk there.

We got into quite a rhythm, and since Cousin Bing didn't like to talk, I amused myself along the way by singing the new songs I had learned on the bus and enjoying the scenery. It was a fairly flat region, with only gentle hills, so I could see a great distance. The houses were all built of big crumbling yellow mud bricks with gray tile roofs, and many of them had slogans painted on them like LONG LIVE THE GREAT PROLETARIAN CULTURAL REVOLUTION and OUR RED HEARTS YEARN TO-WARD THE RED SUN. There were old slogans too, though, like LONG LIVE THE GREAT LEAP FORWARD and LONG LIVE THE PEOPLE'S COMMUNES, from as far back as 1958. I thought this was a very strange place, where old and new were all mixed up together.

Near every group of houses there was a square stone spring with water running from it in a little stream, and the women gathered there to pound their clothes with sticks and rinse vegetables, while others came with shoulder poles and buckets to fetch water back to their houses. When Cousin Bing explained that the water came from the ground, I was very surprised—apart from water taps I knew only about the mountain streams from which we had scooped water at Luojia Mountain.

I was becoming a little tired because of the fast pace, and Cousin Bing stopped and picked a handful of sour jujubes for me from a spreading tree. The sun was starting to set and the scene was getting prettier and prettier: The mist was like a light pink scarf and the smoke from the cooking fires rose purple through the rooftops. Children returning home on the backs of water buffalo and peasants with their twin buckets made silhouettes against the sunset like black paper cutouts. I was content.

Soon we could see a large, gray-walled compound in the distance, and Cousin Bing told me we were almost there. It was very different from the mud-bricked clusters of houses we had passed, and I asked in surprise, "Is that where your brother's Production Team lives? What kind of place is that?"

"The whole thing used to belong to a big landlord before Liberation," he answered. "Now more than seventeen families have moved in."

As we came closer, we saw several young people painting slogans on the wall by the last light of the day. The slogans were huge because they were using brooms as paintbrushes. DOWN WITH THE CAPITALIST ROADERS, they read. DOWN WITH SOVIET REVISIONISM. DOWN WITH AMERICAN IMPERIALISM.

"There's my brother," Cousin Bing said, with the first sign of vitality I had seen in him. "Big brother Han," he called. "You have guests."

A young peasant put down his broom and walked over, wiping his hands on his pants. He greeted us warmly. "This is our cousin Liang Heng from Changsha, Auntie Zhu's son," Cousin Bing said. "We're going to stay with you for a few days."

"From Changsha," Cousin Han echoed, obviously impressed. "Come in and rest, you must be tired." He led the way into the compound. I found out later that aside from one or two young men who had joined the army, the people there had never met anyone from the capital, and had never had any reason to go there themselves. It was only natural that they treat me not as a child, but as an honored guest.

Cousin Han brought us into the small dark room to which he had been assigned when he had moved there from Green Tree Town years before. There was no electricity, but by the light of the coal embers burning dully in the pit stove I distinguished a bed, a large cabinet, and a table by a window. A pot hung over the stove from the ceiling, and there was a huge open water container in the corner.

News of my arrival spread quickly, and I soon had an even larger audience than I had had at Zhu Zhi-dao's. No one could have seen much in the darkness, but that didn't prevent them from coming. Then a tall young peasant made his way through and shook my hand warmly, as if I were an adult. "My name is Zhang," he said. "Cultural Revolution

Committee Leader Zhang. I've heard you're from Changsha. Welcome to our Production Team." I thanked him shyly. I had never before been treated with so much respect.

Zhang smiled and lit a cigarette, and by the light of the match I saw his teeth were as black as if he had never brushed them in his life. "After you rest and eat, we'll talk about the situation in the city. It isn't often that we get firsthand news." He turned and shouted to the crowd, "Our guest is tired, so let's let him rest." At his words, the peasants began to withdraw and he turned to me again. "Please stay as long as you like. We always welcome guests here." Then he shook my hand again, his grip tight, rough, and warm.

Cousin Han had begun to busy himself with our meal. He brought the rice to a boil in a wok, and then poured it into the upper pot to simmer. Next he reached into some crude blue-and-white ceramic jars for some pickled cabbage, turnips, beans, and hot peppers, and put it all together in a bowl. A bottle upended over the wok yielded a few drops of oil. He threw on the vegetables, which were so hot and sour that the steam alone was enough to make me cough and tear. After a moment or two, he announced that they were ready.

"Let's make a soup now," he suggested, and I brightened up, because I was very fond of soup. But his soup was like no other soup I have ever tasted, for he simply scooped up a dipper-full of water out of the container in the corner and swished it around in the empty wok as if there might still be some oil and salt left in it. He added some hot pepper sauce and the soup was ready too.

He served us each a bowl of rice and we began to eat the pickled vegetables. But instead of sharing the dish with us, he took his rice back to one of the ceramic pots and poured some salty pickling water over it. He ate this with a great deal of noise, and helped himself to another bowl.

After this unusual dinner, I had my first lesson in cigarette smoking. Cousin Han brought out a huge leaf of tobacco and chopped some of it up fine with his knife, then cut a strip of paper from an old calendar and rolled it up tight. He lit his creation and handed it to me; I took it like a man, but wheezed and wept when I inhaled like the little boy I was. Cousin Han comforted me, "Cough a bit and you'll feel better. I was that way too at first, but I've been smoking since I was eight years old."

As he put the pot back on to boil, the male peasants began to return to listen to me talk about "important national affairs." The room was soon filled with glowing brown faces, weathered and wrinkled, and the strong smell of fresh tobacco. They asked me all kinds of questions, but I found them very difficult to answer. It was as if the peasants had no previous knowledge of the Cultural Revolution at all, and the gap in knowledge was too great to be bridged by someone like me.

"What's this we've heard about Rebel factions?"

"What about the Capitalist Roaders? We're not really sure who they are."

I told them what I knew about the Work Teams and the students, the "Protect the Emperor" groups and the Rebels, the parades and the criticism meetings. Of course, I left out a lot of the cruelty, and didn't mention a word about my own family.

Zhang sighed. "It's so hard for us to get information here. There's no radio in the Production Team, and we have to go all the way to the commune office to see a newspaper. The County Red Guards came to Green Tree, then the town came to the commune, the commune to the brigade, and the brigade to us. They told us to form a Cultural Revolution Committee of five cadres of poor peasant background. Then they asked us if we had any landlords, and I said the old one was still living here, so they told me to lock him up in the water buffalo shed and he's in there now. They issued some new slogans, too, and told us to write them up, and get ready to go at any time to Green Tree or the county seat for parades and meetings. But that's all we know. Green Tree is doing a lot of things, but we don't have any educated people or Capitalist Roaders like they do. We're just poor peasants here."

"Tell us more about how they do things in the city," asked an old, old peasant. So we talked for a while about the Cultural Revolution, but the conversation soon shifted to the city itself. "We've heard that there is a nine-story building there, and that people sit in buildings to watch movies. Is that really true?" the old peasant asked.

I bragged about how our theaters could seat over a thousand people, had a balcony section, and chairs that were leather in the winter and bamboo in the summer. They looked so amazed that I asked them, "How do you see movies, then?"

A middle-aged man answered, "We usually have a movie around once a year, on the commune threshing ground. But this year there have been more, thanks to the Cultural Revolution. They were all about Chairman Mao reviewing the Red Guards. Chairman Mao knows how poor we are, and he didn't even charge us to see them! So everybody went, some people from more than ten *li* away."

I thought this was pretty funny. The peasants didn't realize that what they had seen were "political movies," compulsory in the cities. Of course they were free! But I didn't say anything; I didn't want to spoil the limited pleasures they had.

In this way we passed several enjoyable hours, until we were all yawning. The peasants left, with warm good-byes, and Cousins Bing and Han shared the bed, while I slept on a bamboo couch they had borrowed for me. Dawn had already broken when I awoke again.

Although I stayed there only ten days, I developed a deep friendship with the local people. No one asked me about my background or why I was there, and they respected me as an educated person. They asked me to write letters for them to their sons in the army and to relatives in other counties; Zhang wanted me to help him figure out the operating instructions for a gas lamp the Team had purchased for evening meetings. A group of young men came to me, too, in the evening after they had returned from collecting manure and picking tea oil buttons, wanting me to help them form a Red Guard group. They had prepared red paper for their armbands, and they wanted me to write the characters "Red Guard." But they had brought only black paint, and I explained that in the city using black for such a serious purpose would be considered counterrevolutionary, and they had to get white or yellow. So they came back again with white, grateful that I had saved them from making such a grave error. I wrote the characters for them and, proud and excited, they stuck their new armbands on their sleeves with paste made of cooked rice.

One day there was a meeting, and Cultural Revolution Committee Leader Zhang read a notice which said that the next day all the peasants were to attend a demonstration at the county seat to criticize the "Protect the Emperor" faction. Furthermore, he read, all participants would receive two *jiao* from the Production Team in addition to their usual work points.

The peasants cheered wildly. Many of them had never been to Shuangfeng before, and now they would be paid to go! They rushed home to prepare, washing their best clothing, figuring out their finances. It was as if they were going to a festival.

Cousin Han looked very sad when he realized he had almost no money to take with him, and I suddenly remembered that Auntie Zhu had given me money and rice coupons for my living expenses. I took the five bills and the coupons from their hiding place within my *Quotations* and pressed them on him. He protested for a long time but finally accepted awkwardly, putting three *yuan* carefully under the cotton pad on his bed and folding the other two deep inside his pocket. We boiled a lot of sweet potatoes to take with us and went to bed early, for it would be a twenty-*li* walk to the county seat.

We awoke before dawn, at around four. There must have been fifty or sixty people, including our new Red Guards proud with their paper armbands. We had torches to light the way, and on the hills all around we saw other torches, as if the whole countryside were covered with giant fireflies. The different Production Teams identified one another from great distances by means of strange birdlike calls, and the calls grew into a chorus as everyone within a twenty-*li* radius converged on Shuangfeng.

At our rapid peasant pace we arrived at dawn, to find the streets already flowing with people. Cousin Han was so excited he didn't know what to look at first, and our mobility was so limited that we just floated wherever the crowd pushed us. There was no organization, just a loudspeaker announcement that at nine there would be a meeting in the square. Perhaps the Rebels just wanted to prove that they had a lot of support among the peasants; the sheer numbers were impressive.

I began to notice a pattern in the way the peasants went shopping. They would go into a store, eyes big at all the wonders offered, and then, as they gradually realized everything was too expensive for them, their faces fell and they went on to another one. Most of the people from our Production Team ended up only with a towel or a small mirror or a comb. Cousin Han was staring at everything, and then he found something he was longing to buy, a white tee-shirt for one *yuan* eighty. He vacillated forever, as Cousin Bing and I urged him to go ahead and get it, wanting it but knowing that there would be only two *jiao* left over afterward. Finally, almost trembling, he took out the carefully folded bills and handed them resolutely to the salesgirl. He accepted the brown-paper-rolled treasure with reverent hands.

It was close to nine and the current of people was drifting toward the square. There were so many people that we couldn't actually get into the square, but we heard the loudspeakers. "We salute the poor and lower-middle peasants," "The Rebels of Shuangfeng County thank the poor and lower-middle peasants for their warm support."

That was about the extent of the meeting and we continued to drift, ending up in a bookstore where Cousin Han bought two posters of quotations from Chairman Mao with his last two *jiao*. Then we spent awhile looking at a bus with some of the others from the team, and I became a lecturer, pointing out the steering wheel and the horn, the windshield wipers and the headlights. They could have stared for hours. They were also entranced by a row of bicycles parked in a row outside an official building. They had probably never seen so many in one place before.

People were starting to go home with their purchases, so we ate our sweet potatoes and started off, too. The way home seemed long because the sun was hot and the crowds had exhausted us, but Cousin Han seemed so satisfied that I felt it had been a really successful day. Then when we got home, he went and got his two-*jiao* supplement from Zhang and he seemed even happier, although Zhang himself didn't seem so happy when I ran into him the next day; he was worried about being able to pay for the Team's chemical fertilizer.

Then one morning Cousin Bing went back to Green Tree Town to see his family. He returned the next day with some money from Zhu Zhi-dao and the message that I should now go home. "Don't bother to stop off and see Auntie Zhu," Cousin Bing reported. "Your bus money's right here."

I was very sad at the thought of leaving, but I knew Father hadn't wanted me to stay away too long. The peasants were also sad, and loaded me with gifts of roasted sweet potatoes, peanuts, and their home-made hot pepper sauce. The young Red Guards I had helped walked the whole eight *li* with us, and I invited them all to come to Changsha to see me. They stood for a long time outside my bus window, the sunlight catching the white letters on their makeshift armbands, and I waved at them through the back window until they were out of sight.

CHAPTER NINE

The New Long March

In early September, all college students and the more Revolutionary teachers and middle school students received permission to travel free throughout the country for what was called "exchange of experiences." Within a short time, trains and buses were hopelessly crowded. At this point a new phase began—long-distance walking. It was started by some students from the Dalian Shipping Institute in Manchuria who hiked all the way to Peking to visit Revolutionary sites. Their journey was heralded as a way for young people to "temper" themselves (and save the country money on transportation fees). Suddenly it was as if China had been turned into a nation of soldier-actors, at least so far as young people were concerned. We were to re-create for ourselves the hardships suffered by the Red Army more than thirty years before, either by marching as they had through the Jinggang Mountain and Ruijing District (where they fought their first successful guerrilla wars against the KMT in 1934), or by following the 25,000-*li* route of the Long March (during which 300,000 men were reduced to 30,000), or by walking all the way from Yanan to Peking, the road taken by our victorious troops in 1949. During all of this we were to wear facsimiles of their coarse gray uniforms and straw sandals, carry heavy burdens as they had done, and travel at the forced march pace of an army at war.

Since I was only twelve, I would normally have had no chance to become involved in such things, but one day the oldest son of the neighbors who shared our kitchen with us came home from Peking, where he was a composition student at the Central Institute of Music.

Our families had always been very close, if only because of the Chinese custom of "enjoying the cool" on the hot summer nights; we'd often brought our bamboo stools out in the front of the house together and chatted idly until the heat had dissipated enough to let us go to sleep. Peng Ming was about eight years older than I, and had always been the person my sisters and I looked up to; he was confident, determined, brilliant, and a little hyperactive; his sentences poured out end to end, as if his mind worked much faster than his mouth could produce the sounds. When I heard he was home again, I felt the thrill of excitement a young boy can feel only when his hero is at hand.

Peng Ming looked taller and bonier than ever, and he now wore thick glasses, perhaps a result of the nighttime hours he had spent filling empty staves with Revolutionary music. He was, of course, a Red Guard, and he soon proved that he knew more about everything than we did, including how to organize a New Long March team. As he talked, he moved his long thin arms as if he were working magic, describing how we would walk from our doorway all the way to the very top of the Jinggang Mountain 800 *li* away (about 240 miles). We would follow exactly in the Red Army's footsteps, suffering every hardship they had suffered, learning from them, turning ourselves into worthy inheritors of the torch of Revolution by journeying to the very spot where it was first lit. Liang Fang decided to go and at last agreed to take me. When Father approved, glad to get me safely out of the house again, I was in raptures. From then on I would have died for the right to follow Peng Ming.

There were eight people on our team, including Peng Ming's younger brothers and sisters and several other neighbor children, all of them much older than I. We prepared for three days, learning how to fold our things inside our blankets in a neat little square of army green, how to tie our Red Army–style straw sandals and wrap our leggings around our calves. We prepared a red flag with yellow characters in imitation– Chairman Mao calligraphy reading "Long March," fitted placards on our bundles with Quotations so the people walking behind us could see them and take inspiration, collected a first-aid kit, a map, and canteens. My proudest moment was when Peng Ming pinned on my red armband, not a makeshift paper one, but one of finest red silk, with the shining snow-white words "Red Guard" painted onto it. Then he attached a beautiful Chairman Mao button to my jacket, a noble yellow profile with metallic red rays emanating from it and Tian An Men Square in red relief below. I think I grew ten inches.

It was a beautiful crisp winter morning when we set out through the gates of the *Hunan Daily,* the eight of us in formation, Peng Ming's younger brother in the lead carrying our red flag. Father and the other parents saw us off, anxious but not regretful, proud but afraid to show their feelings before the small gathering of onlookers. Tears were controlled on my part as well, for I was determined not to show my age. I marched proudly and quickly, without looking back even once.

The people in the Changsha streets stared at us with respect and envy, and this made us walk even taller and faster. We had soon passed through the suburbs and entered the countryside itself. Within half a day we began to encounter other New Long March teams, some from as far away as Guangxi and Guangdong provinces, and I felt prouder than ever to be from Hunan, Chairman Mao's home province and the fountainhead of the whole Communist movement. Some of these other groups had better costumes than we, with real gray uniforms and caps with red stars, and most of the teams were larger than ours, but our excitement and purpose were the same. We struck up an instant camaraderie, singing songs together, encouraging each other, exchanging information about what lay ahead. The walls of the peasants' houses had been painted with slogans like ONLY 750 LI TO THE JINGGANG MOUNTAIN and REVOLUTION TO THE END, so we felt more than ever that we were all engaged in a common pilgrimage, that we were all part of an exalted tide being pulled inexorably toward some sacred moonlight.

The peasants in the communes we passed through were warm providers. There were roadside stands where we could replenish our canteens with boiled water, and each commune had a major hospitality station where there was hot rice in huge wooden barrels, of which we could eat as much as we wanted free. There was never much in the way of meat or vegetables, but none of us complained, since it was our purpose to suffer the hardships of the Red Army. We were probably better off than they anyway, since at most stations there was a shelter in which rice straw beds had been spread for tired wayfarers, and the peasant women prepared hot water for washing and drinking. We must have depleted their stores and taken up an enormous amount of their time, but the peasants seemed glad to make sacrifices for Chairman Mao, and always urged us to eat more as if we were their own invited guests. Many of them already had small collections of buttons and printed slogans, souvenirs of the many groups who had passed before us.

We covered most of Changsha County by the first night and stopped at a district hospitality station. It was an old Qing dynasty meeting hall, with a curved roof and eaves like the flip of the hair of a girl in a foreign movie. We soaked our blistered feet and crawled into bed two by two, one person's blanket below and the other's above, our body heat raising the temperature in our cocoons enough above freezing to let us pass a comfortable night. We had walked close to eighty *li* (twenty-four miles).

The days passed and we soon got into a rhythm, sometimes climbing high mountains where we could see the original slogans of Revolution carved into the rock faces. WE WANT LAND, they read. DOWN WITH THE LANDLORDS. There were pretty little pavilions where we could rest, and the forests rang with the cries of teams calling to each other. Liang Fang and one of our other girls dropped back to walk with a team from Hubei Province, but I kept up with the boys, although I often wept with the pain of blisters and exhaustion. Later we began to follow the Red Army's custom of traveling at night, burning torches to light the way and walking until we were asleep on our feet. The more we suffered, the prouder we were, and some groups even bypassed the hospitality stations to sleep in the open and dig sweet potatoes from the peasants' fields with their bare hands. We saw the ditches where Chairman Mao had lain to fight the KMT, and the towns and villages were like museums, with the Red Army's meeting rooms, guns, sandals, and documents all preserved with faithful reverence. We could get precious Chairman Mao buttons at these sites, those invaluable souvenirs that had become national symbols of fervor and sincerity. Sometimes we were lucky and came upon some town square where an old graybeard, a member of the original Red Army, was speaking to the gathered Red Guards about his experiences in the Liberation. The excitement of such times was tremendous; I had never felt closer to the glorious Revolution, which had saved China from a thousand evils. When Peng Ming stopped our team once so we could carve our names into a thick bamboo, I took the knife and cut as deeply and as beautifully as I could.

I did find one thing strange, though. To judge by the old slogans and by what the Revolutionaries had to say, the peasants seemed to have been more interested in getting land for themselves than in Communism or Socialism. I realized, too, that if they had understood so little about the goals of Liberation, they understood even less about the Cultural Revolution. They were treating us so warmly because they adored Chairman Mao for driving out the landlords and he had told them to welcome us; but they really didn't seem to know why we were there or what was happening in the cities, nor did they really seem to care. This was a little disturbing to me. We were struggling to develop Communist thought and ideals, while it seemed as though they had been selfish and materialistic. And for so many years we had been taught about our great Socialist peasant Liberation!

After four days we descended from the mountains and came to the large city of Pingxiang in Jiangxi Province. From its appearance at night it was nearly as big as Changsha. The time was after midnight, it was raining gently, and we had walked nearly one hundred *li* that day, but our rest was not to come easily. Throughout Hunan Province we had been given excellent treatment, but when we crossed the provincial border, the numbers of Red Guards increased far beyond the peasants' capacity to accommodate them. In Pingxiang, every hotel and hospitality station was filled with pilgrims, all sleeping on the floors like rows of wrapped dumplings. With no place else to try, we were told that the only space available in the last hospitality station was the corridor, which was already wet with rainwater.

In our innocence, we Changshanese would probably have slept in the muck without too much complaint. However, we were traveling with two more experienced teams, and Peng Ming, as a Peking Red Guard, was accustomed to respectful treatment and getting his way. An argument developed, with Peng Ming and the others accusing the station workers of failing to support the Red Guard movement and the workers protesting that there simply wasn't another inch of space to be had. The ruckus aroused the sleepers and they all came to our defense. Pretty soon the whole hospitality station was involved in what promised to be a major incident. It was then that Peng Ming decided to make me his prime exhibit.

"Look at this child," he said, putting his arm around me. "A twelve-year-old boy, wet to the skin, exhausted, but driven by his Revolutionary commitment to surpass his own physical limits. Look, he's already got a cold" (it was true, my nose was running uncontrollably), "but he doesn't complain. But you would make this child, this seedling of the Revolution, sleep in the cement corridor in the rainwater."

There was a murmur of general sympathy, and many cries of "Here, young fellow, sleep in my bed," and "Here's a towel and a dry sweater, take these," but I stood in embarrassment beside Peng Ming, too overwhelmed by all the attention to want to leave his side.

The workers still refused to give in, however, and finally Peng Ming and the others proclaimed a hunger strike. We all sat down in the office and refused to move. This was to tell the inhabitants of Jiangxi Province that the hospitality station was undermining the Cultural Revolution. The rain beat on the roof and slogan-chanting faces flickered in the light of kerosene lanterns. Our wet clothing gave off a musty smell like mildew. My eyes were stinging with exhaustion and my body ached all over. I think I could have fallen asleep sitting right there on the office floor.

This was my first experience with confrontation tactics, and it was short and sweet. The workers hastily yielded us their offices, two large rooms, and we spread our things wherever there was space for a body, on the floors, on the chairs, and on the desks themselves, piling stacks of documents into one disordered mountain. Victory warmed our dreams, and the next day the local Red Guard newspaper criticized the workers, saying their lack of hospitality was "a question of Proletarian Revolutionary feeling." They also said that everyone should learn from the youngest Red Guard ever to visit the city, their twelve-year-old comrade-in-arms from Hunan, who "struggled as resolutely as his older teammates, never fearing hardship, and always placing others before himself." As we left Pingxiang, Liang Fang wiped my runny nose for me with her handkerchief and commented dryly, "You're a Red Guard now. Red Guards blow their noses."

The next part of our journey took us back up into the Luoxiao Range, to the historic village of Sanwan, the site of the famous "Sanwan Reorganization" in 1929, during which the Party had first been placed in absolute command of the Red Army. We climbed with ever greater eagerness, pulling ourselves up by the long branches that hung down like ropes, choosing the hardest routes near the cliff faces, scrambling on all fours amid the rocks and boulders. We arrived in early evening, exhausted and triumphant, with very empty bellies.

Along the road, we had seen a lot of notices urging Red Guards not to stay the night in Sanwan but to press on, because it was only a small Production Team of several hundred peasants and they didn't have the facilities to handle many of us. However, such notices were useless since almost everyone wanted to stay at the Revolutionary site. The place was filled with red armbands, and the peasants were boiling rice frantically, never enough to meet the demand. Every time a pot was finished, the Red Guards squeezed around, pushing and shoving, the camaraderie we had experienced earlier in the trip forgotten in the need to get something to eat.

I was still smaller than most, and I had a green cap that I had gotten from one of the old Revolutionaries in exchange for one of the precious Chairman Mao buttons I was acquiring at each historical site. I snaked my way in through the thicket of legs and emerged in the center by the pot with my cap outstretched, receiving a hot hatful of rice from a harried peasant woman. I escaped proudly back to my teammates with my booty, and we ate from the dirty cap with our hands. Hygiene was the last of our concerns.

The next problem was housing, and Peng Ming thought of a clever way to make use of his musical talent. He spent a few minutes composing simple movements to accompany the songs he had taught us on the road, and rehearsed us for half an hour. Then he announced that we would be holding a performance for the Sanwan peasants on their threshing ground.

Crude as the show was, the peasants loved it, for Sanwan was a culture-forsaken place, and several members of our team had decent singing voices. When we volunteered to teach the peasants some of the songs, they began to regard us as windfalls from heaven. From there it was a simple step to an invitation to spend the night as guests in their houses, and we trooped off two by two.

The houses were wooden and had two floors, very different from the sturdy sprawling mud-brick homes of Hunan. The second floor was made simply of planks laid crosswise over structural logs, uneven enough that you could see much of the floor below through the cracks, unstable enough that an unwary footstep could lift a plank and send you crashing right through the floor.

This is exactly what happened, and I landed in a pile of brushwood on the floor below, my face scratched and bloody. I was more breathless than hurt. Our peasant hosts were in a panic that I was injured, and I was worried that I had broken their house. But when Peng Ming poked his head down through the floor from above and his glasses joined me in the brushwood, everyone laughed. Going aloft again, I was more careful, managed to find myself a comparatively solid stretch of board, and was soon fast asleep.

After Sanwan the mountains were higher, and at times we looked down into swirling clouds and fancied ourselves on fairy islands in a floating archipelago. There were fewer trees, most of them piney and gnarled, and the air was full of frost and moisture, coating the rocks with slippery ice and giving us all a hoary look of premature age. I was soon covered with cuts and bruises from my falls; fortunately Father had insisted that we bring army sneakers and the white gauze face-masks (worn for protection during cold, dry weather), so we were able to discard our straw sandals and warm our frozen mouths and noses. It seemed our urgency increased the nearer we came to our goal, and we were traveling almost at a trot when the road permitted. I thought it strange the way our fingers and toes felt like ice while we sweated so much that our clothing was wet.

There were two major landmarks on the Jinggang Mountain, one the Mao Flatland and the other the Ci Flatland. The second was higher and had been the major Communist base. Most Red Guards spent the night at the Mao Flatland, resting in preparation for their ascent to the Ci Flatland, but like people with an obsession we decided to continue on without stopping. A loosely formed group of about twenty, we marched through the night until we didn't have the strength to sing and there was only the sound of many footsteps crushing dry twigs. Finally, a long distance away, we saw the glimmer of lights, and we knew we had reached our destination, the final stop in our 800-*li* quest.

I don't know how we made it the rest of the way, but the lights got bigger and bigger until at last they turned into the biggest surprise of our trip, a group of five ultra-modern multi-story government buildings every bit as fancy as the Hunan Hotel in the Changsha Martyrs' Park. Perhaps Chairman Mao had built them in memory of his guerrilla days and used them for top-level secret meetings. Now they were packed with Red Guards, and with sleep already a film over our eyes, we were assigned to the back of a stairwell where there was fresh rice grass and enough space for the eight of us from Hunan if we doubled up into four cocoons, two of girls and two of boys.

The next day we saw how clever Chairman Mao was to choose the Ci Flatland as his base. It was ringed all around with sharp peaks, each of which would be as difficult to cross as the one on which we had just expended our final strength. It was a pretty area, and would be fertile enough in the summertime with all the mountain streams and good brown land, but now it was poor and barren, and the peasants had no task but to stare at the newcomers. There were so many Red Guards that the streets were running with them, and more were streaming down from the mountainsides every moment. I suppose somebody should have known that the flatland would become a disaster area, but there was no sign that anyone had foreseen the consequences of sending a nation of young pilgrims to a few square miles of wintry land on one of the most rugged mountains in China.

Our troubles began that morning. Peng Ming suddenly ran to the outhouse and came back half an hour later looking green and yellow and holding his stomach. He lay down on the straw and couldn't get up again. Two of the girls were sick, too. When I went with them to the clinic we found that there was an epidemic, and the clinic was full. There would be rice porridge available for the ill twice a day, while everyone else would be eating boiled sorghum. It was a real nightmare— our leader was helpless, and still more young people poured down like red ants, triumphant and excited, then sober and worried when they learned of the illnesses and the food shortage. And then the worst thing possible happened: It snowed.

It came down in thick, obstructing flakes, the winds blowing it off the slopes and filling the bottom of the huge bowl we were in. It continued for an interminable three hours, and when it stopped a light blanket of snow had blown through the window to cover Peng Ming where he lay; Liang Fang's hands were frozen to a strange red color. It was frightening and beautiful: Snow in Changsha never came this white and thick.

Then in the perfect silence of snow I heard a strange sound like a distant tractor or a nearby fly, and a small helicopter emerged from behind one of the mountains and hovered above us, then descended cautiously lower and lower over a field. We all ran out in the snow waving our hands and nearly weeping with happiness, shouting, "Chairman Mao will save us," "Long Live Chairman Mao." Then the boxes began to drop, big square ones with parachutes, settling with a sigh into the snow.

At first people ran everywhere at once, as if trying to get a box for themselves. Organization soon prevailed, however, and the boxes were carried to the central hospitality station to be apportioned. Soon we heard we were to line up, either bringing our identification cards or sending them with a team representative. Liang Fang took my primary-school photo of me in my Young Pioneer scarf with the others' middle-school and college I.D.s and went to stand in line.

She returned in an hour with a small bag of biscuits and two pieces of hard candy for each of us and the news that the Ci Flatland was being evacuated because of the epidemic. The next day army trucks would be coming up the paved road to ferry us all to a place called Jian County where we would be put on trains and sent home. Teams with illness would have priority over others, so we would be among the first to go.

We heard the news with a mixture of relief and regret. We were miserably uncomfortable and worried about our sick comrades, but this seemed an abrupt and inglorious ending to our Revolutionary travail. During the whole journey we had regarded physical discomfort as a welcome test, always remembering that it was nothing compared with what the Red Army had suffered; in all the ten days of our New Long March, I had never heard anyone complain about his struggle with nature. I had never been so cold or hungry in my life, yet if someone had given me a choice about going down in an army truck or walking, the decision would not have been an easy one. So Liang Fang's announcement took us by surprise, although we realized sadly that evacuation was the only solution.

The trucks came early in the morning, almost a hundred of them, and the soldiers packed us all in, thirty or forty to a truck. It was a beautiful sunny morning and the snow was melting, but we were too weak to enjoy it; even our proud flag seemed to have gone limp. I stood by Peng Ming holding a blanket around us, and the girls leaned against each other with their arms entwined, their hair matted, and their hands still that strange red. The road twisted back and forth like an active snake, which didn't make us much more comfortable; Peng Ming's brother threw up twice and Liang Fang three times. The descent seemed to last forever, four hours, five hours, six hours, but finally the road straightened and quickened and we began to notice army trucks coming back for a second load. We were in Jian County, but we were half dead. We were luckier than we knew, however, for within a week meningitis broke out on the mountain. I've heard that the monument listing the names of the hundreds of Red Guards who died there stands over ten feet high.

CHAPTER TEN

Peking!

When we finally got home, we learned that the State Council had issued a directive announcing the end of the "exchange of experiences" movement and calling on all Red Guards to return to their original units. When Peng Ming recovered, he went back to Peking, but not everyone was as dutiful as he. The more the order was repeated, the more young people feared they would never again have the chance to travel to other places, for under normal circumstances most couldn't expect to leave their home towns in their entire lifetimes. There was a last-minute flood of new departures by people hoping to get in on the tail end of the free train rides, and clever ways to get around the new restrictions were invented.

Liang Fang and I, for example, walked for three days south to Hengyang, and then traded our free tickets back to Changsha for those of a group of agriculture students being sent home to Guangzhou. (They were trying to get to Peking, and every bit of progress north was welcome to them.) In Guangzhou we spent Spring Festival at the home of an old colleague of my father's with a pretty little daughter of my age, who took us to eat as many bananas and sticks of sugar cane as we could manage. Her name was Sha An, and she danced and sang her way into my twelve-year-old heart, weeping when Liang Fang and I decided to give ourselves up at one of the hospitality stations and get free tickets back home again. Later, I would cherish that childish love she had offered me and think of her when I was lonely.

This was just a prelude, however, to my big adventure. I had

nothing to do because the middle schools were so busy making Revolution that they were taking no new students, and traveling had gotten
into my blood. My greatest dream was now to go to Peking, where I
could be with Peng Ming again. I was lucky: Some new friends from
the Peking Machinery Institute agreed to take me back home with them.
I pinned my collection of Chairman Mao buttons in display fashion onto
a large handkerchief, folding it carefully and putting it into the pocket
of the big beat-up cotton-padded overcoat I had borrowed from Father.
I wanted to be ready for anything.

The trains were even more crowded than they had been on the trip
to Guangzhou, and at first we despaired of being able to squeeze on.
There were no conductors (and no tickets), but the Red Guards already
on board refused to unlock the doors. At last we noticed that one of the
washroom windows was slightly open. My bigger friends hoisted me up.
I got my hand inside and released the latch. We pushed the window
open and I crawled inside.

There were two Red Guards sleeping by the open hole in the floor
that served as a toilet, and they weren't happy to see me when my
entrance woke them up. I argued with them a long time before they
finally agreed to let my friends climb in. Then the proprietors of the
toilet opened the door pointedly and showed us out, locking the door
into "Occupied" with a snap.

It had been cold outside but the train was hot. Every conceivable
space was claimed, with people even sitting on the tea tables and
sleeping on the luggage racks. The only thing we could do was stand
and hope to negotiate for a place with someone getting off.

Considering the close quarters, the general mood wasn't bad. There
were occasional fights, though, the major one being with the Guangzhou
Red Guards, who had barricaded themselves into four entire cars at the
beginning of the trip and refused to let anyone else in. Finally their
windows were smashed and there was a redistribution of bodies, but in
Wuhan, five hours to the north, the density was restored again. There
was struggle at every station, the people outside wanting to get in and
the people inside wanting to keep them out.

It was two days and two nights to Peking. Food soon became a
problem, but those with foresight shared with those without. Even worse
was the question of relieving oneself, for the bathrooms had long been

blocked off. The girls developed a system of climbing out onto the platform in groups and encircling each other while they did their business in turns; the boys simply went out and used the tracks, for there was no shame in those days. Leaving the train was a dangerous game, however; there was no guarantee your re-entry would be an easy one. On more than one occasion I saw someone left behind because he had responded to the call of nature.

At Zhengzhou came trouble. The station was full of soldiers checking everyone's identification papers and making those from the South get off. Already a small angry group was being ushered to one end of the platform, and we could hear chanting and quarrelsome voices from the next car. I was really afraid, for it seemed that all my hopes would be for nothing. Then one of my friends urgently motioned for me to follow him out the window on the track side, and walked me along the far side of the train where the soldiers wouldn't see us, all the way back to the last car. It was a signal car, and a worker in an oil-stiff cap was sitting in it, wiping his red and green lantern.

"Old master-worker," said my friend very politely. "This is my little brother. He's very ill and can't bear the crowd any longer. Won't you let him rest in your car awhile?"

The worker looked at us suspiciously. "No one is allowed to ride in here," he said. He looked me over and I tried to seem young and sick, which wasn't too difficult. I could see him softening. "Are you from Peking?" he asked.

My friend showed him his I.D. and I was glad I looked too young to have one. I was glad too that my standard Chinese was better than that of most of my classmates. Screwing up my courage I said in my best approximation of a Peking accent, "If you let me ride with you I'll show you my Chairman Mao button collection." In those days, there was nothing more coveted and more difficult to get than a Chairman Mao button, since few people outside of the Red Guards themselves could make the long journeys to the Revolutionary sites where they were distributed. The worker's eyes gleamed with interest and I pressed my advantage. "I'll give you one. I'll let you choose any one you like."

"All right then, come on up and let me see," he said, his duty quickly forgotten in the face of such temptation. "You can stay for a while but you'll have to go back at the next station."

I climbed on before he could change his mind and my friend waved briefly and left. Then I reached deep into my pocket and took out my handkerchief, exposing my treasures to his greedy gaze.

His hands were big and greasy and I sat in horror as he fondled my prizes, my heart jumping as he paused before each jewel, afraid that that would be the one I would have to sacrifice. While I couldn't bear to part with a single one, I could also hear the loudspeaker calling, *"All Red Guards without Peking identification cards, please get off immediately,"* and I was afraid he might pay attention and make a connection between the announcements and my presence. So I babbled incoherently, trying to distract him, telling him how I had gotten these in Sanwan, those at Pingxiang, and he wavered interminably, hating to lose any of them just as much as I did. Finally he unclasped one of the Jinggang Mountain buttons, a big red one with Chairman Mao's head floating over three golden peaks. "I'll take this one," he announced. "I already have one of Peking, and now all I need is Shaoshan, Yanan, and Ruijing for the complete set of the five major Revolutionary shrines."

I thought I would die, for I only had three from Jinggang Mountain. At the same time I felt I would have given him the whole handkerchief-full if only he wouldn't throw me off the train. So I watched in private agony as he pinned the button onto his blue worker's overcoat, smiling and chatting as if I were his guest for Sunday tea.

I was praying for the train to start but it didn't, and finally the worker hopped off to see what the delay was about. He came back ten minutes later and said, "Some of the Red Guards wouldn't get off, but the Peking Red Guards helped the PLA to move them. We should be moving along in a minute." Sure enough, the train pulled off, and we passed the group I should have been among, Red Guards from Henan, Hubei, Hunan, and Guangzhou, standing miserably on the platform waiting to be sent back where they had come from.

At the next stop I thanked the worker and told him I felt better, and went back to join my friends. They greeted me with a round of applause and made room for me in the now-spacious car. I fell asleep and when I woke up I was in Peking. The loudspeaker was playing "The East Is Red," and it was the sweetest sound I had ever heard.

Peking was cold to my sneakered feet, and the wind was like knives, but to me it was heaven. The avenues seemed five or six times as broad as those in Changsha, the buildings cleaner and more splendid, if a bit austere. I immediately demanded to be taken to Tian An Men Square, and tired as they were, my friends took me, watching with amusement as I stared at everything that was legend—the Great Hall of the People, the Monument to the Heroes of the People, the Historical Museum. Like every other Red Guard coming to Peking for the first time, I took my oath in front of the huge picture of Chairman Mao, lifting my "Little Red Book" in my right hand, sticking out my chest and reciting proudly, "Chairman Mao, Liang Heng has finally come to your side. I will always be loyal to you. I will always be loyal to your Thought. I will always be loyal to your Revolutionary line." I could have stayed there all night, but my friends comforted me saying there would be many other chances. They took me home with them, drew me a map of where to find Peng Ming and the Central Institute of Music so I could go first thing the next day, and found me a bed and tucked me in, their little weary traveler.

It took me nearly a whole morning to find the Central Institute of Music in the Western District. It was so famous that I'd expected it to be on a grand avenue, but it was behind an old iron gate off a small lane. Still, what I saw when I walked in was more than beautiful enough to satisfy me, for across the road stretched an old rectangular building in the imperial style, with a green tile roof, ornately carved wooden windows, and red pillars. I walked through and found myself facing a second building identical to the first, and saw on the right a smaller one—with the sign MUSEUM OF THE HISTORY OF MUSICAL INSTRUMENTS—which for some reason was all boarded up. Beyond the second barrier were the gray cement dormitories.

I learned that my friend Peng Ming was probably in the broadcast station of his Rebel organization, so I went there to look for him. He and his comrades were crowded around a desk on which was spread a group of photographs, and they were discussing them in urgent tones, pointing, and passing them around. I stood awkwardly in the doorway for several minutes, afraid to disturb them. I thought Peng Ming looked exhausted, and much thinner than before, but still close to magnificent in his Red Guard army-style uniform and red armband.

He finally noticed me, breaking into a huge smile and coming over and grasping my hands tightly in his. "You've come just in time. Work in our Red Guard organization and make Revolution with us." Then he

turned to his friends. "Comrades," he announced. "This is my old
neighbor, and the youngest member of my New Long March team. He
has come all the way from Hunan to help us." From that day everybody
knew me as "Little Hunan."

Peng Ming shared his own narrow bed with me, and every night
we squeezed in with a pillow at each end, a blanket, and an odd
assortment of beat-up coats piled up in a small mountain on top of us.
Every morning, he led me in singing "The East Is Red," and every
evening, "The Internationale." If he had a few minutes, he instructed
me in Revolutionary thought, teaching me that we young Revolutionaries
must be willing to give our blood for the Revolution, that we were the
dawn of China, and that we must always be vigilant against our own
individualism and Revisionist tendencies. I admired him more than
ever, although he was so busy he usually had to ignore me. Sometimes
he never came back to sleep at all, or stayed awake in the room all
night writing posters and articles. He lived as if there were a war going
on, and did everything with bloodshot eyes in an aura of emergency.

He let me wander around for a week to get used to the surroundings.
The classrooms were all boarded shut, and signs hung on the doors
reading FEUDALIST-CAPITALIST-REVISIONIST. Pianos had been pulled out
into the corridors and sealed shut with the stamps of the Red Guards,
and broken desks and chairs lay about everywhere. Sheet music of
classical European composers was scattered all over the floors, some of
it in charred remnants, and from ceiling to floor, from wall to wall,
sometimes more than ten layers thick, were the words of struggle and
criticism. The existing walls weren't enough for all these words, and
additional bamboo partitions had been erected all over the grounds of
the institute, slicing flowerbeds in two and blocking alleyways between
dormitories. Sometimes the characters were so large I could hardly
imagine how they had been written with a brush, sometimes so small I
had to bend down to read them.

Often when I went to the bathroom I would notice two men sweeping
the corridors and cleaning out the toilets. One day another child told
me that the old one was Ma Si-cong, the President of the Institute and
a famous violinist, and the youngish one wearing heavy leather shoes
and traditional clothes with cloth buttons was Liu Shi-kun, the famous
pianist. I had seen enough of this kind of thing by then not to think

much about it, but when Peng Ming explained to me that the pictures in the broadcasting room the first day had been of Liu Shi-kun accepting First Prize in an International Youth Competition in the Soviet Union, I assumed that he must be an unusually bad man.

After about a week, Peng Ming told me that I could help the organization. Because I was so young, he asked me to sell their newspaper, *The Red Flag of Art*, around Wang Fu-jing, Xi Dan, and Tian An Men Square.

I didn't know my way around, so a fat little girl pianist became my guide and special friend. Like most of the other children selling newspapers she had been something of a child prodigy and a student at the Central Institute of Music's Attached Middle School. We took turns riding each other to work on the back of a bicycle. She had an unusually piercing voice, and could outsell the rest of us hands down.

I worked like a madman, sometimes not getting to sleep until two or three in the morning. Latest of all was probably the evening Peng Ming asked me to help the group hang a cloth slogan on a propaganda wall on Xi Dan Street. The slogan was nearly two stories high, and we had to use two ladders fastened together to climb to the top. When we had it unrolled and straight it said in huge gleaming black characters, DOWN WITH XIAO WANG-DONG! DESTROY THE MINISTRY OF CULTURE!

In this way I gradually got to know what was going on at the Central Institute of Music. The situation was basically the same as it was all over China, and the Rebel groups were deeply involved in factional struggle. The old "Protect the Emperor" group had been disbanded, but some of its members had formed a Rebel group called the "Mao Ze-dong Thought Struggle" group under the famous scholar Guo Mo-ruo's son Guo Si-hong, and it remained a major conservative force. The Rebel group was led by Peng Ming, and it was called the "Red Cliff Struggle" group, after the book about a pre-Liberation KMT prison. There was also a new group, which had splintered off from the Red Cliff Struggle group, called the "Peking Commune." Each of these groups claimed to be the most Revolutionary, and it was always attacking the others in big character posters and broadcasts as "protectors of the Reactionary Capitalist Road."

These factional struggles were so absorbing that the Revolutionaries had little time for anything else. Then one day, a month or so after I had arrived, disaster struck. The Mao Ze-dong Thought Struggle group plastered up a huge poster announcing the bad news.

> The Red Cliff Struggle group has released our Institute's stinking Capitalist Roader violinist and helped him to escape. Last night a Japanese radio station reported that Ma Si-cong and his family have already left China. This counterrevolutionary incident was planned and effected by the Red Cliff Struggle organization, which must bear the consequences.

I shall never forget the look of incredulity on Peng Ming's face when he read that poster. He looked as if he had just been told that he had forgotten to go to his own father's funeral. Then he shouted for a truck to take the group to Ma Si-cong's house to prove that the poster was a lie.

I hitched a ride on the back of somebody's bicycle. It was all true. Although none of the belongings had been removed, there wasn't a Capitalist Roader in the house. Everything was in great disorder, for there had been many search raids, and the Red Cliff Struggle Red Guards were standing in the middle of the chaos saying that they had been tricked, and that the Mao Ze-dong Thought Struggle group must have let him go. Then they hurried back and put up a poster saying *eren xian gaozhuan:* EVIL PEOPLE ARE THE FIRST TO MAKE ACCUSATIONS. The two groups fought for nearly a month about this, but nobody ever established how the famous violinist got away.

One evening late at night, I was lying in bed watching Peng Ming writing posters. He had a brush in one hand, and he was eating two steamed yellow sorghum buns and some pickles with the other. His hair stuck out like fire all around his head, and his frame was like that of a skeleton in glasses. For a long time I had wondered about why he wanted to drive himself to that condition, and screwing up all my courage, I asked, "How did you get to be so dedicated and enthusiastic?"

He stopped writing and looked at me sharply. Then he put down his brush and began to talk with me. I think it was the first time he had seen me as anything more than a child. "I want to exercise myself," he said. "I want to collect experience. Supporting the Great Cultural Revolution is a great chance for us young people to develop ourselves."

I thought to myself that in a way that was what I was doing, too, since the struggles in Peking really had nothing to do with me. And I thought too that I should try to understand more about what was going on around me. "Why do you sometimes say that you want to turn the Central Institute of Music inside out?" I asked.

"Because I agree with Chairman Mao. The Ministry of Culture is full of 'emperors and generals, beautiful ladies and gifted scholars.' Our institute has been a castle for musicians who care about works only a small number of people can understand. It shouldn't belong only to a small number of people, but to the worker, peasant, and soldier masses." He looked at me with excitement and conviction. "There's a role for everyone to play, young and old, in every corner of China. You're lucky that you're doing so much to help while you're still so young. When you remember this when you're all grown up, you'll realize how very glorious it all is."

After that conversation, Peng Ming brought me to meetings and let me help do propaganda work. But the first time I had real responsibility was the day of the meeting to criticize the pianist Liu Shi-kun. They were holding him in Peng Ming's room prior to the meeting, and I was allowed to stand guard. I was very proud. I had a big green army-style coat and a greenish hat that looked almost like a real soldier's cap. They gave me a big, stout stick to use as a weapon.

He was already sitting in the room, head bowed, looking far from being a great musician. He had a horse's thin white face and hard, angry hair, and he was pushing the cloth ties of his blue cotton folk jacket open and closed nervously with his long white fingers. He looked up when I came in, but immediately bowed his head again, while I marched proudly over to the window and I stood with my hands at my waist, guarding him fiercely.

The window opened on the square where the criticism meeting was already in session. *"Down with Liu Shi-kun"* echoed clearly from below, and then there was relative silence as the speeches began. Liu Shi-kun looked up and inclined his head slightly as if to listen, but I immediately barked, "Don't move," and he returned to his original position.

After a while, he licked his lips and half whispered, "Please give me some water. I'm thirsty."

I didn't know what to do. A Revolutionary shouldn't give water to his enemy, but I couldn't just stand there with water in the thermos only a few feet away. But what if someone saw me? I went to the doorway to listen to see if there was anyone coming, and then I quickly poured a cup from the thermos.

But the water was too hot, and Liu Shi-kun could barely sip it. I was afraid someone would come. So I took another cup and scooped up some cold water that had been used for washing dishes and poured a little of that into Liu Shi-kun's cup. As he drank it down I said fiercely, "You can't tell anyone about this, or next time I won't give you anything at all."

After a while he looked at me and asked, "How old are you? You must be only a bit over ten."

My pride was offended. I pointed to my red armband. "What's this? A ten-year-old can't be a Red Guard."

Liu Shi-kun only said softly, "You're too young to know better," and was silent.

Then the sound of slogans started up again, and the stairs rang with footsteps. Four strong Red Guards threw the door open and barked, "Liu Shi-kun. Let's go." They were carrying a heavy iron placard and a big paper hat labeled COUNTERREVOLUTIONARY MUSICIAN LIU SHI-KUN. Liu stood up, bowing nervously as they placed these roughly on him and shoved him out the door.

I started to follow, but realized I had forgotten to lock the door and went back. Then I had a queer thought. Perhaps later he would be thirsty. So I poured out a glass of clean hot water and let it sit there to cool. Then I went out to join the meeting.

The crowd was throwing stones and spitting. Liu Shi-kun had been placed on a platform for interrogation.

"Are you a counterrevolutionary musician?"

"I, I—"

Someone kicked him onto the floor and made him kneel.

"I am, I am."

"Did you play stinking Revisionist music in the Soviet Union's World Youth Piano Competition? Did you win a prize? Did you shake hands with Khrushchev? Did you smile and surrender to the Soviet Revisionists? Did you?"

"I, I—" It seemed as if he were trying to remember something. Someone kicked him again. "Speak. Quickly."

"Yes, yes. I surrendered."

Then someone led the crowd in a chant: "Down with the Soviet

Revisionist Spy, Down with Liu Shi-kun." Next they sang the special song they had made up for the occasion:

> Liu Shi-kun you bastard,
> Now you can surrender,
> If you do not tell the truth,
> You may quickly die . . .

Everyone was excited, and I sang with all my heart.

It was cold, and the dust was blowing. The speeches were long and inspiring. Some said Liu Shi-kun was an individualist, that he had tried to become famous; others, that he had lived a Capitalist life-style and hoarded money under his pillow. Then at last it was time to conclude the meeting with the collective study of the sayings of Chairman Mao.

According to custom, the worst counterrevolutionaries had no right to listen to the sayings of Chairman Mao. There ensued a rather lengthy discussion to ascertain which, if any, of the ten-odd counterrevolutionaries present could stay. Only two of the musicians and composers were determined worthy, and the rest were led away.

I went to unlock the door for Liu Shi-kun. When everyone else had left, I handed him the cup of water before he had a chance to ask for it. After he had drunk it down, he asked to be taken to the bathroom. He trembled all over as he walked, and his urine was a queer dark yellow. I felt funny as I led him back, thinking about how Father was criticized, but I tried to push my thoughts away. When they came to take him away he thanked me, in a soft weary voice.

Later, whenever I saw him sweeping the floors and cleaning the toilets I felt embarrassed and tried to avoid him. It was almost as if there were something personal between us.

If there was any single thing that meant ecstasy to everyone in those days, it was seeing Chairman Mao. Ever since I had been in Peking, the possibility had been in the back of my mind, and, like every other Red Guard, I would have laid down my life for the chance. Liang Fang's Red Guard detachment had come to Peking and been reviewed a few months earlier, and I remembered her description well. They stayed at hospitality stations run by the PLA, and the soldiers trained them especially in preparation for the great day. They learned how to march in formation, how to stand at attention. They prepared their cleanest clothes, and traded Revolutionary paraphernalia madly among themselves in an effort to get the largest possible Chairman Mao buttons. When the day came, everyone took out their "Little Red Books," their canteens, and folders full of postcards imprinted with slogans from Chairman Mao and their organizations' names to trade with members of other Red Guard groups from different parts of the country. Everyone knew Chairman Mao always showed up in the morning at ten, but by five, Tian An Men Square was a human sea of red and green. There were big red billboards, red balloons, red armbands, red flags, red placards, red books, and red buttons. And their clothing was PLA green, either real, or the closest imitation. While they were waiting there were singing competitions among the various groups, each one trying to demonstrate greater love of the Chairman and greater Revolutionary ardor. Despite the fact that there were no bathrooms and that it was so crowded that some Red Guards fainted, everyone agreed that it was their happiest day on earth.

By the time I reached Peking, Chairman Mao had already reviewed the Red Guards specially more than eight times, and those glorious days of particular notice were over. However, everyone knew that on May 1, International Workers' Day, and on October 1, National Day, the leaders of China would go to the gate-tower to watch the fireworks. Therefore, as May 1 approached, everyone's mind and conversation were on one thing only: Would Chairman Mao watch the celebration and would we have a chance to see him? Of course, nothing was certain, but I didn't know a single person who wasn't going to Tian An Men Square to find out.

Since the Central Institute of Music was, after all, a performance unit, its Red Guards gravitated naturally toward propaganda work. On May 1, Peng Ming was planning to go with a small group to conduct performances of Revolutionary songs at the Summer Palace during the day, and then go in the evening to the Square. By this time, I had been taught some of the simple dances like the "Loyalty Dance" for Chairman Mao, and I was sometimes asked to carry drums and other instruments, so I went with Peng Ming's group to the park. We were completely unprepared for what happened.

In the middle of singing a song that Peng Ming had composed

himself, we heard the great news: Chairman Mao was in the park! Gathering our instruments together hastily, we ran gasping to the spot, but it was too late. He was gone. All that remained of him was the touch of his hand on the hands of a few who had been lucky enough to get close to him. But we didn't leave in disappointment. That trace of precious warmth in the palms of others seemed to us a more than adequate substitute for the real thing. Those Chairman Mao had touched now became the focus of our fervor. Everyone surged toward them with outstretched arms in hopes of transferring the sacred touch to their own hands. If you couldn't get close enough for that, then shaking the hand of someone who had shaken hands with Our Great Saving Star would have to do. And so it went, down the line, until sometimes handshakes were removed as much as one hundred times from the original one, spreading outward in a vast circle like waves in a lake when a meteor crashes into its center. The joy of touching the hand that had touched the hand that had touched the hand was indescribable, and there were tears in my eyes when I received the gift and turned, shouting, to Peng Ming, "Shake it, shake my hand!"

He grasped my hand passionately in his, nearly weeping. "I'm happy. I'm so happy."

The handshake didn't end there. All fourteen of us piled back into the truck and banged on our drums and cymbals all the way home to the Central Institute of Music, shouting out the news as we drove through the gate. Soon much of the institute had turned out to join in the handshaking. I must have stood there pumping for more than an hour, as the loudspeakers blared out what had happened and played triumphal music. I don't think it occurred to anyone that none of us had been anywhere near the man.

Of course, after this we wanted to see Chairman Mao even more, and our hopes for the evening were high. Finally it was time to go. Once again, we brought our instruments, for we would go from one group to another accompanying them and leading them in song. Everything was as Liang Fang had said, except that it was night. There were tens of thousands of black heads facing the gatehouse. With the exception of propaganda teams like our own, everyone was seated in Revolutionary regiments, singing the slogan songs, chanting, "We want to see Chairman Mao!" There were frequent rumors that the Chairman had arrived, and then everyone would break rank and rush forward in a giant wave, while the soldiers shouted, "Keep Revolutionary order, go back to your places and sit down!" By nine he still hadn't arrived. Then the loudspeakers began to play "The East Is Red" and everyone rushed in a great swell toward the bridge, for this time they were sure he was really coming.

Because of our relative mobility, at that moment we had the misfortune to be at the very rear of the crowd. We were rushing desperately forward, craning our necks to see, when suddenly a line of soldiers ran up behind us and made a passage right through our group. It seemed Chairman Mao had not been in the gate-tower after all, but in the Great Hall of the People behind us, on the opposite side of the square. Now a line of cars was making its way toward us, and I had a front-row view!

Chairman Mao's car was first, a Peking-brand army jeep. As in a dream, I saw him. He seemed very tall to me, magnificent, truly larger than life. He waved his hat as the jeep drove slowly through the throng. The soldiers forming the passageway stood at attention, but the tears poured down their faces in rivulets. Nevertheless they managed to sniffle their refrain, "Please keep Revolutionary order! Please keep Revolutionary order!"

I was bawling like a baby, crying out incoherently again and again, "You are our hearts' reddest, reddest sun!" My tears blocked my vision, but I could do nothing to control myself. Then Chairman Mao's car was past, and Premier Zhou's followed.

The people in front hadn't realized what had happened, and were still chanting "We want to see Chairman Mao!" with their backs turned to all the action. As they discovered him in their midst, however, they nearly mobbed the car, obstructing its passage completely. The Chairman actually got out, then, and shook hands with as many people as he could. It was only when the crowd was told that the Chairman wanted to climb the gate-tower to see the fireworks that they separated and let the car go through.

All the lights in the gate-tower were lit. You could see the silhouettes of everyone inside, although it was hard to tell which one was his. The loudspeakers were still playing "The East Is Red," and the fireworks were more splendid than any I have ever seen. They went on steadily for half an hour, a succession of the most dazzling lights the land that invented fireworks had to offer. There were showers of silver daggers, cataracts of vermilion foam. And with every burst, the hearts of tens of thousands of young people working for the salvation of China opened with reverence for the blessing they had been shown. There were two final miracles, a Revolutionary red rocket, which burst into the words *"Long Live Our Great Leader Chairman Mao,"* and a purple one, which read *"Long Live the Great Communist Party."*

When it was all over everyone ran to the post office to telegraph the good news to their families all over China. I waited more than two hours to trace out the trembling words, "This evening at 9:15 I became the happiest person in the world." I knew my father would need no further explanation. We were awake all night talking about our deep joy. We remembered every detail of what he had looked like or done, although no one could have seen clearly in the darkness. People were still talking the next day, hurrying to buy the newspapers to see if their friends were in the pictures. And leaders like Peng Ming looked to see which Red Guard groups were mentioned by name, to see if there were any new clues about who was in favor.

A couple of days later, I got a letter from my father, who said he missed me and wanted me to come home. My heart was heavy, but since everyone said that Chairman Mao wouldn't be making any more public appearances, and since I had been away for close to half a year, I knew it was time for me to go. Peng Ming's sister (who had reached Peking too late for the great event, and in her disappointment decided to return to Changsha) offered to take me with her.

Before we left, we went to the Gold Water Bridge, and scooped up some of that "Happiness Water" and put it in our canteens. Then we scraped up little piles of dirt and put them in envelopes. Finally, I took out a clean piece of white paper, pressed my hand firmly against the chalky red wall of the Square, and fixed my red handprint to the white paper forever. These mementoes were to be my greatest treasures in the years to come, my solace in times of trouble, and the envy of all my friends.

I had been free in Peking, and had achieved everything I had dreamed of when the Cultural Revolution had first begun. Now I was returning to that old arena of hurts and troubles. I hoped that the situation in Changsha would be as confused as in Peking, and that the Rebels and Conservatives would be too busy struggling among themselves to pay much attention to my family. Still, I had very mixed feelings about going back. It was especially hard to say good-bye to Peng Ming, my protector and teacher. He assured me over and over that he would write to me, but even my Revolutionary will could not control my tears as he grasped my shoulders in a final farewell.

Little Peng and I had to jump a freight train from the suburb of Fengtai to get home since there were no longer any free tickets. We ended up in an open logging car, more fortunate than some of the other Red Guards who had to ride on piles of black coal. It was bitterly cold and the wind hurt, so most of us huddled together at the bottom of the car at the front of the logs. Suddenly a girl perched up on top cried out, "Look, look, how terrible!"

We stood up and saw in the coal car ahead, barely twelve feet away, a male Red Guard raping a female Red Guard while another boy sat on her upper body and held her arms down. I didn't really understand what was happening. I could see she was struggling and crying out, her face all twisted, but her cries were faint in the wind. My friends screamed, "Stop it, stop it!" but if her attackers heard them they must have known there was no way to cross over from car to car.

They switched places right in front of us and the second boy forced her legs apart. Little Peng and her friends were weeping with what I later understood to be horror, fury, and shame, but the attackers were as indifferent as if we weren't there. The girl was black with coal dust and seemed to be getting weaker.

Not long after the second boy finished, we pulled into a station. The boys ran away before my companions could think of what to do, while the girl crawled out and fell onto the platform, weeping soundlessly. We climbed out and went to her.

We were completely unequipped to deal with such things, and had no idea that in such situations the victim should be taken to a doctor. Ignorance is the only excuse for what we did for her, which was nothing. My companions asked her her name over and over, asked who the boys were, asked where she was going. She just lay there, moaning miserably. When the train whistle sounded, my friends seemed torn between their desire to do something and their desire to catch the train. I suppose it was their inability to think of a single way to help that pushed the balance in favor of selfishness, and we left her. I don't think there was a single one of them who didn't feel guilty, though. As we pulled out of the station Little Peng said the girl would never have the face to go home again and would probably kill herself. A boy said over and over again, "They couldn't be real Red Guards." We hardly spoke at all the rest of the way to Changsha.

This incident made such a deep impression on me that it changed me in some fundamental way. I became much more aware of others in trouble, as if always trying to atone for that first failure to help.

CHAPTER ELEVEN

A Gory Climax in Changsha

It was wonderful to get back. As I had hoped, Father was at home, and he embraced me tightly with tears of relief and pride. When I took out my treasures, he found a glass frame for my handprint and hung it up where the Xu Bei-hong horse had been, and poured the water into the prettiest bottle he could find, an old medicine container washed clean. He placed this and the dirt on a little stand before the picture of Chairman Mao, neatly labeled for all the world to see.

Father wanted to hear everything about Peking, for it had been years since he had been there as a reporter. I was anxious to hear about the family fortunes, so I spoke quickly and interrupted myself with questions for him. Now that Father didn't have to go criticize himself and was free to stay at home reading Chairman Mao and talking with people, he was really quite well informed about the situation in Changsha.

In February and March of 1967, the Rebels had suffered a turn in their luck. Worried about the chaos of the preceding autumn, Chairman Mao had ordered a local army unit into the conflict, but to his dismay, many of them had supported the Conservatives. The Cultural Revolution Directorate, bowing to pressure from old Peking Party leaders, had acquiesced to the suppression of the Rebels. In Hunan, the army had labeled as counterrevolutionary the major coalition Rebel groups, the Xiang River Wind and Thunder group and the Workers' Alliance. They arrested a lot of the Rebel leaders. The struggle continued, of course, but in a more subdued manner. Liang Fang, my father sighed, certainly hadn't given up. She was enraged at the setback suffered by her group. The old Provincial Committee structure may have been destroyed, but many of the old leaders had their power back again as if nothing had happened. The student groups which had spearheaded the Cultural Revolution, meanwhile, had long ago disbanded and were no longer a force in their own right.

Many people had come to hate the old leaders for their bureaucratism and abuses of power, and the majority supported the Rebels. The Conservatives were nevertheless all but untouchable, for they had been given weapons by the army and were secure in their bases in the colleges and universities on the West Bank of the Xiang River. There was no bridge in those days, and attackers in boats were very vulnerable, so for the most part people contented themselves with shouting at each other angrily through huge megaphones. For several months the city was split in two, no one daring to cross the river for fear of being taken as a scout for the other side. There had been skirmishes, however. Liang Fang's group had been involved in some fighting, and she was now carrying a gun seized from the Conservatives. Although Father's own life had become quite peaceful, he had been extremely worried about her, especially since the night her group had gone across the river to attack the Institute of Mining and Metallurgy and two of her classmates had been killed.

Soon after my return, the power suddenly shifted in favor of the Rebels. Chairman Mao and the Cultural Revolution Directorate broadcast their support and sent in the national-level 47th Army to help them. The Conservatives knew it was all over; most of them fled on foot to Xiangtan, Zhuzhou, and other outlying towns, while the Rebels flocked to the West Bank to recover the universities and sweep away the last holdouts. Liang Fang was going over every day, but Father urged me to stay at home with him and Liang Wei-ping. Since the army's involvement many people were armed, and there were numerous accidents because nobody knew much about using guns. Father promised that we could read together every day, but he didn't realize that I had already outgrown that kind of thing. There was no way I was going to stay indoors with political action going on.

One morning I had just left the newspaper compound when I noticed a large crowd standing around the propaganda case by the gate. There was a photographic display of what the Rebels had found on the West

Bank, including pictures of corpses beaten to death by the Conservatives, bruised and disfigured faces, and something so horrible I could hardly recognize what it was—a male body with a bloody stump where its sex organs had been. There were also pictures of the Conservatives' instruments for beating their captives, and others of their barricades with guns at the ready.

The exhibit shocked me, but it made me even more curious to go to the West Bank and have a look at the Conservatives' old headquarters for myself. After half an hour's walk down May First Road, I found myself at the passenger dock.

It seemed a lot of others had the same idea I did, for there were hundreds of people waiting to go across. The West Bank had traditionally been Changsha's pride as a scenic area, for the Yuelu Mountain turned red in autumn, and the Lovely Evening Pavilion where Chairman Mao had discussed Revolution with his classmates was even more of a tourist attraction after the temples had been destroyed. Most of the city's institutions of higher learning lay in a three-mile string of red brick compounds nestled between the mountains and the river; then the countryside began, with its green rice fields and thatched peasant homes. But during the past few months, the West Bank had been a forbidden zone.

I could see it was going to be an hour if I waited my turn, so I went instead to the car ferry, where a group of Rebel army trucks were lined up to go across. I was inconspicuous enough, and when the ferry arrived I walked on board along with the armed and helmeted Rebels. We transferred at Orange Island, subject of the famous poem by Chairman Mao, and by listening to the conversation, I heard how these Rebels were on the way to Xiangtan to capture fleeing Conservatives. It was all very exciting to a thirteen-year-old boy. In Peking I had seen plenty of angry demonstrations, but here in Changsha the Rebels were actually engaged in armed combat. It seemed amazing that the Revolution had changed so quickly.

The ferry pulled up at last at the little town of Rongwan, a ramshackle collection of deserted-looking peasant houses, all covered with slogans calling on the Conservatives to give up and turn in their arms. The Rebels piled into their trucks and drove off south down the road. I followed on foot with a crowd of curiosity seekers to the first college, the Hunan Teachers' College.

The Rebels were having their revenge. All the Conservatives' office windows were broken, the broadcast systems had been knocked down and wires were lying about, and piles of paper and flags lay smoldering everywhere. I followed some people into a classroom building and peered into rooms where unlucky Conservatives were being beaten with leather belts. The Rebels' hatred frightened me. Some of the captives seemed nearly dead and were bleeding heavily. But I knew how much the Rebels detested the Conservatives for the way they—and the army—had used their power to suppress their enemies. The ordinary people were at last taking their revenge—rightfully, no doubt—on that collection of toadies, model workers, people with good political performances, and Party members.

I had planned to go on to Hunan University, but a Rebel with whom I struck up a conversation warned me not to. Some of the Conservatives were still hiding out in the basements, and they had guns they were not afraid to use. He seemed friendly, so I decided to ask him about what the Rebels would do with the Conservatives when they captured them and brought them back from Xiangtan.

"Oh, we'll beat them up for a while, just as they did to us, but then they'll be given a second chance. We'll lock them up somewhere and give them a chance to study for a while, and then if they want to, they can join us and carry on the Revolution."

I knew this was standard policy. People were always given a chance to choose again, but they had to choose something; they couldn't stand by uninvolved or they'd risk being labeled counterrevolutionaries.

Then the man told me about someone who had been buried alive, a Conservative leader in a factory and an old Party member. "A lot of Rebels died because of him and his cruel practices. When the tide turned and we were allowed to bury our dead, we decided to give them a real martyrs' funeral. It seemed only right to let their murderer go down into the grave with them."

This tale made my flesh creep, but the Rebel told it matter-of-factly, and when he noticed the way I was staring at him he said simply, "Oh, they've done the same thing to us. He deserved it."

I took my leave and walked off to think about things. Whether the story was true or not, it had jolted me and I wanted to calm myself. It looked to me as though this revenge-taking had gotten out of control, but there was no way to put on the brakes. As horrible as the Red

Guards' treatment of Father had been, I could understand it because he had made errors and it was Party policy that he be criticized. But this kind of violence was more than I could stomach, and it seemed so illogical. The fortunes of the different factions were in the hands of others, and the Rebels who were doing the beating today might themselves be beaten tomorrow. It was as if someone were playing games with us all, but there was no time to figure it out, the play was too dramatic, the action was happening too fast, and too much information was missing.

That summer, things got even worse in Changsha: The Rebels began fighting among themselves. Those who had once been comrades became mortal enemies, and the streets of Changsha ran with blood in the hundred-degree heat of August. The Cultural Revolution lost all connection with its original crackdown on anti-Socialist elements, now long forgotten. A civil war was going on, with each side claiming to love Chairman Mao better than the other, to be protecting his Revolutionary line against the policies that threatened it. Both sides were willing to die for the right to wield power under Chairman Mao's name.

The Rebels had guns now, and more. They had grenades and bayonets and machine guns and cannon and tanks and anti-aircraft missiles, all the weapons that China's military arsenals had to offer. Jiang Qing and the Cultural Revolution Directorate's slogan "Attack with Words, Defend with Guns" had been interpreted throughout the country to mean that all questions should be settled through armed struggle, and since Chairman Mao himself had said that the Rebels should have arms, they felt they were entitled to all the weapons they could get. The guns distributed to the Rebels' small official militia by the 47th Army scarcely satisfied them. They added what they had seized from the Conservatives, stole from the local militias, stopped trains for weapons shipments, broke into arsenals, and attacked military bases. Then they started shooting at each other in order to decide arguments about who was going to be in charge. The "moderate" Workers' Alliance was the huge faction cooperating with the army; their opponents were the Xiang River Wind and Thunder group, which wanted to seize power from the military. But the real issue was the apportionment of power, the power to run the Great Proletarian Cultural Revolution in all of Hunan Province. Hundreds of thousands of Hunanese workers and students found themselves caught up in a battle for very confused goals, with our wise and beloved Chairman Mao at the center of the conflict. It was during this gory climax that people began to realize that the Cultural Revolution would never make sense.

It was absolutely terrifying. Bullets whistled in the streets, and the roar of a motorcycle or the wail of a siren meant violence and tragedy. The gateways of many units had broad white lines drawn across them, and armed guards waited on the other side to shoot anyone who stepped across without permission. There was a 9 p.m. curfew, and no one wanted to go out during the day unless he had to; there were many reports of the deaths of innocent vegetable-buyers by stray bullets. People crisscrossed their windows with tape to prevent their shattering as the city shook with explosions and gunfire, and at night the sky flashed light and then dark with the passing of rockets.

Every evening Father pushed a heavy bureau up against the door and sat down in his old bamboo chair with a volume of *Chairman Mao's Selected Works* open on his lap, his broad brow knitted in concentration. But he never read anything, for the sounds of war in the city beyond disturbed him. Then some alarm would sound, warning us to turn off all the lights, and we would wait in darkness wondering if this time the newspaper would succumb to attack, and what our fates would be.

Every unit was claimed by one of the factions, and the Workers' Alliance controlled ours; they wore white handkerchiefs tied to their arms so we could recognize them in times of trouble. When the lights-off alarm sounded, I used to go to the glassless windows, which hadn't been fixed since the Rebels' children had thrown their rocks, and in the moonlight or by the light of the flares, I would sometimes see a sentry or a band of Rebels going somewhere, the light glinting off their helmets and guns, their white handkerchiefs like luminous shades.

Beneath his immediate terror, Father was profoundly troubled. It seemed impossible to him that Chairman Mao could approve such violence, and he couldn't understand why it was that everyone seemed to have guns, or why they were fighting at all. There was no social order, he complained again and again. Those who were supposed to be protecting the peace were contributing to the chaos; even the police and procuratorial organs had gone to war.

One blazing morning I went out to buy kerosene to use when there were shortages of electricity. Father wanted to go himself but I insisted, for I had been cooped up inside for days and was itching for a look at the city. Cautioning me to stay near the walls when I walked and to run home at the first sign of trouble, he finally let me go.

The road just beyond the gate was usually a busy thoroughfare, but normal traffic had ceased and it was empty except for an occasional army truck and a few fast-pedaled bicycles. I was glad to be outdoors and felt more excited than nervous; I walked the few blocks to the straw and bamboo products store and with a ringing voice I called for the salesperson. The old woman emerged reluctantly and quickly filled my glass bottle, disappearing again into the brooms, mats, baskets, and feather dusters like a rat into a pile of rice straw. She didn't dampen my spirits though, and I whistled as I rounded the corner back onto the road, swinging my bottle in my net bag.

Then suddenly, too suddenly, fifty or sixty men carrying machine guns ran past the gate of the *Hunan Daily* toward me. A short man in black carried the flag with the words "Young People's Bodyguard Squad" on it, the name of one of the groups in the Xiang River Wind and Thunder faction. I instinctively flattened myself against the wall and a number of people leaped for their bicycles in fear; when the men were almost abreast of me they opened fire, aiming off down the road into the distance, shaking with the vibrations of their guns.

The enemy was out of sight, but it responded with force. The bullets whizzed through the air and, as if everything were in slow motion, the flagman fell in front of me and rolled over and over like a lead ball. The flag never touched the ground. Someone caught it and raised it, hardly breaking stride. Then he crumpled and rolled and someone else seized it and carried it forward. They never hesitated to take their places in the front line, always running erect and proud, then falling and rolling. The pool of blood widened to within a few feet of my bare toes. I thought I would vomit.

At last there was too much blood for the Young People's Bodyguard Squad, too, and they retreated to the nearest shelter. This happened to be the *Hunan Daily*, now apparently abandoned by the Workers' Alliance, which must have been behind the invisible guns at the other end of the street. Those of us on the near wall were actually lucky, for we could inch our trembling ways toward the gateway ourselves, but those on the other side were stranded, and I recognized a neighbor of ours across the way, clutching her sack of rice in terror.

I didn't dare to run home. Instead I cowered by the tall office building with the other noncombatants. Other Bodyguard Squad members were waiting inside our gate with trucks and stretchers. As wounds were staunched and bandaged, those still unharmed reloaded madly, breaking open huge wooden crates and spilling the long pointed bullets in random hillocks on the ground. There were a number of army men at the gateway, but since official policy was neutrality, they neither helped nor interfered. Still, when they saw the foolish way the young Rebels were planning to march out into the street to retrieve their fallen, they couldn't restrain themselves. "Crawl, you fools," they cried. "Do you want them to be able to pick you off with their eyes closed?"

So the dead and dying were dragged back, and some of their comrades wept and threw themselves on their friends' bodies while others grabbed machine guns and ran out and shot wildly and pointlessly into the distance. Then one of the Rebels turned a machine gun on the group of us huddled against the building and cried, "Blankets, we need blankets! Where are the Capitalist Roader families in this unit?"

My heart almost stopped, but no one spoke. Unbelievably, our tormentors of the preceding months didn't betray us. We children with "problem" parents froze there with white faces, but no one was heartless enough to loose on us these fanatics, driven mad with grief and fury. The man shot a warning burst of bullets into the air, then cried impatiently, "All right then, where's the clinic?"

"I'll take you," a worker said, and they were gone.

In the meantime, three shining black cannon had been taken off the trucks and the Rebels were trying to get the soldiers to show them how to use them. The soldiers were refusing, and voices were loud and angry. The cannon looked splendid and terrible, of the sort intended for use in Vietnam against the American Imperialists. Finally the Rebels despaired of enlisting the aid of the military and decided to go ahead without instruction.

They shot three times, but each time the shell went wildly astray, one exploding through the roof of the black tiled roofs across the way, another landing in the road, another smashing directly into a car parts factory.

At the time, I found this vaguely amusing, but later it seemed much less so. A worker in the factory where I worked years after told me how he had shot and killed his best friend at a distance of two feet because he didn't know how to use a machine gun. Children were run down by drivers who couldn't tell the difference between a brake and an accelerator, men blew themselves up with bombs and grenades, groups set fire to their own headquarters. The people were unaccustomed to dealing with even the simplest machines; sophisticated weapons were like death-dealing toys in the hands of babies.

With the failure of the cannon, the enemy began its offensive afresh, and spent cartridges bounced off the ground like rain. The soldiers ordered us inside the office building for protection, and at the same time the Bodyguard Squad got the idea of climbing to the top and shooting from the roof. There must have been about twenty of us trapped by the fray, weeping old grandmothers, the workers from the newspaper, terrified people of all shapes and sizes. I was as frightened as the rest but I was still a boy first and foremost, a passionately curious boy of thirteen, so I followed the machine gunners up to the roof and took cover on the first level while they went on to the very top.

They had only one heavy machine gun, and four of them carried it while two followed with ammunition. Three of them left the others to set it up while I looked out over the city and saw everywhere under the perfect skies the white smoke of explosions, the red tongues of fires. Bullets echoed from all directions, many from the Martyrs' Park with its glistening white monument taller than anything in the whole city. The machine gunner aimed not toward this but down along the road, toward the site of their original skirmish.

He would have done better to reconsider the situation, remembering that the Workers' Alliance's cooperation with the army had brought them expertise and better weapons. Perhaps he didn't know that the Monument to the Martyrs was in the hands of his enemies. He had been in place less than a minute, firing in the direction of his vanished opponents, when he was struck in the belly with a shell and came tumbling down to my level, his guts spilling out in midair and falling back more or less into place as he landed. His helmet fell off when he hit and came rattling to my feet. I was too petrified to realize that I ought to have picked it up and put it on, but I had the brains to know that the man was dead and I should stay right where I was.

Someone had already moved in to replace the dead man, but he didn't have time to realign the gun before he was shot in the head. Fortunately I was spared a second view of airborne death, but I was sure I should be the next to go. How I regretted my adventurousness now! I couldn't even weep, and the urine was running down my legs, hot and acrid.

Fortunately the third gunner was no seeker of death, and he crawled down the steps muttering "Terrible, terrible" to himself. He was utterly astounded when he saw me, and stared for a moment with red eyes before gasping, "Do you want to get yourself killed? What the hell are you doing here?" Then he threw open the door and shoved me inside.

The stairwell smelled musty and ever so safe after my brutal vulnerability under the hot blue sky. I collapsed numbly onto the steps as the gunner shouted for help, and within moments people were running up from below carrying guns and stretchers. They brought in the two bodies, and I saw the face of the man who had died so close to me; one eye was open and there was blood flowing from his nose and mouth. His intestines had fallen out again and I bent over quietly and was sick.

"Here, kid, lend a hand," someone said, and I clutched the smooth round bamboo of the stretcher and moved my legs numbly one step below the other down down down and around, down down down and around, until we had reached the second floor.

Someone they called Commander Tang was there, a distraught young man with two guns in his belt and a small contingent of body-guards. "Quickly, quickly," he was saying furiously. "Retreat, retreat." Everyone clattered down the stairs after him asking each other, "Where's the back gate?" as they ran.

They piled into the trucks, a bloody collection of bandages and filth, the motors roared, and they were gone.

That day was a nightmare sprung up from the darkest place in the human mind, full of terrifying images that flashed and faded but never held still enough to be grasped, just melting on and on into new ones, each more distorted than the last. The city shook the whole day, and that evening the skies glowed a queer orange, as if buildings were burning after an earthquake. The next day we learned that members of the "Changsha Youth" organization had leveled anti-aircraft missiles at the Xiang Embroidery Building on May First Square in an attack on the Workers' Alliance. The entire block-long four-story building had burned to the ground.

CHAPTER TWELVE

The Family Scatters

The factional violence had to be brought under control. In September 1967 Chairman Mao visited Hunan and other provinces and, disturbed by what he found, issued calls for an end to the fighting, a return of all students to their schools, the surrender of weapons to the army, and above all, unity. Each province was exhorted to strengthen the Preparatory Revolutionary Committee he had ordered formed in August, to be made up of representatives from all the factions; this was to provide the structure for post–Cultural Revolution government.

Of course, there was a great distance between the edicts and their realization, for the factions were not about to forget their differences so easily. People recognized that in the so-called Great Alliance, the real power holders would be the army, and the army was not popular because of its conservative bent. A propaganda campaign was launched to improve relations between the army and the masses, with slogans like "The People Support the Army, The Army Loves the People." In Hunan, it wasn't until April 1968 that the Revolutionary Committee proper was actually formed, but by the previous October the Preparatory Revolutionary Committee had made a good beginning. Its stated purpose was to "Struggle, Criticize, Change"—that is, to attack the Capitalist Roaders in each unit, and reform the old government structure. In this way the Cultural Revolution was supposed to be turned back to its original targets.

All cadres with "problems" (like Father) were to have an opportunity to attend a Chairman Mao Thought Study Class at the old Party

School across the river. They could remold their thought while a thorough investigation of their cases was being made; then a final judgment would be passed and they would perhaps be "liberated" if their failings were judged not serious. The cadres were to go in groups according to what system their units belonged to. Finance and trade were together, the artistic and cultural troupes, industry and transportation, education, and so on. Of course, there would be overlap since not everyone would be released at once. Father was to go in the ninth wave, made up of members of units controlled directly by the old Hunan Party Committee, such as the newspaper, the radio station, the Hunan Publishing House, the Minority Nationalities' Religions Committee, and the Hunan People's Committee.

Father was overjoyed when he heard about this plan, for he was still convinced that he had committed no serious crime and was the victim of a misunderstanding. He saw it as a chance to settle things once and for all, to resolve this confusing series of events, to learn what his future would be. It would be quiet at the study class, and he would be protected from the abuses of society. He would have a place to study the works of Chairman Mao in peace. Of course, he wasn't happy to leave us, for the few months of family life we had had together since the girls had returned to their schools had meant a lot to him; not having to lose sleep over Liang Fang was a great comfort. He wasn't happy that his residence card would be transferred to the study class and his rice coupons issued there, either, for it was a bit frightening to be separated from his beloved *Hunan Daily*, where he had spent more than half his life. Still, he never thought of the separation as final. He would surely be given work to do again later. So when it was time for the ninth group to go, Father was ready in a few hours, his bedding folded up neatly like a soldier's, his tin cup and towel, toothbrush, toothpaste, and soap all he needed for his indefinite stay.

That morning, Father went and knocked on the Peng family door and Peng Ming's father came out, all ready to go too. Peng Ming's mother and sister came along, all of us marching to the basketball court behind the two men, looking a bit bedraggled, sad to say good-bye, but happy that our relatives were being given a second chance.

We were a bit early, but already there was a large group gathered in front of a notice that assigned the cadres to different groups, on a military model. The whole group was to make up a company, but below that there were platoons, and below that, squadrons of seven or eight. A Rebel worker was to supervise each squadron, and a number of military officers would be in charge of the platoons and the company.

Soon about ten green army trucks arrived, and the cadres were told to line themselves up and stand at attention. There were more than a hundred of them, journalists, editors, photographers from all of Hunan Province. Each one had a Chairman Mao button on his chest and a "Little Red Book" in his hand; each one carried a square green bundle on his back.

A tall thick army officer walked back and forth in front of them, looking them over. Suddenly he cried out, in a Northern accent, "Right face!"

The poor intellectuals didn't know what to do. Many of them looked about in confusion, while others shuffled vaguely toward the right. Father turned left.

I roared with laughter, but at the same time I couldn't believe Father could be so stupid. I knew more about discipline than he did.

The commander said, "All right! What would you do if there were a war, not knowing left from right? When you've graduated you'll be real soldiers, every one of you. Now let's recite Chairman Mao's most recent announcement together!"

So they recited, in strong proud voices, the statement saying that they were going to struggle against themselves and criticize revisionism. Then they were asked to sing "The Great Helmsman," and someone pushed Father forward to conduct, as he had in the old days before the Cultural Revolution. His back was bent a little, and his short "Revolutionary" haircut had none of the looks of his carefully styled editor's cut, but there was spirit left in the way he moved with the music, and his arms still held command and confidence.

The Loyalty Dance was next, and we all danced, the soldiers too, hundreds of people on a small basketball court, using simple movements to express our love for Chairman Mao. I felt submerged in the happiness of the group, in the pleasure of mass action.

There was one small group that was not so happy, though, for they were not allowed to participate, but stood on the side under guard. These were the Capitalist Roaders, including Senior Assistant Editor Meng. When Father and the others piled into the trucks, making a splendid picture in their dark clothing dotted here and there with military green, standing behind the pictures of Chairman Mao and the huge red flags, the Capitalist Roaders were ushered into cars and driven away.

We three children wept a little as we watched Father go. Now there was really no one to care for us, and we had no way of knowing when we would see Father again. Liang Wei-ping had been taking Mother's role for a long time, and now she would have to take the part of Father, too.

On the first Saturday afternoon I went to the gate to wait for Father, because everyone said that those whose questions were not too serious would be allowed to come home on weekends. Liang Fang and Liang Wei-ping stayed behind to cook a splendid meal, not something from the dining hall but a real dinner, with the new spring vegetables the peasants were bringing in, and fat pork, and steaming rice. There were many at the gate besides myself, talking among themselves, convincing themselves that their fathers, mothers, husbands, wives, sons, and daughters would surely be coming home.

Almost all of us were disappointed. Seven or eight cadres showed up in a group and their rejoicing families swept them away; the rest of us waited for nearly an hour before we gave up. That night the three of us cried, leaving the beautiful meal sitting there on the table untouched. We couldn't understand what was wrong and why he hadn't come home.

It was the same every week, but it got worse, for now the cadres were coming back in groups of twenty and thirty, and then forty and fifty. The families could no longer bear to wait at the gateway, but walked all the way down to the river and stood at the dock waiting for the ferry, stepping right next to the edge where the cold wind blew off the water, picking their relatives out at great distances among the peasants with their baskets of vegetables and the "commuters" with their bicycles. Even after the group of cadres got off and we knew Father wasn't coming we always waited for the next boat, and then walked home in silence, not even bothering to pretend we weren't miserable.

Finally one day we got some news, although it wasn't worth much. The worker in charge of Father's squadron came by our house on Sunday and gave us twenty-four *yuan*, which he told us we would be receiving every month. He was nasty to us, telling us that Father was very busy and had no time to come home. He would say nothing about his situation or when we might expect him. In a way, this made us feel even worse.

Even what little home I had left was about to be destroyed. I had lost my mother through a political movement, I had lost my father through a political movement. And now I was to lose my two sisters. This time it was the movement to send Educated Youths to the countryside to live and work with the peasants.

The Cultural Revolution at this stage had turned inside out. Where at first the students had gone to the factories to spread Revolution, now the Workers' Chairman Mao Thought Propaganda Teams had moved to take over the schools. According to Chairman Mao's directives, they were to seize power on the educational front and supervise the intellectuals, and, as it turned out, they stayed there until Chairman Mao's dying day. One of their main tasks was to put into effect Chairman Mao's call for lower and upper-middle school graduates to "go up to the mountains and down to the countryside." They delivered "mobilizing reports," saying that the peasants were waiting for the students warmly, that in the countryside fish could be scooped out of the flooded rice fields with a hat and wild turkeys were so numerous that they could be killed with a stick. They said it was the students' duty to turn Chairman Mao's home province into a beautiful park, that this was a great opportunity to achieve Revolutionary glory, that those who went would become the true Red inheritors of the Revolution, tempering themselves and building the Revolutionary cause just as Chairman Mao himself had led the Red Army to do in the Yanan region during the Anti-Japanese War. Those who signed up early would be proving their loyalty to Chairman Mao, whereas those who hesitated would be considered politically backward. Middle-school students from Changsha would be able to choose among three different districts, but if they preferred to make separate arrangements to join relatives in other places, that would also be acceptable and praiseworthy. The main thing was to go, to leave the crisis-ridden cities and begin a new life.

The young people signed up excitedly for many reasons—because the Cultural Revolution had exhausted them, because they wanted to escape from their unhappy lives at home, because there was nothing to do at school, because they yearned for something fresh and romantic, and above all because Chairman Mao had told them to go. Later, after the first groups sent back reports about what it was really like, nobody wanted to go anymore, but by then the program was no longer voluntary, and there was no choice in the matter.

In January 1968, Liang Fang signed up to go to Jing County in

Western Hunan, a rugged, mountainous district that was the choice of many of the older and earlier Red Guards whose parents were under criticism and who wanted to get as far away as possible to avoid society's scorn. She had given up all hope of figuring out the Cultural Revolution, for she had been right one day and wrong the next too many times. She regretted the violence and excesses to which she had contributed; too late she saw the futility of such acts. But she hadn't lost her interest in social change and the nature of society. She thought that by going to the poorest area she could really investigate China and learn something about Marxism-Leninism and Revolution. She truly believed she could help create a new countryside, a mechanized Communist utopia.

Liang Wei-ping chose the Yuanjiang District near Dongting Lake and Hubei Province, for she wasn't sure that she could handle the tough life in Western Hunan. She was among the first to sign up in her whole school, and she persuaded Peng Ming's sister and some other good friends to register with her. In their imaginations, they saw their country destination as a lovely place—a sweet dream where they could amuse themselves. Neither of my sisters worried about the details of how they would live, for they weren't leaving much behind them. However, they did want to say good-bye to Father.

Liang Fang's group was scheduled to leave first, and the day before she was to go she announced that she was crossing the river to see him. I heard this with great excitement and a little trepidation, for I longed terribly to see him myself, but I had never heard of anyone at the study class being allowed to have visitors. I begged Liang Fang to let me go too.

I think she was glad of my company, as if she were clinging to the last bits of family she had left. Liang Wei-ping had an organizational meeting to attend, and saw us off regretfully at the bus stop, thrusting two of Father's shirts into our hands, newly mended. It felt strange to board the boat we had gone to meet so many times. I felt almost as if we were crossing a forbidden line. The ferry groaned and creaked, and the Xiang River seemed broad and fierce, autumn having restored the fullness that summer baked away. Liang Fang and I stood close together, looking at the narrow junks with their patched square sails as they rocked and plunged over our muddy wake.

Rongwan Town had restored itself since I had last been there, and it was bustling with people doing their marketing. The narrow cobble-

stone street twisted among the old wooden houses until it straightened
and broadened into a country road. It was about four *li* to the study
class but we didn't take a bus. For some reason we wanted to avoid
asking directions.

We knew immediately that we had arrived when we saw a red brick
compound laid out neatly and symmetrically at the foot of the Yuelu
Mountain with STRUGGLE AGAINST ONESELF; CRITICIZE REVISIONISM in white
paint on the walls. We hesitated several minutes, afraid to approach
the armed soldiers on duty at the gate-house, but at last Liang Fang
walked firmly up and said, "We've come to see our father."

The soldier looked surprised, but he led us into the gate-house
asking, "What's his company and squadron number?" Fortunately we
remembered, and he made a call reporting our arrival and asked us to
wait a few minutes.

From where we were standing we could see a small sportsground
on which a group of men were being drilled by a soldier. From the looks
of them they were intellectuals, for many wore glasses, but I didn't
recognize any of them. They were running in place with great precision
and an air of experience.

At last the phone rang, and we were told we could go in to the
office. Following the soldier's directions, we walked past the dining hall
where we saw several hundred tables set up in one huge room, bowls
and chopsticks laid neatly at each place, and past the dormitories where
through the windows we could see the cadres studying along the long
tables between their bunks, smoking as they read. The whole place was
perfectly silent.

For a while I couldn't figure out why things looked so nice, and
then I realized that it was the first place I had been in more than a year
where there were no big character posters. However, on each dormitory
there was what looked like a festive display, a series of big pictures of
Chairman Mao and below them vertical rows of bright red paper hearts.
We went up to look at one of the displays and read the words "Loyalty
Board" and saw that each heart was labeled with someone's name, and
beside it was a row of little red stars and flags. Then we understood
that this was a record of each "student's" monthly performance, for the
stars and flags corresponded to a long horizontal list of categories: "5:00
Oath of Loyalty," "Early Military Exercises," "Personal Hygiene," "Personal Appearance," "Collective Study of Newspapers and Documents,"

Liang Heng at five with his younger sister, Liang
Wei-ping (left), his mother, and older sister, Liang
Fang. His parents were divorced two years later.

Grandmother and
Liang Fang stand behind
Liang Wei-ping and Liang
Heng (center) in a
photographer's studio in
Changsha in 1957.

Liang Heng (right) and fellow *Hunan Daily*
rebels.

Guo Lao-da, one of the peasants with whom Liang Heng lived and worked in the countryside. Liang Heng took this picture of him during a return visit to the Production Team in 1980.

During his search in Peking for his lost friend Peng Ming, Liang Heng stands in front of the Temple of Heaven.

The oil refinery basketball team in Martyrs' Park in Changsha, after winning a match, in 1974. Liang Heng is #7.

On a winter vacation from
the refinery, Liang Heng
visits with his sisters in
Martyrs' Park.

Visiting Shaoshan, Chairman
Mao's birthplace, in 1975

Liang Heng on a catwalk
of the cracking tower that
he helped build at an oil
refinery in Changsha's
northern suburbs

Factory workers surround Liang Heng in a formal portrait taken at a party honoring him. The Chinese characters at the top of the photograph read: "Congratulations to Comrade Liang Heng on being admitted to college. From Work Team #2."

Liang Heng's father with Judy in his home in Shuangfeng County

Judy and Heng at their wedding, 1980

"Physical Labor for Thought Reform," "Speaking During Criticism Meetings," "Self-criticisms,". "Loyalty Activities," "Memorization of *Quotations* and *Works* of Chairman Mao," "Singing Revolutionary Songs on Entering the Dining Hall," "Evening Oral Reports to Chairman Mao on Daily Conduct," and so on. All the spaces were filled with either flags (good) or stars (excellent), so everyone must have been trying very hard.

At last we found the reception room for the *Hunan Daily* company, where an arrogant-looking military man was waiting for us. He told us that Father was very busy studying and could not be disturbed. We should go back home and Father would come see us when he wasn't so busy.

We argued with him for nearly half an hour, explaining that Liang Fang was going to the countryside and might not be back for years, that it had been months since we had seen Father, that we had brought a few things for him. Finally the man agreed to go get him, but the interview would have to be restricted to no more than ten minutes.

Father came in looking tired and thin, but his face lit up when he saw us, his eyes shining behind his glasses. Then Liang Fang explained all in a breath that she and Liang Wei-ping were going to the countryside, and Father suddenly seemed wearier than I had ever seen him.

"This family will be scattered all over the place," he sighed. "But 'The home of a Revolutionary is the four seas.'" His smile was bitter. "I'm to blame for everything. I don't even have any money to give you, and now you're going so far from home with no one to look after you. Liang Heng," he took my hand, "what will you do now? You must promise me to stay at home and study." Suddenly he looked cheered and said, "I think there are a few rice coupons tucked away in my copy of *Das Kapital*. Maybe that will help."

We knew time was pressing and wanted to know so much. "Why haven't you come home?" I asked. "Is your question serious?"

Father glanced nervously over at the soldier, who was occupying himself at the desk. "Oh, no. I'm just very busy. I'm so sorry not to be with you now, but I want to use every minute to study. Maybe soon I'll come back on Sundays, and after that I'll graduate and can be at home all the time."

I felt like crying, because it was obvious that Father had been suffering a lot; he just didn't want to tell us, or couldn't tell us. Liang Fang pressed the shirts Liang Wei-ping had mended for him into his hands. "We thought you might be too busy to wash your shirts every day, so Liang Wei-ping fixed these for you. I'm sorry we couldn't bring—" she broke off awkwardly, not wanting to reproach Father for our poverty. It seemed there was nothing to talk about that wasn't painful.

Our time was already up, and the soldier interrupted us. But Father insisted on seeing us off, and begged him to let him accompany us part of the way. The soldier finally left to consult with other leaders and returned with the worker in charge of Father's squadron, the nasty man who brought us our monthly twenty-four *yuan*. Father could go, they said, but this man was to walk a few feet behind us the whole way.

Our footsteps spoke out what our voices could not, that the family ties of a lifetime were now about to be stretched to their outer limits. In these final moments together, we thought over everything the family should have been but was not, of all the happy futures we had envisaged that were now the shattered dreams of the past. Now Father was like a prisoner and Liang Fang about to become a peasant. How unlike anything either of them had imagined for themselves! How Liang Fang had wanted to go to college, how Father had wanted to join the Party and go to the top of his profession. How I needed a family! The peasant houses tucked into their clusters of trees looked so protected and home-like, almost a mockery of what we needed so much but could not have.

Father wanted to come right down onto the dock with us, but we urged him back, afraid that we might start to cry in front of all the other passengers. Father himself kept back the tears with a supreme effort. He knew his supervisor was watching him and that a lack of control might have unforeseen consequences. So he was the first to turn away, and we watched his close-cropped head, taller than the others in the crowd, until it dwindled and was lost in the distance.

Liang Fang left the next day, and Liang Wei-ping and I went to the No. 1 Middle School to see her off. She had almost nothing to take with her, just half a mosquito net and a badly worn old army-style jacket. The trucks were decorated with flowers and banners saying "The Farther from Home, the Nearer to Chairman Mao" and "The Poor and Lower-Middle Peasants Are Closer Relatives than Mother and Father." All the students were wearing huge red paper flowers on their chests, but Liang Fang's face was ashen and many of her classmates were weeping. As the motors started up, there was a roar of cymbals and drums and firecrackers, and the Propaganda Team led us all in shouting "Learn from the Educated Youth," "Salute the Educated Youth." Then the trucks pulled out on a farewell parade throughout the city; Liang Fang was leaving Changsha for good.

Liang Wei-ping's departure was scheduled for the following week. She went across the river to see Father in her turn, but her request was denied and she came home in tears. Her last days at home were spent cleaning everything one more time. She patched the windows where the cardboard had fallen out and darned all my clothes extra in the places they were likely to tear. She even scrubbed the walls and washed the floor, but the house looked just as barren when she was finished. Then she took down our framed family photographs. She polished the glass over and over again, and finally opened the back and took out a little picture of the three of us with our Nai Nai, me fat and frowning on a tricycle, Liang Fang in overalls, with bows in her hair and her big white smile, Nai Nai hunched over, draped in black, staring at the camera with big eyes, Liang Wei-ping herself with her hair cut short because of the scalp disease, but looking plump and pretty. "Liang Heng," she said, "would you mind if I took this with me? I want to have something to remember the family by."

At last she too was gone. That evening I discovered she had left a note for Father saying, "Father, I love you. I miss you." It wasn't until I was lying in bed trying to fall asleep that I realized how terribly, terribly lonely I was. Her ironic last words to me echoed in my ears: "Oh well, maybe in the countryside they'll let me join the Communist Youth League."

CHAPTER THIRTEEN

On the Streets

The house was too empty. At thirteen, I couldn't make myself stay indoors and read the works of Chairman Mao no matter how much I wanted to please Father. Something had changed inside me, too. All the violence had numbed me, and I didn't care if I never participated in the Revolution again. My family had sacrificed so much for it but it had given us nothing in return. If there was no one to care for me, why should I care for myself? I found myself wanting excitement, even danger to throw myself against, and I didn't care whether I came back dead or alive.

My adventures began in the cold spring of 1968, a few months after my sisters left, with the return to the newspaper of my clever friend Little Li. It was his mother's turn to attend the study class, and there were no facilities at her unit for a child on his own, so although his father had left when mine had, Little Li came back to the apartment where he had grown up. Now we had two empty apartments to play in.

He had fallen in with an unusual crowd, the sons of some of the highest-ranking cadres in all of Hunan Province. Normally, we would never have met such privileged children, but Little Li had gone to the exclusive Heroes' Training Primary School after his four years in the newspaper school. By rights he should never have been there, but his mother had connections with the principal, so he was admitted "through the back door" to the training ground for Changsha's elite. Now the Cultural Revolution had brought these lofty scions of power down to our level, for they too had lost their parents. They came every day from their homes in the Hunan Provincial Party Committee compound and the restricted Hunan Provincial Military District to Little Li's house. We formed a kind of gang, an alliance of blood brotherhood sworn before a picture of Chairman Mao but based more on outside threats than real fellow feeling. There were a lot of gangs in those days, for the city had lost all semblance of order. The notorious professional gangs from pre-Liberation days had made their reappearance, and there were thousands of other young people on the streets. There were no schools to instruct or control them, and many of them had lost their parents to some form of re-education. So they banded together as a means of survival. Our group was one such example, but we were unlikely bedfellows.

Our completely different reactions to the fall of our parents showed how far apart we really were. I wanted only to defend myself, but the high officials' children were planning revenge. They were used to power, and they were just as arrogant as they had been before the Cultural Revolution. Now they spoke constantly of what they would do to punish those who had written big character posters about their parents and beaten them in public. They noted down names and waited confidently for the day they would have their power back again. Their calm assurance was entirely foreign to me.

We spent most of our time together learning how to fight. We really trained ourselves, practicing all kinds of martial arts. We hit bricks with our hands day after day until they bled, and then we fought the pain until the scabs hardened into calluses. I was growing now, shooting up like a young bamboo. The cuffs of my pants reached only to my calves, my shirt was tight across my chest. It felt good to hit things, to feel my new muscles harden and swell. My body demanded to be tested.

The high-ranking cadres' sons often brought liquor to Little Li's. Then we'd drink and fight among ourselves, seven or eight of us in a small room, not angry but using our full strength because we loved to feel the hard thud of our fists in flesh, loved the comforting pain and the bruises we wore as emblems of our toughness. When at last the wine bottles glittered in pieces on the cement floor and our bodies ached, we would shake hands and light cigarettes for each other, expensive cigarettes purchased in the exclusive hotels and shops for high-ranking cadres only. It was a good life.

The sixteen-year-old leader of the group was the son of the Hunan Military Region Assistant Commander. His name was Cheng Guang and

I liked him very much, perhaps first because he was tall like me, but also because he was frank and open, and had a tremendous tolerance for pain. I learned my discipline from watching him continue to work out when the rest of us could take no more, always slicing and kicking into the air with the force of real battle. He was dark and handsome, with white Northern skin and a suggestion of a mustache, and he never took off his real military clothing even when the sweat had soaked through to his jacket. I remember how he used to laugh at the Red Guards for their imitations of army uniforms, and he would show me the diagonal weave of his green jacket and say, "That's real PLA quality." I learned from him that you could always recognize a high-ranking cadre's son by this jacket and the wide blue pants, white gloves, and black corduroy Peking-made shoes they liked to affect. They wear that kind of informal uniform to this day.

Cheng Guang shocked me a bit at first, for he had a girlfriend. This was unimaginable, not to say dangerous, for someone of his age. Everyone knew that you had to be at least eighteen to begin even to think about such things; a classmate of Liang Fang's had been thrown out of school for his audacity. But Cheng Guang didn't even try to keep his girl a secret. He carried her photo in his breast pocket, and we saw she was plump and pretty, and had a fashionable short Revolutionary haircut. When I had conquered my embarrassment I discovered another emotion: envy.

Little Li wanted to have nothing to do with teenage love affairs, for he had been well brought up and was even slightly stuffy. So when Cheng Guang asked us to correct a love letter he had written (elitist school or no, the children of intellectuals were still the better students), Little Li refused almost rudely. However, I sensed that one of the reasons Cheng Guang had cultivated our friendship was in hopes of just such help. In any case, I didn't care what I got myself into, or what my reputation became. I ignored Little Li's frowns and invited Cheng Guang to come with me to my house.

I felt shy to be alone with this boy I admired so much, and a bit ashamed of our bare-looking apartment with its broken windows and layer of dust. I unfolded his letter a bit awkwardly, but gained in confidence as I discovered that at least in studies I was his superior by far. He had written many wrong characters and his handwriting was poor. Blushing a little, I added the "mouth" to the character "kiss," and rearranged the strokes in "embrace." Remembering the Western stories I had read before the Cultural Revolution, I suggested it might be better to say that his girl's eyes were like the stars rather than like the moon, and he happily agreed. Then I recopied the whole thing for him. He was so grateful that our friendship entered a new phase. At the same time, cautious Little Li had set disappointing limits on how far he was willing to go for excitement. We drifted away from each other and, like many children who had nothing to do, he took to learning Revolutionary songs on the violin. The musicality of many young people today is a direct result of this phase of the Cultural Revolution.

For more than a month Cheng Guang and I were like body and shadow. He often slept at my house or invited me to stay with him at the military headquarters. I had to climb over the wall because only army personnel were allowed in, but we were never discovered. I wasn't lonely anymore, and felt safe for the first time since Father's posters had gone up more than two years earlier. No one would dare to hurt me with friends like these.

One clear winter afternoon the gang was to meet at my house to go to the Martyrs' Park. Cheng Guang was late. We were joking about how he must have been delayed with his girlfriend when he came storming in, his fair skin flushed with anger and cold, his smooth brow creased in fury. "My brothers," he announced, "if you really are my brothers—remember, we swore with our blood—now is the time to prove it. My girlfriend and I were just riding our bicycles by the river and a bunch of hoodlums knocked her over and insulted her. And goddamned if I wasn't alone. But I promised them we'd get back at them. We'll have our revenge!"

Defending the honor of a lady love was a bit alien to me but I felt a thrill of excitement at the seriousness of his tone. Some of the other boys smiled a bit, though, and asked, "What did they say, that she was pretty?"

"Pretty, nothing!" exclaimed Cheng Guang. "They called her '*mantou* mountain,' that's what!" He lifted his huge white gloves to his chest as if squeezing two large imaginary breasts.

At this even I laughed, but Cheng Guang shouted, "What's so funny?" and we were instantly silent. He said, "We're meeting them tonight at seven at the back gate of the park. It won't be easy because they're real 'black society' and there are a lot of them. We'll attack them hard and run for it, and they won't know what hit them."

The high-ranking cadres' sons had organized themselves into ranks according to their fathers' positions, and Cheng Guang was commander-in-chief. Despite their bravado, when they heard we were to fight real hoodlums they were all afraid, but none of them raised a word of protest. I drew a deep breath. This was a far cry from our usual escapades, the most extreme of which had been grabbing a handful of oil cake tickets when a girl cashier wasn't looking. We had been practicing so long; this was the real thing. I made a fist and felt the strength coursing through my body.

The shadows were long and the yellow moon hung low when I reached our meeting place in a wooded corner of the park that night. Someone handed me two iron spikes to grasp in my fists; most of the others carried sticks and heavy tools. Cheng Guang had a bundle with him which he shoved at me. "Put these on," he whispered. "Don't ask any questions." I took out a green military jacket, a pair of white gloves, and a white face mask.

The hoodlums were standing in the shadow of the trees beyond the gate. The street light caught the cigarettes hanging from the corners of their mouths. They seemed to be a motley group in dark work clothes, and most of them reached into their pockets when they saw us. My heart pounded. Maybe they were from the most terrible gang of all, the "Five Liu Family Tigers!"

A voice came out of nowhere. "Stinking black cadres' sons! Dogs relying on the strength of your masters!"

"Don't worry," Cheng Guang whispered hoarsely. "Our victory lies in our escape. Listen for my signal to run." Then he called out with all his strength, "Fuck three generations of your ancestors!"

He ran forward with us at his heels. I was hitting in all directions, the iron spikes propelling my fists and making them powerful and heavy. Sometimes I connected with something and sometimes I didn't. I didn't even care. It was a terrific feeling.

But not twenty seconds into the fight I heard Cheng Guang's call for retreat. I escaped before our opponents were able to land a single solid blow. They chased us, but the gate of the military headquarters was less than a hundred yards away; Cheng Guang had laid his plans well. The startled sentries let us by with a flash of confused recognition and then stood with bayonets raised against the tattered flood of hoodlums. Our cheated pursuers came to a furious halt. We were safe.

Cheng Guang's tactics—and his military background—saved us that time, but the conflict was far from over. Our enemies outnumbered us, and they lay in wait for Cheng Guang outside his unit day after day until he hardly dared to go out at all. At last he sent an emissary to negotiate with them, and a price of fifteen cartons of the best cigarettes was named. We talked them down to eight, which still came to more than sixty *yuan;* I contributed my remaining fourteen *yuan* to help my friend out.

The odd thing was that in the course of these discussions hostility died away. We discovered we had bought peace and friendship. Even today there is a comfortable liaison between the sons of high-ranking cadres and the "black society," dating from the Cultural Revolution days of gang wars and alliances. I found myself unexpectedly drawn to these people, for coarse as they were, their feelings seemed natural and sincere, whereas Cheng Guang, I knew, would forget me when his father regained his high position. I actually had a lot in common with these "hoodlums"; the better I knew them and the hundreds of others with whom they associated, the less I saw them as hoodlums at all.

Among the younger ones there were orphans, delinquents, peasants come illegally from the countryside, children like myself whose parents were in the study class or away in the countryside for thought reform, "Educated Youths" who were trying to avoid their stints among the peasants, and an odd assortment of other misfits who had found their way to the lowest reaches of society. Then there were the older people, the garbage collectors, cart pushers, outhouse cleaners, sellers of roasted sweet potatoes and green-onion pancakes deep-fried in spattering oil. There were the key-makers, the rice-wine hawkers, the shoe and pot repairmen, the rat poison sellers. They did everything that lay beyond the reach of a normal government job.

At first I was merely curious about them, and then gradually I became one of them. I had hours to spare for their complaints and stories, and in the spring and summer of 1968, when I was fourteen, I was always with them in the tea houses, hardly bothering to go home anymore, sleeping at the railroad station or anywhere else I ended up late at night. Although they were miserably poor and their lives monotorious, they were truly free. In some way they were beyond political life. Of course, they were occasionally arrested for conducting their illicit businesses or disturbing the peace, but as long as they didn't break any major law, they could curse the police, swear, complain, and speak their minds without repercussion. Movements came and went, but they always scraped up their few *fen* and drank their tea. They cared about each other, too, and they came to care for me. They knew what had happened to my parents, and they sympathized and spoke out the things I hardly dared to think to myself. They said that the Cultural Revolution was a mistake, that my father had done nothing to be punished for, that children like myself shouldn't be living out on the streets with them, that we should be in school. I was deeply moved. Theirs were the first meaningful words of consolation I had heard since the Cultural Revolution began.

It was a bitter freedom for me, though. I returned to the work of pushing carts, this time with no sense of stepping down in society. I saw the son of one of the most notorious Rightists on the *Hunan Daily*, an old chief editor. If he had been pushing carts since 1957, why should I be ashamed? I got to know all the prices, learned how to help myself if I got a load of apples or bananas, learned what it was to sweat for a living.

It was hard to earn enough, though. Even if you pushed until you were exhausted, there might be only one or two *yuan* a day. I had expensive new habits, too: Wine and cigarettes sustained my friendships and dulled my pain. So I sold my family's leather suitcases for eight *yuan* apiece, and sometimes I crawled into the newspaper's dining hall window at night and stole *mantou*, potatoes, eggs, chicken. After I had filled my belly I always felt wretched, for I knew how sad Father would be if he knew I was a thief and a hoodlum. I couldn't help myself. My life was like a feather to me, floating on thrills, wine, cigarettes, and curses.

One of those who befriended me was an old man we called "Pock-mark Liu," a bony fellow with sunken, cratered cheeks and tobacco-stained teeth the color of grasshopper juice. A scar on the back of his neck stretched partway up his scalp, cutting a taut white swath among the gray stubble of his hair. His dirty undershirt stretched over the sharp curve in his upper back, and his sandals always looked so large

I couldn't imagine how he kept them on his feet. He had a touch of asthma and his voice rasped when he made his crude jokes, but through his vulgarity and ironic cynicism he was among the kindest of the whole lot.

I met him pushing carts. When he saw that I was new he yielded a job to me, and then when I returned to thank him he told me all the places where I could get free boiled black tea, the kind that's so bitter that you want to grimace, but that can restore the life in anyone. Later, when he switched to selling oil pancakes at the gate of the Martyrs' Park he always urged them on me free of charge, but I never allowed myself more than one because I knew he needed money just as much as I did. Then I didn't see him for a month or so, and finally ran into him at the Northern Station, where he was just coming out of one of the offices.

He looked filthy, and from ten yards away I could smell something overpowering and distinctive, very familiar but not quite identifiable. He greeted me enthusiastically, but waved me back, calling, "This pig slop'll crawl right over to you if you don't watch out!"

"What've you been doing with pigs?" I asked, keeping my distance.

"Mothering them along to Guangzhou, twenty *yuan* a shot," he answered. "Got to get them there alive or Hong Kong won't buy. Say," he said, grinning his copper-colored grin. "They might take you on if I backed you. How about it?"

I would have been a fool to say no. Twenty *yuan* was more than I'd seen since Father had been sent to the study class. We agreed to meet that afternoon, after he'd been to the bathhouse.

My height proved useful. Pockmark Liu told the railway official that I was eighteen and had some experience with animals; after a warning about not trying to sneak out to Hong Kong with the pigs, I was hired. The next morning Pockmark Liu led me past the dozens of cars of oxen, chickens, ducks, geese, rabbits, and fish toward the pig section. Each car had its own particular stench and noises, its own particular collection of eyes staring through the slats. There were at least thirty pigs in our two-level car, huge monsters any one of which weighed twice what I did. They had beady, intelligent eyes that followed us as we walked to the entrance, and a spectacular and varied range of vocal expression. Our narrow bunks at the end of the car were separated from our charges by a thin slatted wall with a little doorway in it, but we were to spend most of our time inside with them, feeding them, changing their water, hosing away their shit, making sure they didn't get sick and die on us. Suddenly I wasn't sure if it was all worth it, even for twenty *yuan*, but Pockmark Liu had already uncurled the hose and handed it to me, and I was at work.

Worst of all was feeding them. You had to crouch over nearly double, their slop in wooden buckets on your shoulder pole, while they rushed at you grunting and screaming, each trying to be the first to eat. The train shook and rattled so they were unsteady on their feet, and I was terrified that one of them might fall over and crush me: I might be stamped into their muck before Pockmark Liu even had a chance to notice what was happening. My back ached after only an hour and I stank as if I had rolled in the stuff deliberately. It was frightening to think I had four feedings and five changes of water ahead of me during the two-and-a-half-day trip; the brunt of the labor would be mine because Pockmark Liu was old and I owed him his rest.

Sleep was impossible that night. The stench was so pervasive I felt I was gasping for air, and the noises were insistent and always changing. Thirty pigs never piss at the same time. Every few minutes came the hard, swift, hissing sound, punctuated by the pigs' continuing grunts and screams and the lowing of oxen from the car behind. Not even the gentle rhythm of the train in motion could rock me to sleep.

It must have been well after midnight that we rumbled to an unscheduled stop. In the relative silence I heard Pockmark Liu toss on the bunk beneath mine, and I realized he couldn't sleep either. "Old Liu," I called out softly. "Are you hungry?" I waved half a *mantou* down into the blackness below, and felt the touch of his gnarled hand.

"Thank you, Tall Fellow," he answered. "I could use a bite. It's hard to eat when everything stinks so, though."

I leaned over the edge of the bunk and looked down. "Aren't you used to it yet?"

"I never will be. Heaven knows I've done everything in this life, from beekeeping to teaching school, but this is the worst. You can never wash yourself clean."

"I didn't know you were a schoolteacher," I said. So Pockmark Liu told me his story.

He had once been a worker in a towel factory, supplementing his income by renting out two rooms. After Liberation, the rooms were confiscated and he and his wife sent to the countryside because they belonged to an oppressing class. There, because he had read a few books and could write a fair hand, he was asked to teach primary school. Then in 1958 during the Great Leap Forward when the People's Communes were formed, he had complained about the food in the new collective dining hall, and he was severely criticized. His teaching job was taken away. "Your mother's!" he swore. "What a fool I was to complain. Actually, if only they'd kept up a few more of those stupid policies we wouldn't have an overpopulation problem."

I remembered Father's description of the peasants lying dead in the fields during the early 1960s disasters that followed the commune movement, and I understood his humor. "Where's your family?" I asked.

"The world is my family. When my wife was in the countryside she picked up a lot of the local superstitions and one of them killed her," he said, laughing again, but bitterly. "One day she heard a crow cawing in the eaves and an old neighbor woman told her it meant that an army would be passing soon. My wife repeated the news everywhere, and it got to the brigade leaders. Three weeks later we heard Chiang Kai-shek was invading. So the leaders decided to make an example out of her for welcoming the enemy. They locked her up in a dark room and beat her." Pockmark Liu paused for a moment and resumed in a huskier voice. "A few days later she got out and jumped into the pond. . . . A lot of people have died, all of them good people."

I didn't know what to say and I stammered, "Well, I guess my family is pretty lucky."

"Oh, I don't know about that," he said. "My wife's free now, and even though I'm the lowest of the low, so am I. I don't have to answer to anybody. Sometimes it's even worse if you try to believe in it all. So many fools give thanks for getting shit thrown in their faces. Don't be duped like them, Tall Fellow. The more you believe, the more you've lost and the more of a sucker you are."

His words made me think of Father. Although I didn't say anything, I still thought it was good that his beliefs were so strong, that he was so patient. If Father's convictions were any less, he might well kill himself like Pockmark Liu's wife, and I wasn't ready to look at death as freedom. I felt confused, but comforted myself with the thought that most people were like my father and there were only a handful like the old man in the bunk below. I changed the subject. "I wonder why we've stopped?"

"It's probably the fish. The water spills or a tank springs a leak and someone has to fill it up again. Last time we stopped for more than three hours."

His words made me drowsy, and the pigs too seemed to be sleepy at last. "Let's sleep, shall we, Old Liu?" I said.

"Good dreams, Tall Fellow."

But that night I dreamed of thousands of pigs with thousands of eyes, all staring at me hungrily. . . .

At last we arrived in Guangzhou. I had been looking forward to calling on my pretty little friend Sha An, for I had not forgotten her tears of farewell when she saw me and Liang Fang off at the station years before. I was wondering, too, about her family's fortunes during the Cultural Revolution, for her father, like mine, made his living with his pen. It wasn't until after I had been to the bathhouse and bathed until my fingers were white and wrinkled with absorbed water that I realized I couldn't possibly go. The odor of pig piss, shit, sweat, and slop lingered, and even the fresh clothing I had placed under the tattered quilt was permeated with it. I got sadly onto the next train home with Pockmark Liu, two ten-*yuan* bills burning like hot coals in my pocket.

"Now I can come home every week. Why weren't you here? Next Sunday I hope the place is cleaner. It looks like dogs have been living here. Your father."

I found this note one Friday afternoon in the winter of 1968. It had been more than a week since I'd been home. That morning I had been drinking harsh "white liquor" with my friends, throwing it down my throat as if it were the fire we were too poor to buy. Father's elegant characters looked incongruously graceful on their scrap of faded newspaper, and they sobered me instantly. I sank down on my dirty crumpled quilt and burst into tears.

What must he have thought when he smelled the acrid dust and saw it lying thick and gray over my bowl and chopsticks? Had he noticed the disappearance of the leather suitcases and the mosquito net? Had he shivered as the wind blew through the unplugged windows? I trembled to think that he might have guessed at the life I was living, and realized frantically that I had less than two days to put my affairs in order and think of a plausible explanation for where I had been.

Not even Liang Wei-ping could have worked like I did, and by the following afternoon the dust was gone. Almost every sheet and quilt cover flapped wetly on the communal clothesline, and a few rays of winter sunlight shone down to dry them. My hands were icy red from scrubbing and I ached from strange new exertions, but I couldn't rest. I sat down to make up all the entries I had missed in my study diary, copying down titles of articles and chapters from the *Works* that I had meant to read. I knew Little Li would coach me. At last I was ready.

He arrived early Sunday morning. It was an odd visit, since we were intensely curious about each other's lives while defending our own secrets fiercely. His temper was worse than I'd ever seen it. Sometimes he paced back and forth like a tiger in a cage, sometimes he lay on the bed, sucking furiously on his cigarettes, sighing deeply. I told him I'd been staying at Little Li's and he looked at me sharply and then lectured me on the importance of study. He told me about a colleague's daughter who had been living on the streets. She had become pregnant and been arrested and sent to a labor camp. He said he hoped I wouldn't bring him shame and trouble. I protested vigorously but he looked at me with those stern, deep, suffering eyes as if he already knew everything.

I was able to gather that he was home because his "historical question" had been resolved. In fact, his problem was no worse than most, but he had been kept in the study class without visiting privileges because there had been some uncertainty about his motivation in joining the KMT Youth League, and the matter of his brother and sister who went to Taiwan with the KMT had to be investigated. Now he had been cleared, and it was only a matter of time before he was "liberated" and sent to the countryside. He had written about his "historical questions" so often that it had aged and wearied him, and now that his exoneration was in hand, he seemed too broken to enjoy it.

On subsequent Sundays I learned more about his life in the study class and came to understand why he was always so irritable when he came home. Everyone was part of a "Red Couple" and had a partner to whom he had to report the thought of every moment, even his dreams. If his thought was Revolutionary and loyal, he was encouraged, but if he felt homesick or missed his children or his wife, he was guilty of "private thought" and was criticized. Father's partner was an old colleague named Tang, and they knew each other's thoughts more intimately than lovers, and ruled one another with iron hands. When Father came home, all the worry and discontent he had to hide from his partner spilled forth. "What do they want from me?" he used to mutter over and over to himself. "I've told them everything a hundred times."

Father's return put an end to my wanderings. I called on Little Li, and discovered he had been studying at home the whole time and had also become a rather accomplished violinist. I joined him and his friends in their studies, and we read the works of Marx and Lenin as well as those of Chairman Mao. Like my father, I took copious notes and was thorough in my readings. Everything I read told me Socialism was glorious; perhaps there were so many inequities in our own society simply because people hadn't carried out Chairman Mao's directives. Despite what my fellow students and I had been through, none of us had lost our faith. When we weren't working hard, we learned to play instruments, raised pigeons, and waited dutifully for our parents to come home.

CHAPTER FOURTEEN

We Become Peasants

At last Father was "liberated" to become a peasant. The cadres had made errors, Chairman Mao said, because they had been away from the grass roots too long. Now they were to settle in the countryside for prolonged re-education; at the same time they would help to "cut off the tail of Capitalism" by bringing Revolutionary knowledge and construction to the most isolated regions of China. I would naturally go too.

Father believed he would now be a peasant to the end of his days, yet he was remarkably cheerful about it. He seemed to have lost all desire to resume his career. "It's too dangerous to live by the pen," he joked. "I'd rather have peasant bones. And you'll be a peasant's son, so no one will accuse you of having a bad background anymore." Another reason his spirits were so high was that after nearly five years of a marriage that was a marriage in name alone, he was going to be able to live together with his wife. A transfer from her small town to the big city had been an impossible dream, but their request to settle in the same barren region in the countryside was readily granted. So Zhu Zhidao came first to Changsha from her own Chairman Mao Thought Study Class, bringing her life's possessions with her on a shoulder pole.

The Spring Festival of February 1969 was a joyous time in many units, although none of the traditional feasts and family gatherings were permitted. In every theater we saw propaganda workers dressed as cadres and Educated Youths marching, carrying knapsacks on their backs and "Little Red Books" in their hands. They sang:

To the frontier, to the country,
Where the Revolution needs us most,
Great Party, Beloved Chairman,
We are ready at your command.
To the frontier, to the country,
To the harshest places in the land.

Rouge-cheeked peasants greeted them with cardboard pigs, chickens, and sheaves of rice singing, "How we welcome you, how we have longed for your Red gifts . . . " The two groups clasped hands warmly, then turned to the audience for a finale of praise for our great Socialist motherland. Our criminal fathers had become heroes.

Father, Zhu Zhi-dao, and I attended training sessions at the newspaper. We had to sit up perfectly straight, holding our "Little Red Books" over our hearts. Everyone was expected to speak, rows upon rows of disciplined soldiers of the Revolution showing their enthusiasm for becoming peasants. If there was an awkward silence, Father would elbow me out of my erect concentration on the peanuts and cigarettes for which I had come, and I would remark dutifully and briefly that I yearned to inherit the torch of Revolution. By that time I had learned how and when to recite the slogans printed in the newspapers.

In fact, I was genuinely pleased to go, although I knew we were going to an extremely poor area, Changling County in Hengyang District to the south. This time we weren't running away from anything, but settling down to make a living. I imagined how we would plow and plant, eat what we grew, and have some dignity again.

The worst problem for the cadres was their lack of furniture. Most families didn't even have a bed to call their own; what they had in their apartments was included with the rooms, water, and electricity for five *yuan* a month. The wood shortage in Changsha was terrible, since the province had never recovered from the massive deforestation of the Great Leap Forward. Hammering something together was out of the question, and there was nothing available on the market. At last the newspaper rescued us, agreeing to sell a bed to each family for seventy *yuan*, a reasonable price. Father was feeling rich since the study class had repaid part of the salary they had confiscated during the sixteen months he spent there, so he also paid the newspaper for our table, and bought all the other things he imagined we would need: conical peasant hats against the sun and rain, vegetable seeds, kerosene lanterns, books on agriculture, extra shoulder poles and baskets. . . . He knew that where we were going stores would be few and far between.

Only one thing shadowed my happiness. As I have said, Father had officially left the *Hunan Daily* when his file was transferred to the study class. The salary he was now receiving was issued by his cadres to the Countryside Military Company, to which all cadres going to the Hengyang District belonged. His file was to remain at the study class in Changsha, but our Changsha residence cards would be canceled and new ones set up at the commune to which we would be assigned. There was something frightening about surrendering all claim to the city where I had spent my whole life.

I had known many people who wanted to move into Changsha, from my wet nurse to Auntie Zhu, and the controlling factor was always their lack of a Changsha residence card. If we had no residence cards, we would not even be able to visit without a letter of introduction from our units to a Changsha hotel; if we tried to stay in the homes of friends there might be a residence card check. Before the Cultural Revolution, these had occurred only on major holidays, but now they seemed to come every night after twelve, a loud knocking on the door and a quick perusal of the family's papers. You were supposed to report all guests to the local Public Security Bureau where, if there were good reason, they would be issued a temporary residence card. Without such a card, they could be arrested. The Public Security Bureau said the frequency of the checks had been stepped up to catch Educated Youths who were coming back illegally from the countryside, but they were also a good way to arrest just about anybody.

There was nothing glorious about the night two Public Security Bureau officials came to confiscate our residence cards. They were tough and cold, and it was no wonder: In effect, they were throwing us out of the city. Father was in the inner room when they came so they asked me for the papers, and with an instinct I could not have explained, I said, "We lost them." But Father came out and without hesitation took the red plastic booklet from the drawer where we kept our meal tickets and rice coupons. He placed it in a big white glove and it disappeared forever into a blue padded policeman's overcoat. My father is paying the price for his trusting honesty to this very day.

.   .   .

The reality of my situation was suddenly clear to me, and a restless sense of unfinished business pressed with an urgency that I could not ignore. I went to see my mother.

As I turned down the familiar lane, the first person I saw was Waipo. She was crouched by the communal faucet, rinsing rice in a pot. The back of her faded black padded jacket was turned toward me, and I stood behind her for a moment, watching her tiny, bony hands turn the rice in icy clouds until the water cleared. She looked like a small rodent at work.

"Waipo," I said, but she didn't hear me over the sound of running water. "Waipo, it's me. Liang Heng."

Her head came around and I saw the familiar buck teeth in the little face, which was now covered with new lines like the marks of a hundred birds in rich brown clay.

"Little Fatso," she cried, rising and embracing me. "Hard-hearted child, why haven't you been to see us? Who brought you up? Aren't you ashamed of yourself?" Then she burst into tears, smiling all the while. At last she sniffled, "Your poor mother misses you so terribly. She dreams of you constantly. Why, your sisters are much braver than you. They came here often before they went to the countryside."

This was astonishing news to me. So that was why Liang Wei-ping had behaved so strangely when I asked her where she had been the afternoon before she left! My sisters had tricked me with all their talk of Revolutionary purity. I need not have stayed away, after all, any more than they did.

"She'll hardly recognize you, you've grown so tall," said Waipo, reaching up and putting her cold red hands on my face. "But look at your clothes, they're all too small for you. Your poor father can't take care of you."

I found my voice. "Where's Mama?"

Waipo led me down the narrow alley and into the dark wooden corridor to the smoky cooking area. Mother was bent down to the coal stove beneath the wok, taking out the burned lotus briquets on the bottom to make room for a fresh one on top. Even in the darkness I could see her hair had gone gray.

"Zhi-de," called Waipo. "Look who's here."

Mother stood up, looking massive in the small room. When she recognized me she made no move toward me. She just stood there and wept.

Ten minutes later, I was seated inside on the wooden bed shared by Mother and Waipo. Their words tumbled out as they bustled about pouring hot water and shaking spicy-sweet "strange taste beans" out of a biscuit tin to serve me. The family was much changed, they told me. The older girl cousins were long gone to the countryside; they hadn't been permitted to go on to upper middle school because of Uncle Yan's Rightist question. Uncle Yan's "cap" was off now, and he had a job at his old unit, the No. 1 Hospital, in the Reference Room. "He's come down a lot," sighed Waipo, "but at least this way he doesn't have to talk to anyone, so he stays out of trouble."

"The other big change is that Uncle Lei has taught me a lot," said Mother.

"Uncle Lei?" I asked. She seemed to assume I knew who he was.

Suddenly Mother blushed fiery red. "Don't you know?" she asked.

"Uncle Lei is Mother's husband," said Waipo. "He'll be back for supper."

The enormity of our separation hit me. Of course, Father had married again and it was only natural that Mother do the same. But it was astounding to me that I had heard nothing about it, especially since everyone loved to gossip, and Mother lived so close to the newspaper. If Father had known, he didn't think it worth mentioning to me.

I learned that Uncle Lei was an accountant in a tea-packaging factory, and that they had been married soon after Father's wedding to Zhu Zhi-dao. His background was even more dangerous than Father's, for he was a real intellectual with an economics degree from Peking University. His older brother, now in Taiwan, had been Kuomintang ambassador to France, Cuba, and Canada, and had a Ph.D. in International Law from the University of Paris; his younger sister and her husband were scientists at the Shanghai Institute of Botany and Physiology and were graduates of the University of Pennsylvania in the United States. Mother and Uncle Lei were extremely worried about them, since they were being attacked as U.S. spies (why would they have returned if they had no mission to fulfill?), but had had no word from them for many months. A second brother, an engineer, had been killed by a stray bullet the previous year in Guangxi Province, where the Cultural

Revolution had been even bloodier than in Hunan. "We've been very lucky, though," said Mother. "Uncle Lei's very careful. He never offends anyone, avoids going out, and speaks his mind only at home. And I've learned enough from him about keeping my thoughts to myself that there really hasn't been much trouble for me either. It's been as if we were under an umbrella of safety." As Mother spoke, I realized she was a changed woman. There was none of the energetic determination that had once marked her character. In its place I found something tiny and timid despite her physical bulk.

The conversation shifted to what I had been doing, and when I finished, Mother said, "I've missed you so much, but I never blamed you for staying away from me. Perhaps it's much safer that way. But now you've come to see me and I see how tall and strong you are, all grown up, and you tell me now you're going away to the countryside to live. It's almost more than I can bear." She got up and fumbled through a drawer to hide her tears, then turned and shoved five *yuan* into my hands. "You'll be needing this. I'm already an old woman and my needs are simple. . . ."

I didn't want the money because I knew I would never be able to explain where it came from, but I took it to please her. In some ways I felt worse and worse the longer I sat there. It was clear that our separation had been even harder on her than on me, and I regretted my cruelty in staying away so long and my hard feelings toward her during the seven years since the divorce. It was something of a relief when Uncle Lei came home and I could concentrate on meeting my new relative.

He was a soft-spoken, thin, self-effacing man with a receding hairline and glasses. He seemed overjoyed to see me. It was evident that he didn't like to make idle conversation, but the pleasure in the way he clapped his hand on my shoulder and looked me up and down spoke more than words. I felt even more sorry now that I had not come to them when I was wandering the streets. They could at least have provided me with some kind of home.

Waipo made me my favorite fried rice with eggs, and hot pepper soup, and we ate together, although I was getting increasingly nervous about what Father would think about my long absence. When I could stay no longer, Mother and Waipo insisted on seeing me to the back gate of the newspaper, and as I walked inside they stood motionless at the mouth of their little lane, like graven images of the Buddha, one bony and wise, the other fleshy and dispassionate.

Feeling was good among the cadres and their families as we made our two-day journey. We had people from the Provincial Communist Youth League Committee and from the Minority Nationalities Committee as well as from the newspaper, so we must have been close to 350 in all. Standing as we were in the open trucks, jostling together by accident and by design (body heat was precious warmth), we could not help becoming intimates, and our good spirits made us friends. We stayed a night in Hengyang, ten people to a room, and drove the next day through the mountains, arriving at dusk at Guanling Prefecture in Changling County.

But how different was our reception from those in the propaganda performances! It was true that the peasants stood at the mouth of the cobblestoned street with their gongs and firecrackers, but they chanted their slogans of welcome listlessly. And as our trucks jounced down into the town itself, I saw to my horror that in every doorway there hung a corpse! It looked like some kind of eerie mass suicide.

Moments later I realized that the twilight had turned straw effigies of Liu Shao-qi into dead flesh. But the shock had broken my happy mood, and when we finally pulled to a stop, I climbed over the side with a feeling of impending unpleasantness. A small group of skinny-looking peasants had gathered there on the threshing ground to greet us, and we looked at the barren surroundings with dismay: They hadn't even prepared tea or hot water.

Our hosts seemed more interested in admiring the fine painted furniture than in helping to unload the baggage trucks; the little children who had followed us from the town were everywhere underfoot, making faces at themselves in the wardrobe mirrors and staring at us. There was no organization, and in the confusion, lotus briquets spilled and shattered, thermos bottles cracked and were cradled by distraught grandmothers. Fortunately, Father was more alert than most, and was able to climb up and hand our belongings to us directly over the side. Meanwhile, some of the old ladies had started fires with the broken briquets and were boiling rice right there on the cement threshing ground.

By the time everyone found their things I was feeling cold, anxious, and hungrier than ever. I knew we might still be miles from our destination, and I worried about how we could possibly transport all our things in the darkness. Our Company leader, Old Dai, a cadre from the newspaper with a strong Revolutionary political performance, was standing with an important-looking man who someone said was the commune Party Secretary of the Goose Court Commune, where we were all going. They seemed to be comparing lists. Finally they shouted for order, and the pairing off began.

First Old Dai would call out a cadre's name, then the commune Party Secretary called out the name of a Production Team (see appendix, page 294). Evidently each Production Team would be assigned only one family, so we would be leaving our newfound friends to live alone with the peasants. When the cadre's family raised their hands, a peasant representative from the Team walked over and conferred with them. A few families with lighter burdens gathered their things together and disappeared immediately into the darkness, but most stood and talked together with apparent agitation, for it was obvious that there was too much luggage.

We were among the last named, and when Old Dai called "Liang Shan!" Father leaped to his feet calling "Here, here!" The commune Party Secretary read, "Gold Market Brigade, Number Nine Production Team!"

A shortish peasant strolled out of the crowd, nonchalantly rolling a cigarette as his shoulder pole teetered unsupported by his neck. "I'm Accountant Wang," he said, walking up to Father. "You're alone?" Father gestured to Zhu Zhi-dao and me, and he frowned. "We didn't expect so many. We took in a cadre during the Socialist Education Movement in 1963, but never a whole family. We can't possibly manage all these things."

Father pushed a good cigarette into Accountant Wang's hand. As he lit it with his own, Father asked, "What's to be done, then?"

"Let's go to the brigade leader, Party Secretary Li."

Apparently the brigade leader was the man at the center of a group of peasants, and we could hear him shouting and cursing from some distance off. "Pigs!" he was yelling. "If you can't carry it yourselves go back and get help then. Your mothers are all whores if you can't figure it out for yourselves!"

I was amazed at his arrogance. At least we had been spared the embarrassment of a direct confrontation.

Accountant Wang shrugged and said, "I'll be going then, it's not far."

I was familiar with distances in the countryside and was not much reassured, but there was nothing else we could do. By that time the local people had gone home for dinner, and the officials seemed to think that now we were all matched up, their work was done. So we waited miserably with the other families and their furniture, abandoned in the damp darkness of our new home.

Our peasants came back an hour and a half later, strong young men with baskets and shoulder poles. They were all named Wang or Guo; the entire Production Team of over a hundred people was descended from the same two families. They hooked our things up with remarkable efficiency, leaving us with only the centerpiece of the double bed, a wooden frame with straw woven across it. Of course, they were much faster than we, but they left behind a little boy of around nine to carry a torch for us.

The child was very patient, and smoked cigarettes as we walked. Father couldn't see well at night because of his glasses, and he had never had much exercise. The bed was heavy, so we had to rest every few hundred yards. Little Boy Guo, as we were told to call him, stood there with the torch, moving on dutifully when we picked up the bed again. At one point he sang a little folk song, and Father asked him to stop and repeat it. By the flickering torchlight, Father noted down this pearl of folk culture, more animation on his face than I had seen in years. Another time the boy asked us if we were afraid of tigers. I said no, of course, and then he handed me the torch saying he wanted to run ahead to go to the bathroom. When Father and I came to a large boulder, there came a terrific high-pitched growling and yapping, startling in the darkness. Then the boy stood up behind the rock. "I knew you were afraid," he announced triumphantly.

It must have been close to midnight when we arrived. Little Boy Guo took us immediately to the Team leader's home. A crowd of shaved heads was already waiting for us around the fire.

Team Leader Guo came to the point. "Old Liang, Chairman Mao has sent you to us, so we should welcome you. But this Team has many members and very little land. If we have a good harvest, each person has only three hundred to four hundred *jin* per year, and that's including sweet potatoes."

Father knew his figures, having been an agriculture reporter so many years. He was astonished. "Then how do you live during planting time?" he asked.

"Sometimes the government helps, but it's never easy. Old Liang" —the Team leader drew a breath—"maybe you should speak with the commune leaders and ask to go somewhere else. We simply can't support you."

The others chimed in. "There are so many of you."

"You have no experience."

And an angry voice: "Damned brigade leaders don't assign anyone to their own Production Teams!"

Father spoke gently. "Countrymen. You must understand that we have come not because we wanted to but because others wanted us to. We cannot ask them to send us anywhere else. Please forgive us. We'll help with the work as best we can."

"Help with the work? We've got to give you food, find you a place to live. What kind of help is that?" came the chorus.

Father was silent a moment, and then said, "We can't go back. We don't have city residence cards anymore. But tomorrow, if you like, I'll go to the leaders and explain your difficulties."

The peasants seemed much mollified, as if they saw that Father was a good man and would do his best. "No need to discuss any further tonight," announced the leader. "Let our guests eat!"

They ushered us into another room where they had prepared big bowls of food in the traditionally hospitable manner of the countryside. My eyes bulged when I saw the thick chunks of pork. No sooner was I seated than I helped myself to two fragrant mouthfuls.

For some reason, the peasants weren't happy about this. One of the women standing by the side watching the men and boys eat reached over and covered the pork with cabbage while another tried to distract me by urging me to drink some soup.

As we were led off to sleep, Father whispered to me, "That meat was Spring Festival meat for their gods. It was only on the table to show their hospitality. If we are to live here in peace, we must be careful to respect their customs." Then he and Zhu Zhi-dao were taken to one house and I was led to another, where I shared a bed with a peasant boy.

Father didn't have to go look for the leaders the next day. They came to the Production Team, the Party Secretary of the commune, foul-mouthed Brigade Leader Li, and our Company leader. Old Dai was the only one who didn't seem drunk, and he looked very professional with his red star on his military cap.

To our surprise, the peasants had lost all trace of their unfriendliness of the night before and now seemed strangely stolid. Team Leader Guo brought out rice wine and poured it into big teacups, urging the leaders to drink, and other people filtered into the meeting room, hanging back toward the walls. Father began to speak his piece on behalf of the peasants, but he had hardly finished his opening sentences when the commune Party Secretary exploded.

"What kind of attitude is this?" he demanded, slamming his thick hand against the table and addressing the crowd. "Is this the way to respond to Chairman Mao's call? Is this the way to understand his edicts? He teaches us, 'Do not fear hardship, do not fear death'—so what does it matter if you add a few mouths to your dinner tables? Chairman Mao sent them here. If you don't welcome them, you're opposing our great leader."

Brigade Party Secretary Li was even fiercer. "Filthy cocks raised by whores! If everyone else can manage, what's the matter with you? If you have rice to eat, you receive the cadres. If you don't, you receive the cadres. That's just the way it is."

Our discomfort at being thus forced on the peasants was acute. There wasn't a word of protest from them in the face of these imprecations; in fact, they didn't seem to be affected much one way or the other, mules under the whip who know they must eventually obey. No wonder I had heard so much about the autocratic "work style" of the leaders in the countryside! They were despots in their little kingdoms, armed with the sayings of Chairman Mao.

When they had gone on to another Production Team, Team Leader Guo took us to a room in his younger brother's house. "Guo Lucky Wealth and his wife have no children," he explained to Father, "so this room will be yours. You can set up a small bed in the kitchen for the boy." I wasn't too pleased with the thought of sleeping in the smokiest room in the house, but I was in no position to choose. At least the peasant couple, on first impression, seemed kind.

"Now I'll show you your vegetable plot," said Team Leader Guo, pleased by the satisfaction Father had expressed with our sleeping quarters. He led us out into the fields and I discovered the area looked familiar and lovely, a real, typical Hunan countryside, with iron-rich red earth and mud houses to match, yellow rice fields, and blue-silhouetted mountains not too tall in the distance. It was bitterly cold, of course, as Hunan is in February (there is no central heating south of the Yangtze, even in cities), but I was used to feeling always slightly chilled during the winter. When we came to our plot, I reached down and broke a piece of the cold, dry earth in my fingers. It was hard to believe this was to give us our cabbage and our sweet potatoes, our beans and our turnips. Then Father's freshly polished leather shoes caught my attention and I looked up past the tidy city clothes on his elegant frame to his bewildered intellectual's face behind its thick glasses. He looked bizarre in this place where everything was tinged with the color of the land. I suddenly wondered how we were ever going to make it.

In fact, although Father was a peasant in name, his situation was quite different from that of a peasant. It was more like that of the local leaders we had met, for he earned a government salary (issued by the study class and distributed by the commune) and he was given rice coupons, a meager but sufficient twenty-six *jin* a month. These entitled him to buy rice at the town food exchange, to which the peasants turned in their government quotas for shipment to the cities. Father's labor in the fields was expected as part of his re-education, of course, but it was not to be rewarded in any way. Thus, aside from this small vegetable plot that had been carved away from some other family, Father was not really a financial burden.

The problem was us, the family members. The coupons we received for twenty-one *jin* of rice were not enough and, like the peasants, we received no salaries. According to policy, we were to be allowed to earn work points with them when we labored in the fields. The system worked like this: A day's work brought a certain number of points, ten for a man, seven for a woman, three or four for a child or an old person. At the end of the year, the accumulated value of all a person's points was calculated; in our Production Team ten points were worth only fourteen *fen*, an indication of the extreme poverty of our region. From this hypothetical sum of money was subtracted the value of the rice and sweet potatoes that had been issued to the person, leaving him or her either with a small amount of credit, which might be paid if the Production Team had funds, or in the Production Team's debt (an attempt could be made to work this off during subsequent years). Our participation in this system was unwelcome because the Team was already at peak production level, and more hands would not grow more rice or sweet potatoes. Even if it could, our inexperience made us all but useless. The collective wealth of the Team was thus fixed, both in terms of food and of cash. By stepping in we would be impoverishing everyone just a little bit. It was no wonder they hoped we would be transferred.

Ultimately, we bought our acceptance. The peasants' dissatisfaction was so widespread that a new edict came down ordering all cadres to "invest" part of their savings in their Production Teams, according to their own financial situations. In our case, the price was fixed at 200 *yuan*. It was steep, but it proved worth it. The Team members were delighted, since they needed to buy fertilizer and had found their own resources inadequate; Father's contribution bought a year's worth of chemicals. At the same time, the peasants were beginning to realize that we had really come to stay. It was Father's mission, as an educated man, to help "blow the spring wind of Chairman Mao Thought all over the land," and he devoted all his feeling and energy to it. Through this work, we became a real part of the community.

Normally, during the bitter early spring, the peasants closed their leaky doors tight against the wind. Families would sit bunched together around the brushwood fires in their kitchens, their hands reaching up their opposite sleeves to their elbows, their heads withdrawn into their ragged jackets like cautious turtles. In this way, they waited for the brief daylight hours to pass so they could retreat once again beneath their warm bedding.

Father's arrival interrupted this hibernation. Now the doors stood open to the whistling wind, and eager purple hands pasted up the red paper couplets Father had written, one on each side. The peasants seemed to feel that the slogans created a pleasingly decorative effect, and Accountant Wang, as the only adult who could read, was more than pleased with his new status as translator. Then one day, Father organized a few strong men to clean the big dark Wang-Guo family ancestor-worship room, pushing the brushwood and threshing wheel to the side and sweeping away the twigs and dust of years. He put up fresh posters of Chairman Mao and Lin Biao wearing soldiers' uniforms, explaining patiently that the great Revolutionary Marshal Lin was co-leader of the Cultural Revolution and Chairman Mao's hand-picked successor. The peasants clicked their tongues against their teeth in admiration at the twin splendor, although they had no idea what Father was up to. Next he rubbed his hands together to roll away the dry paste, and took a pack of Chairman Mao quotation cards out of his book bag, issuing one to each person as a symbol of the "Little Red Books" they did not have.

"Fellow countrymen," he announced to the fascinated crowd, "from now on we are going to be like the people in the city. In the morning we are going to ask for strength, in the evening, make reports." In the murmur of confusion that followed, he self-consciously buttoned the top button of his jacket, touched the Chairman Mao button on his chest as if to reassure himself that it was still there, and held his *Quotations* out exactly in front of his breastbone. Then he turned to face the Great Helmsman and the Revolutionary Marshal and bowed, with utmost gravity, three times to the waist.

There was a general titter of nervous laughter. Father looked so serious, and the peasants had never seen anyone bow to anything except the images of their own ancestors. But they were eager learners, for they loved Chairman Mao. At last they had an earnest teacher to show them how to express their love.

Every morning when the cocks crowed at the pale white light an hour before dawn, Father went to the threshing ground to blow his whistle. The sound flew to the distant mountains and bounced back again, and the peasants hastily emerged from their homes, tying their pants up with bits of rope, thrusting suckling babies under their shirts. We all crowded into the ancestor-worship room to face the two shining images flickering like living shadows above the kerosene lamp.

I hated it. I was used to sleeping through the 5:30 loudspeaker back home in the newspaper, and I had been through so much, politically, it seemed unfair that I should have to take part in these primitive rituals. My head always weighed on me like a heavy stone, but I was Father's son and an example, so I stood there, asleep on my feet, with weariness deep in my heart as well.

We opened with a verse of the weighty "The East Is Red," Father conducting with a stalk of sorghum. The heavy voices sounded as if they were being addressed to the interior of a jar of pickles, and it was all I could do to force myself to join the cacophony. Then Father led us to repeat one of the three famous essays, "The Foolish Old Man Who Moved the Mountain," "In Memory of Norman Bethune," or "On Serving the People." Everyone in the whole country was supposed to memorize these and I had done so long ago. The halting process of helping the peasants learn without texts seemed interminable. I bowed to the Chairman and his righthand man, of course, when the time came, and droned along with the rest, but I was unconscious of anything much until the litany, when Father asked, "What do we wish for Chairman Mao?" and the answer resounded, "Long life, long life, long life!" "And for Vice-Marshal Lin?" "Good health, good health, good health!" This was the signal that it was over. I could go back home to sleep.

CHAPTER FIFTEEN

The Spring Wind of Chairman Mao Thought

The time came for the peasants to teach us. Poor Father. He was totally unaccustomed to labor and made a fool of himself over and over again. In the early spring, the only major work was spreading fertilizer, mostly night soil and the chemicals bought with Father's "investment." The mucky pond bottom was another rich resource though, sticky and black with dead fish and plant life. We were supposed to carry our shoulder poles down the dirt steps that had been carved in the bank and go right into the stuff up to our knees. There we'd hook on two baskets loaded with mud and carry them back up and out to the fields, running with that low, even stride which is the only comfortable way to carry an extremely heavy burden. I was strong and learned quickly, but Father never mastered it. I remember him the first day, arriving serious and earnest, his pants rolled up above his knees and his soft feet red with cold, eager to learn from the peasants. But before he made it safely into the muddy slop at the bottom, he slipped on the rounded little steps and flew ingloriously to his destination, bottom first. Everyone laughed, of course, but Guo Lucky Wealth reproved them, saying, "What would you do if you were asked to make speeches like Old Liang? We could beat your asses with a stick three times and wouldn't get a fart out of you." Father smiled good-naturedly. "Never mind," he said. "If I work hard, eventually I'll get it."

After this first fall, he went all the way home to change his pants. He did so again after the second, but after the third he had nothing more to change into and worked as he was, muddy from head to toe, but safe on the pond bottom loading baskets.

Despite such blunders, Father seemed more at peace with himself and the world than I had ever seen him. He became talkative again, smiled often, and sometimes even hummed under his breath. The exercise was evidently good for him, for he looked younger than he had since before the Cultural Revolution began. He was a little sad though, as he discovered the depth of the peasants' day-to-day misery. Theirs was a poverty he had only touched upon as a reporter; he had been shielded from it by being shepherded from place to place by cadres who treated him as an honored guest. It was a cruel reality, very different from the one he had envisaged as he read documents and newspapers in the comfort of his office. Where was the liberation from suffering the Revolution had advertised so proudly?

Living in the No. 9 Production Team was a shock for me, too, for neither Uncle Hou's nor Cousin Han's Teams had been so poor. The Goose Court Commune had a long history of misery, and in the early 1960s many had died there. The land had been exhausted by years of intensive cultivation and inadequate fertilizers; it grew barely enough rice to feed the Team, but even so the peasants had to turn most of it over to the government. They had a saying that summed up the situation very neatly: "During the first half of the year, we grow rice for the government; during the second half, we wait for emergency relief." Many things made more sense to me now. I understood, for example, that the peasants produced babies the way a chicken produces eggs because their basic food allotment would be increased with each new family member. Then the rice could be redistributed to those who needed it most, the active men. The women and children sacrificed their portions to keep the best laborers fit, and made do with sweet potatoes and sweet potato leaves.

The peasants' only real source of income was the paltry twenty *yuan* they received for each pig they sold to the government. If this money was hoarded carefully for ten years or more, it might conceivably buy someone a bride; even in those days, 300 or 400 *yuan* was a minimum price. In our Team, marriage was out of the question for at least eight of the middle-aged men, and a new house, even one with a straw roof at only 800 *yuan*, hadn't been built for years. The only other money came from the chicken and duck eggs, which sold for five *fen* apiece at the commune center; with this there might be enough for a little oil or salt. No wonder Cousin Han had rarely cooked with oil!

We didn't have to look beyond our own hosts and neighbors, Guo Lucky Wealth and his wife, for constant reminders of the desperation of these lives. The man's name was a mockery. How embarrassingly splendid our ordinary city furniture suddenly looked! The couple had only an old wardrobe, a rickety table, and a bed that looked like it would collapse at any moment. They slept under a cotton quilt that they had inherited from Old Guo's father; it was black with grease and age, and most of the stuffing had fallen out. Between the two of them, they had only one whole pair of pants, which they shared and reserved for days when one of them went to market in the commune center. As for food, they often put the rice hulls the government issued as pig feed on their own tables, giving their own sweet potato leaves to the pigs. It was not surprising that the government often complained that their pigs were underweight. Every time Old Guo took a pig to market, he fed it watered-down slop to bloat its belly and plugged its anus with cloth to keep it from losing precious poundage. Even so, officials usually sent it back again. But none of this poverty was unusual. Things in the house across the way had reached such a crisis that the old man in the family, feeling himself too much of a burden, had killed himself the previous summer during planting season, hanging himself from the storage ledge.

There was little opportunity to see better worlds, much less move away from this one. Less than a third of the people had even been to the town only eleven *li* away, and perhaps a tenth had been farther, to the county seat. The only possible means of escape was to become a soldier, the coveted—though temporary—honor given to a few strong young men. Military service took them to Peking, Shanghai, the border areas . . . and then, when it was over, thrust them cruelly back into their misery. Back at home, they were authorities on everything, but sadly unsatisfied. They looked enviously at the young men coming up who had not yet served, and cursed those still on active duty as "ankle-rubbers"—toadies of the military commanders.

Father fully expected that officials would criticize his work during the first few weeks, but he was shocked and a bit hurt by Old Dai's complaints. "Other cadres are doing much more than you," asserted the

Company leader. "Weren't you told that the peasants were to 'make reports' in the evening as well as 'ask for strength' in the morning? Weren't you told to establish a study room?"

Father shifted unhappily in his seat, and took a hard swallow of hot tea. "But the peasants don't even eat dinner until nine," he said. "They'd be exhausted."

Old Dai looked Father up and down, his red star prominent over his small face. "Chairman Mao teaches us to bear hardship," he replied dryly.

So the next morning after the "asking for strength" ceremonies, Father had the peasants move the sweet potatoes in the storehouse up to the second level. With Zhu Zhi-dao's help, he cut paper "loyalty hearts" for every member of the Production Team and pasted them up on the wall with spaces next to them to record punctuality and participation at meetings. He put up new posters of Mao and Lin, and painted a slogan on every wall. Then he announced that beginning now, according to commune directive, everyone was to attend evening study meetings or their work points would be docked.

To his surprise, the peasants were delighted to come despite the lateness. The storeroom became a center of life for the Team, a forum for working out disputes and making plans. Father read every evening from the newspapers and answered questions about what he read; for people who had never been past the mountain barriers at their doorsteps, it was a rare chance to learn about what lay in the world beyond.

I enjoyed Father's status as teacher, and I had my opportunities to show off as well. I recounted countless times the story of my glimpse of Chairman Mao in Peking, elaborating new details for the pleasure of my rapt audience. Of course, sometimes the peasants asked questions that neither Father nor I could answer, like why Chairman Mao wanted to attack Liu Shao-qi. Liu was a long-standing favorite in the countryside because his policies of "more private plots, more free markets, more enterprises with their own responsibility for profits and loss, and quotas fixed on a household basis" had stimulated the economy and made the peasants richer after the natural disasters just after the Great Leap Forward. But how could we defend him when the whole country was mobilized against him? Still, the discussion was always lively, often ending after midnight. We finished with our "reports," and made three more bows to Mao and Lin, babies awakening and gurgling on their sisters' backs as if they were being given a water buffalo ride.

But a few weeks later, Father was told it still wasn't enough. Why wasn't he using every moment of the day to instruct the peasants in Chairman Mao Thought? demanded Old Dai. In the other Teams, the cadres brought their work into the fields. . . .

That evening, in front of more than a hundred pairs of eyes, Father turned to Chairman Mao and said, "I'm sorry, Great Helmsman. I have wronged you. I haven't done enough to bring the spring wind of your Thought to the Number Nine Production Team."

Before he could go on, a chorus of voices interrupted him. "No, Chairman Mao, it's not true. Old Liang is a good man."

"He's made our Team very beautiful, putting up quotations from your work everywhere."

"He's brought us a lot of knowledge and never asks us to feed him or bring him wine to drink like the other cadres."

"He's come from such good surroundings all the way to our poor Team to teach us. . . ."

It wasn't until that moment that I realized how deeply the peasants had taken Father into their hearts.

By that time, the rice seedlings were a hand high in their carefully tended beds, brilliant yellow-green like an emperor's coverlet. They were now being tied in bunches with pieces of straw, carried away in baskets, and thrown out into the big fields to be transplanted. The peasants took a bunch at a time in one hand and, using the fore and middle fingers of the other as pincers, planted the shoots in the mud under water six inches deep. They could stand with bent backs for hours, working at the rate of two plants a second. Father, Zhu Zhi-dao, or I worked more slowly than a peasant child of five or six.

After Old Dai's second criticism, Father was spared an aching back but waded through the fields now, making his way from one person to the next, reading in his loudest voice from the works of Chairman Mao. Sometimes he recited slogans rhythmically so as to set a pace for all the workers:

> Xia ding juexin,
> Bu pa xisheng!

Pai chu wannan,
Zheng qu shengli!

(Make a resolution,
Don't fear sacrifice!
Drive out ten thousand troubles,
And achieve victory!)

At noon when the peasants rested, Father had them all sit together and listen to recent edicts. He became an expert in the application of the *Quotations* to all situations. If there was an argument, it was "Unite to seek even greater victory!" If people were tired at the end of the day, it was "When comrades are in difficulty, they should think of their achievements and of the light ahead so they can summon up all their courage."

Father never took rest even in bad weather. "Political work is the lifeline of economic work," he would intone, holding his "Little Red Book" up near his glasses to shelter it from the rain under his conical peasant hat. Or, beneath the midday sun: "Under no circumstances should one forget class struggle, the dictatorship of the proletariat, reliance on the poor and lower-middle peasants, the policy of the Party, and the work of the Party," he would declare, his face red from the heat, his white shirt so wet with sweat that it stuck transparently to his chest.

It wasn't until we had been in the countryside several months and I had turned fifteen that Party policies forced Father once again to wrestle with himself. This time, it was the final battle.

The tension was between his loyalty to the Party and his sympathy for the peasants. The first step in "cutting off the tail of Capitalism in the countryside" had been to instruct the peasants in Revolutionary thought; the second step was to apply that thought by enforcing specific policies. It was in the early summer that he was summoned to an old landlord's moss-covered brick home in the town. For four days he listened to leaders from the Changling County Revolutionary Committee sum up the favorable situation in the countryside and outline the rules for the work that lay ahead. He came home looking a bit unhappy, and after a few evening meetings, I realized why.

As it had been in the city, the main slogan was "struggle, criticize, reform," but here the emphasis was somewhat different. "Struggle" meant to struggle against Capitalist thought—Liu Shao-qi's notions of big private plots and more economic freedom, for example. "Criticize" meant to criticize Capitalist tendencies, like the desire to make money by raising pigs, chickens, and ducks, and by selling things at farmers' markets. "Reform" meant learning from Dazhai, the model agricultural commune in the North, where work points depended on good political performances, and "class struggle" was life's main theme.

Those first few days people always came to our house after the meeting. "Old Liang," they said. "We don't understand. Why is raising chickens and ducks rotten Capitalism? How can we buy oil and salt if we don't sell eggs?" One thirty-five-year-old bachelor complained, "I have almost two hundred *yuan* now. But if I can't raise more than one pig a year, I'll be sixty before I can look for a wife. Do they want me to dream about women for the rest of my life?"

Father inhaled deeply on his cigarette. I could see him fighting himself, his forehead raked with worry. He had no answer.

Suddenly Guo Lucky Wealth exclaimed, "I know, Old Liang. You're an educated man. You can write a letter to Chairman Mao. Explain it to him. Maybe he doesn't understand."

Father smiled ruefully. "My countrymen. I've been around trouble for many years, but I've never been able to do anything about it." He sighed deeply and was silent again. The weathered faces fell and moved back, murmuring among themselves. But I was staring at Father in astonishment. It was the first time in my life that I'd ever heard him fail to defend the Party.

Suddenly every courtyard became a slaughterhouse and every man's hands were bloody, for the news spread that the commune had formed an "Attack the Evil Winds of Capitalism Team" to enforce the new policies. Pig chases were held in and out of all twenty mudbrick houses; twenty upon twenty screams of defeat echoed off the mountains. Frantic clucks bubbled up to the sun in thousands. Better to eat a laying hen yourself than surrender it to the government, the peasants reasoned. But of course they couldn't really bear to eat that precious flesh. They smoked it and salted it and packed it away in earthenware jars to keep the way an old woman saves her pre-Liberation dowry earrings by sewing them into her rice straw pillow.

It was nearly a week later that Party Secretary Li, the brigade leader, came to conduct the evening meeting. He had gone first to our room to hear Father's report, and they were walking together to the meeting hall, taking the long route so he could check the newly transplanted rice seedlings. I was trailing behind. Suddenly Old Li came to a horrified stop. Six pretty white ducklings were swimming merrily through the water, feeding on the fresh green plants.

"What incredible gall!" he exclaimed. "Old Liang, class struggle is everywhere! But this time they won't get away with it. Tonight, we'll make this a living example." They continued walking, the brigade leader punching Father excitedly on the shoulder as he made his plans.

The ducks were Guo Lao-da's, of course, the most intransigent member of our Team. A thirty-eight-year-old bachelor and an orphan, he had been in trouble ever since the early 1960s, when the floods had been so bad that he had gone to the county seat to beg. The Public Security Bureau had caught up with him because he had no residence card, and he was arrested and sent back. Ever since then there had been a black spot on his history, and whenever there was a new political movement, he was dragged out and made an example of, because in our Team the ex-landlords had died long ago.

So tonight he was to be the first on the chopping-block. I felt a rush of pity, for he often came to our house and I liked his eccentric ways. He was in Father's debt by many *jiao*, but he was an expert at the art of borrowing, and never asked for more than two at a time, making up the modesty of his request in the frequency of his visits. He always held the bills tightly in his hand as if he could squeeze oil out of them, saying, "Wait until my ducklings are big. Then you'll have a feast for an emperor!" Father always answered him smiling, enjoying the ritual. "Don't kill any of them, let them lay eggs. Then you can pay me back in cash."

I found I had fallen quite far behind Father and his companion, and on a sudden impulse I made for Guo Lao-da's house at a run. He was blowing his cooking fire with a mouth bellows.

"Guo Lao-da!" I cried. "Get your ducks out of the field! The brigade leader's seen them and he's going to criticize you!"

Old Guo put his bellows down slowly, his shaved head gleaming in the firelight. "His mother's," he swore tonelessly, as if stating a fact.

"Can a Party Secretary eat me up? If my ducks like the fields, let them stay there. They're not bothering anyone."

"You should go," I insisted. "This is serious."

"Six ducks have a nibble on public land. Well, who knows how much public food that farter has eaten, dropping in everywhere at mealtimes. We poor peasants don't know how to write, but we keep our accounts with our bellies!"

I didn't dare stay away any longer. "My father would want you to go," I said, and slipped out.

That evening Old Li seemed even more pleased with himself than usual. "In our movement to cut off the tail of Capitalism we have achieved great victories," he announced, "but there are still many problems. The situation is especially grave in the Number Nine Production Team." He paused, and looked around for emphasis. Then he bellowed, "Guo Lao-da's ducks are an example of rotten Capitalism!" He paused again. "Guo Lao-da, stand up and ask Chairman Mao for forgiveness!"

Guo Lao-da had been sitting in the front row. Now he got slowly to his feet. He looked big and gawky up there in front of everyone, but his rage gave him a strange kind of grace. "What makes you think your cock is any bigger than anyone else's?" he shouted in his thick regional dialect. "If I'm going to kowtow, I'll kowtow. But it's to Chairman Mao, not to you!" And in a flash, before I had time to decipher his words, he was down on all fours in front of the posters, knocking his head on the earthen floor with three loud thumps that could be heard all over the room.

We all had to laugh. He had stood up to the brigade leader so bravely, but he looked so foolish down there on the ground. Old Li was furious. "Guo Lao-da! Don't think it's over just because you kowtowed! If you don't kill those ducks tonight, we'll bring your case to the entire commune!"

I never dreamed that this uneducated peasant could render a Party Secretary speechless, but he did. "Do you know whose ducks these are?" he demanded, shaking his finger. "These ducks are Chairman Mao's ducks. One is for Old Liang, to repay my debt to him. But I'm sending the other five to Peking for Chairman Mao to eat. And whoever is crazy enough to try to kill my ducks, well, he's the one opposing Chairman Mao!"

We roared again with laughter. This was better than a comic performance. The brigade leader was absolutely helpless. Finally he said, "If we can't settle this matter tonight, we'll settle it soon enough!" But as the peasants filed out of the meeting room I heard him mutter to Father, "Old Liang, this business. I'll put you in charge of it." It was his admission of defeat.

Father and Auntie Zhu were about to go to bed when Guo Lao-da came to our house, a changed man. The bravado was all gone. "Old Liang," he said, his voice deeply troubled. "What shall I do? My ducks have supported me my whole life. Do they want us to starve to death to fight Capitalism?"

"Hush," whispered Father. "They could blow out your brains for saying less." Then he spoke softly with him until the fire burned down very low. I was already asleep in the kitchen when Guo Lao-da went out to kill his ducks.

Although Father resolved this incident peacefully, the next one was worse. It was the hungry time when "green and yellow don't meet"— one crop was gone and the next still unripe. Even our family ate squash, for none of us wished to be the only ones with rice on the table. We loaned out what we had, and tightened our belts like everyone else.

Most of the "Capitalist" hogs had already been turned into preserved meat, the twenty *yuan* each had represented now a dream of the past. Only our hosts still had two pigs grunting in their attached sty, plump, lively, and nurtured like babies. Old Guo's wife still spent hours carrying in wild grasses and the special vegetables to which they had devoted part of their plot, chopping them fine with a cleaver in each hand, and simmering them lovingly into an edible slop. Perhaps it was because the couple had been so generous to us that Father closed his eyes to this violation of the rules.

Then one night after we were all asleep, a loud explosion shook the house. Cooking utensils fell off the kitchen wall by my bed, and I was showered with mud-brick dust. The bed itself trembled. Clad as I was in my undershorts, I ran outside.

A loud wailing came from the pigsty. "Murderers! Dog-lungs! Wolf-hearts! Oh, my precious pigs!"

Father was holding up a lantern. Half of the sty was gone, and the pigs were lying bloody in the debris. Old Guo's wife had thrown herself over their bodies, sobbing as if she had lost the sons she never had.

The neighbors came running, the women's breasts bulbous and

luminous in the dim light, the men's ribs patterns of light and dark. Guo Lucky Wealth stood there dazed, clutching the broken wall where it came to his shoulder. He seemed not to hear the angry words of the crowd. "Damned 'Attack the Evil Winds of Capitalism Team!' So they're helping themselves to the militia's grenades now!"

Then Zhu Zhi-dao came out. She had taken the time to dress, and, surprisingly, seemed more self-possessed than anyone else. "Come, Sister Guo," she said, pulling the weeping woman up. "You won't bring them back that way."

In her distraction, Guo's wife's attention was drawn to the lantern Father was holding up, and then to Father himself. "Old Liang!" she cried, grasping his hand in her bloody ones. "You must speak for me, be my judge. How can we live now?"

It must have been the immediacy of the trouble and his concern for the people involved that blinded Father to the fact that this was a question of Party policy. Or perhaps it was the fact that he had been awakened from a deep sleep and his censors were not functioning properly. Something exploded inside him, something that he had been trying to silence for more than twelve years. "I'll go!" he cried. "I'll go find the commune Party Secretary this minute!"

Four of us started out, Guo Lucky Wealth, his older brother, Team Leader Guo, Father, and myself as lantern-bearer. It was a journey full of stumbles and falls for Father in his nearsighted fury, and when we came to the nearby No. 10 Production Team, he paused and announced, "We'll get Company Leader Dai to come with us. Then they'll really listen!"

Company Leader Dai was not happy about being awakened, but even so he expressed his sympathy for the peasants. Four cadres had already come to see him, he said, to protest the "Attack the Evil Winds of Capitalism Team's" use of weapons to kill animals. "We can use persuasion," he said. "There's no need to use terror and violence."

Father shocked me by disagreeing even with that concession. "That woman didn't have a grain of rice," he said excitedly. "She's been ill for a long time and never had money to see a doctor. Those pigs were so close to being fat enough to sell—within a week she could have had forty *yuan*, enough to pay her debts and more. Why shouldn't she raise an extra pig? Old Dai, Chairman Mao didn't mean for his policies to harm the peasants, did he? Come on, let's go to the commune Party Secretary."

Old Dai looked at him as if he were crazy, and assumed an official tone. "Let me remind you that we are cadres who have been sent down to the countryside for re-education. We have no right to interfere with local affairs. Control yourself, Old Liang. Calm down. Here, smoke a cigarette and maybe you'll see things more rationally."

Father looked back at the men who had rested all their hopes on him. They were standing well back in the shadows, defeat already on their faces. He mopped his dripping face with his handkerchief.

"We'll do things according to established precedent," said Old Dai crisply. "We'll report the situation when we have our meeting next week. It's senseless to go running around in the middle of the night. Now go home and go back to sleep."

It was an order from a superior. Father had done his best.

Of course, no one did anything to compensate Guo Lucky Wealth's wife for the loss of her pigs. Chairman Mao's policies had been carried out, and that was all that mattered. Finally Father took forty *yuan* out of his own pocket and made Guo Lucky Wealth's wife take it. "For rent and services," he said.

It wasn't long before the country leaders realized the city cadres were not dependable enforcers of policy. Like Father, they were all too likely to sympathize with the peasants they knew. But if they couldn't be trusted to carry out policies in their own Teams, they could be reassigned in groups to Teams where they had no personal relationships. There they could supervise each other and still be of use in cutting off the tail of Capitalism. So in late summer, when we had been in the countryside for more than half a year, the cadres were organized into "Struggle, Criticize, Reform Propaganda Teams." Father was among those drafted.

Father's happy days were really over, now. The economic situation was getting worse and worse, yet he was responsible for overseeing the ruinous policies. He spent months at a time with other Production Teams, while other cadres came over to our Team. It worked; fearful of receiving bad reports themselves, the cadres spent their time ensuring that no extra animals were raised and full government quotas were turned in, keeping records of each peasant's political enthusiasm, making sure that rice shoots were arranged with the government-prescribed distance between rows and between plants, and, of course, continuing and strengthening the Chairman Mao worship activities. They were in charge of punishing those who sold things privately and those who went up to the mountain to cut firewood on government land; criticism meetings and docked work points were now the order of the day. Finally, they sat in judgment over those who began to steal because they were too poor to feed themselves. This phenomenon, the Propaganda Team announced vindictively, was the ugly head of class struggle revealing itself.

CHAPTER SIXTEEN

"It's Going to Be Tough Here"

When we heard that arrangements had been made for the cadres' children to go to school at the Changling No. 4 Middle School in Guanling Prefecture, Father and I were overjoyed. It had been almost three years since I had graduated from the Three Mile Primary School, and now, at fifteen, I was eager to renew my studies. Granted, I would now be receiving a "Revolutionary" education, as provided for in the Cultural Revolution's educational reforms, but at least I wouldn't be spending all my time bent over in the fields. People said the town was like a country Shanghai, with shops, a post office, a bus stop, a clinic, and occasional movies and theatrical performances. To me, the idea of living there was a reprieve arranged by fate.

So it was in good spirits that I wrapped my few belongings in a bedroll and walked the eight *li* to school. It was a simple cluster of dirty buildings within a walled compound, the typical red star over the gate. A group of boys were playing a game of after-school basketball, and I felt a rush of happiness at the thought that now I would be able to join the activities that had once given me so much pleasure. I walked up eagerly to ask where I could find the school office.

To my surprise, the boys drew back sullenly and none of them would answer my question. It wasn't until I had repeated it for the third time that one of the youngest pointed silently to the front building.

I was no more than a few yards on my way when I heard behind me the familiar words that struck more fear in my heart than any others. I had believed I would never hear them again. "Stinking intellectual's son!" "Five black type!" Then, distinctly, I heard the sounds of six throats collecting spittle and depositing it wetly in the dust.

A teacher showed me to my narrow wooden bunk bed, one of more than fifty in the single room that was the boys' dormitory. The boy sitting on the bed below mine was Little Wu, the son of the Provincial Communist Youth League Party Vice-Secretary. He had a big round head and sun-dark skin, and he greeted me happily; we knew each other rather well since his family had been sent to the adjoining No. 8 Production Team.

He explained the situation. The students at this school had passed level upon level of political test to be permitted to attend, getting approval from their brigades, their communes, and the town itself. All of them were the children of poor and lower-middle peasants, so it was no wonder they were suspicious of us. And if their superb Revolutionary backgrounds didn't make things difficult enough, the school Revolutionary Committee had told them that we new students were sons and daughters of cadres who had made serious mistakes in the city. We were coming to school for re-education. They were to supervise us and criticize us, but to avoid becoming friends with us at all costs, lest we contaminate them with our "bad thought." Even in the dormitory we were segregated. We twelve boys were all to be together in six bunk beds set a little away from the rest. Little Wu sighed. "It's going to be tough here, really tough. Maybe even worse than in Changsha."

This was hard for me to believe, coming as I did from a Production Team where our relationship with the peasants was so good. But it was true. The peasant students jostled us when we stood in line to fetch hot water for washing; they mocked us as "city dogs" when they saw the soft patch-free cotton gym pants we slept in. My disappointment was so sharp that I could hardly sleep that night. It was like sleeping in a room full of enemies.

Things got worse over time, and the fact that, as resettled cadres' family members, we received three meals of rice, didn't help. The peasant children came back every Sunday night carrying their week's worth of sweet potatoes and their jars of salted peppers on their shoulder poles. Before each meal they filled their metal bowls with three or four tubers and turned them over to the dining-hall workers to be steamed. When the huge wooden crate opened and released its cloying sweetness into the air, they snatched their own bowls and hid away to eat their meals as if they were starving. But we lined up somewhere else entirely, at the teachers' window, handing over the coupons that symbolized the huge gulf between our worlds and receiving our fluffy white rice. Of course, at only three *liang* a meal, about a bowl, we were still ravenous.

The peasant children also hated us because our grades were so much better than theirs. After our training in the city schools, we quickly memorized the simple political texts and sat bored through the elementary math and physics lessons. We even showed better coordination in gym and in our "Revolutionary performance" classes. But there was never any homework and we had no books to read, so after school let out at two o'clock, we were equals in idleness.

All this contributed to making us little better than wild creatures. Most of us cadres' children already had substantial street knowledge, and our classmates' persecution and our hungry bellies forced us to use it. Although the girls tended to suffer in silence, we boys were a gang before we realized it.

Our first adventures were at the farmers' markets, now tightly controlled by the government for the sale of collectively produced goods, but still crowded and lively. Production Team representatives came for miles around to sell everything from rapeseed oil to dogmeat to snakes, and the local officials walked about importantly, checking credentials and collecting taxes. At the height of the day, there were performances of Jiang Qing's "model operas." We loved them, as we loved the chance to supplement our miserable diets.

We had our techniques down to perfection. A group of us would approach some poor vendor and someone would haggle with him about prices until he was blind with fury and had lost his usual vigilance. Then the rest of us went into action. Preserved eggs disappeared into eager pockets and peanuts vanished in greedy fistfuls. We were never caught; we were much too experienced for that. To us, stealing wasn't a moral question, but a question of survival.

It was too easy, and we were too hungry. So we started to go out at night as well. After the dormitory was quiet, the twelve of us picked our way through the complicated structure of intersecting beds where our forty classmates lay near-naked and snoring. Headed for the sweet potato fields, we ran silently into the night, trained now to use the moon shining in the rice paddies as our torchlight. We went farther each time, to fresher and safer territory, recognizing the potato plants by the dew glittering on their tangled leaves.

Even today, I want to cry when I think about that life, how I wriggled down between the rows, nearly burying myself, and scrabbled in the earth with my fingers until I felt a hard tuber. Fear and barking dogs made me greedy: I wiped off as much dirt as I could and devoured the potatoes raw, right then, as I lay there on my stomach with the clinging earth grinding like metal in my teeth, the pulp tough, juicy, and bittersweet, creating revolutions in my belly. It wasn't until we were nearly sick that we filled up the extra pair of pants we had made into a sack by tying the ankles with string, always urging each other "That's enough, that's enough," in our terror of being discovered. Then we hoisted our loot around someone's neck, the crotch at his nape, and he led the run back, anchoring the elastic bottoms in his hands, gliding with those little, even paces we had learned from the peasants.

We still had to hide our plunder in the back of the deserted storeroom, where it would stay until we pretended to have bought it the next market day. And we had to wash ourselves in the pond, our splashing setting off all the dogs in the town. It was often near dawn by the time we lay back in our beds, our swollen bellies already aching and cramping with their strange burden. I was grateful many times over for the precious mosquito netting that had hidden my absence.

Our classmates brought back word from their Production Teams that there was an infestation of wild pigs around that year. In a sense, I reflected sadly, they were right.

I was particularly wretched during that time because I still had no family. My father was away and my stepmother was indifferent to me. I didn't know whether she didn't know how to take care of me or didn't want to, but when I went home on a Sunday she didn't even leave any rice for me if I went out into the fields to work. So I often stayed alone in school, lying all day on my straw bedding. I cried a lot. During the days I was very fierce, but at night when I was alone I cried soundlessly into my pillow.

Gradually the peasants in the Production Team came to notice the way Zhu Zhi-dao treated me, and gossiped about it in the fields in their good-hearted way. Guo Lucky Wealth and his wife were especially kind to me during my vacations, and often shared their few sweet potatoes with me. Finally I just gave them my rice coupons and the twelve *yuan* monthly allowance I had from Father, and the relationship became official. I moved my bed out of the kitchen and into their part of the house, where they cared for me like their own son.

Guo Lucky Wealth's wife's hands were busy from the moment she woke up to the moment she went to bed. It was through living with her that I learned to have compassion for peasant women. Not only did she have to work with the men in the fields (and for fewer work points), but she was also responsible for the hundreds of household tasks: hauling water from the pond, washing vegetables for pig and human food, feeding the fire with brushwood, cooking, scrubbing clothing, repairing the grass roof when it leaked, spinning thread from cotton for mending, and cleaning the kitchen so that not even a fly could feed itself in it. Although she was still young, her hands were rough and cracked like old boards, and her bare feet were much larger than Father's. She wore her hair in two shining black braids, and her coarse round face reflected the humor that was her only answer to her misery. Life was a burden that she accepted and bore patiently, loving to talk about its sorrows as she smiled through her own sad words.

Her great tragedy was that she was barren. The couple had no children to share the work, add to the family work points, and take care of them when they were old. Guo Lucky Wealth's wife talked about this constantly, and soon I had memorized the story. It seemed that a movie had been shown at the brigade soon after her marriage, illustrating the life of a young Communist heroine. Afterward, Brigade Leader Li told all the women that they should learn from her, a childless woman of more than thirty. During the next few weeks, barefoot doctors would visit every home to insert intrauterine devices. Guo Lucky Wealth's wife had been so inspired by the film that she consented to the procedure, but afterward she found herself so racked with pain that she could hardly go to the fields to work. Perhaps, she said, it was because the doctor was inexperienced, having been trained for only half a year. It was women's misfortune that men couldn't risk birth control because they were the main labor force!

The commune clinic had refused to remove the IUD because of its family-planning campaign, so she had been forced to turn to a woman who made a business of doing such things illegally, for the price of a few eggs. This woman had performed the operation with a wire bent into a hook, but had made a wreck of both her uterus and her bladder, so that now she had to wear cotton pads to absorb the constant flow of urine, laying them out in the sun to dry when they became saturated and had to be exchanged for another. "Aiya!" she said often, smiling at her own folly, "I should never have gone to see the free movie!" I suggested many times that we save some money for her to see a doctor, but she said it was useless, she was already in debt to the Team because of doctors. She said, "The only person who can help me is a witchdoctor, but they're all afraid to come now because of the Propaganda Team."

Then one rainy day when we were all at home, a small child came running with the word that the witchdoctor was coming. We saw her coming up the road under her leaky umbrella, an old woman, gray-haired, with triangular sightless eyes and headache medicine stuck to her temples with black paper. She began her muttering when she entered the room, her plump assistant at her heels. "This village is full of ghosts. Ghosts and demons in every house."

Guo Lucky Wealth's wife ran immediately to a ceramic jar under the wardrobe and brought out five eggs, a usual price, babbling out the history of her complaint as quickly as she could. Meanwhile, I had three *jiao* in my pocket, and I quickly resolved to have my fortune told; I had been buffeted about too long by circumstance not to believe in fate.

First the blind witchdoctor took a stick of incense from her bag and stuck it unerringly in a crack in the wall. She had Guo Lucky Wealth's wife lie in bed, and burned paper money on the damp earthen floor, a preliminary attempt to buy off the ghost. The plump assistant had disappeared to find a branch from a peach tree, that potent anti-ghost weapon that can also be dangerous if you sit under it too long in the springtime, and returned with a healthy sprig. Many peasants were crowded into the doorway now, staring with curious, frightened eyes.

I had never seen anything so impressive. The old blind woman danced about the room, chanting and threatening, using the peach tree branch as a sword to strike out at the invisible ghost. The ghost was clearly struggling bravely, and the assistant represented its moans and taunts for the audience's benefit. The two women sang a kind of litany of attack and retreat: "Where are you?" "Here I am!" "You have to go now!" *(a slash of the branch)* "But I haven't had my supper yet!" *(groan)*

This went on for about fifteen minutes as Guo Lucky Wealth's wife lay sweating and terrified in her bed, submitting to the lashes, even those that fell on her face, as if she didn't feel them.

At last the witchdoctor announced in despair, "The ghost won't leave!" and her ghost-assistant cackled in triumphant confirmation. Guo Lucky Wealth's wife burst into tears. "It wants to eat something, maybe four more eggs, and then it will go," continued the old woman. "I've never seen such an evil ghost." Guo Lucky Wealth's wife turned to look at her husband in mute appeal, and he bent down once again to the ceramic jar. There were only two eggs.

"I have money!" I cried. "I can give it two *jiao!*"

The old woman grinned delightedly. "Money works even better than eggs, with ghosts," she said, and she ran to the kitchen, once again unerringly, and picked up two cleavers. She swung these through the air by the bed, jumping and whirling as if being attacked on all sides. Then she paused, apparently victorious, and the ghost whimpered, "I'm going, I'm going, don't beat me anymore!" The old woman fumbled in her bag and brought out a glass bottle full of clear liquid. "This is water of the Immortals," she announced, sprinkling it around the room and on Guo Lucky Wealth's wife, who seemed to have fainted away. "Now the demon won't dare to come back. But you tell the sick woman not to have a drop to drink for three days, or she'll break the charm and ruin all our work. Now," she sighed and waved her arms as if to feel out new ghosts. "Who's next?"

Everyone had crowded into the room to catch a drop of the water of the Immortals, and the old woman did a brisk business. There were no more exorcisms, but many, like myself, wanted their fortunes told. It was more than an hour before my turn came. The witchdoctor had me sit down on a stool in front of her and placed her ice-cold hands on my face. I shivered all over, remembering that these hands had grappled with ghosts, but I kept my wits enough to answer that I was born in the morning and in the year of the horse.

"You are about fifteen years old," she crooned, "and your family is scattered North, South, East, and West. You are now in the sea of bitterness, your two older sisters, your parents, and yourself, but this is the worst time. Many people have tried to harm you, and will continue to do so in the future, but when you are about twenty, you will be very lucky. People may try to keep you from enjoying this luck, but they will only partially succeed. As for your father," she frowned and her cold hands tightened on my face, "it will be many, many years before he leaves the bitter sea."

I thought all this was astoundingly accurate, and well worth a *jiao*. I waited for years for the truth of her predictions to reveal itself, anticipation of my good luck a continuous consolation. But Guo Lucky Wealth's wife's experience did not end so happily. It was true she stopped urinating during the days she didn't drink anything, but the water came again immediately afterwards. "I was so thirsty that I began again too early," she wailed, holding her wet pants and weeping.

It was nearly Spring Festival, the Lunar New Year, February 1970. My classmates had gone home and I slept alone in the damp dormitory, waiting to meet my sister Liang Wei-ping at the bus station and take her to our Production Team. Her leaders in Yuanjiang County near Dongting Lake had granted her a week's leave.

I hadn't seen her in more than a year, and I hardly recognized the sweet-potato-puffy young woman who got off the bus. Her girlish braids were gone and her hair was short now, like a peasant's. Perhaps she no longer had time to comb out her hair, or perhaps like me she had discovered that in the countryside no one washes his hair except incidentally, while swimming during the summer. She was wearing the same baggy blue clothes that she had on when she left, but they seemed tight, and they were patched. She looked much older than her seventeen years.

I was overjoyed to see her, but even happier to see two long, dense loaves of glutinous rice in a basket hanging from the pole on her shoulder. Years later she reminded me how I begged her to break off a piece, and then crouched down by the road and devoured it ravenously, washing it down with ditchwater. She described how she had cried as she watched me, squatting there in my rags, stomach distended, but the fine winter sleet must have hidden her tears, for I have no memory of them.

Zhu Zhi-dao was in the kitchen by the fire when we arrived several hours later. The paths had been slippery because of the weather, and our feet ached from being clenched up inside our torn army sneakers; it was the only way to get enough traction to keep from falling. Our stepmother acknowledged us only when she saw Liang Wei-ping's long rice *babas*, but then she smiled and got up slowly to fetch the hot water thermos and a basin for us to soothe our feet.

Guo Lucky Wealth and his wife were more hospitable, and news of Liang Wei-ping's arrival spread quickly. The peasants commented on how pretty she was, and many of them urged her to visit their homes. Most of all, they were interested in hearing about conditions in the Team where she lived, such as the value of a work point (seven or eight times its worth in our Team) and the yield of a *mu* of land (about .16 acre; see appendix, page 293). When she talked about the problems of fertilizers and preparing pig slop, she sounded just like an experienced peasant. Liang Wei-ping had always been generous, and she divided one of her long *babas* among her many hosts, ignoring Zhu Zhi-dao's admonishing frowns. The peasants now accepted her completely.

It was from them she learned about how Zhu Zhi-dao had treated me, and she told me angrily that she had her own grievances as well: She had begged for five *yuan* a month for oil and salt and been refused. Although Auntie Zhu was kind enough to Father, she just didn't see us as her own children. Once I even overheard Liang Wei-ping ask her for sanitary paper for her monthly; she was told to use old newspaper instead.

Things were better after Father came home because Zhu Zhi-dao seemed more cheerful. Father looked older now, with a hint of a shuffle in his walk. At first I thought he was just weighted down with coats, for he was wearing everything he owned. He glued himself to the fire, however, and continued to shiver; we learned he had been sleeping on floors with only rice straw between himself and the damp earth, and had been rheumatic for several months.

Spring Festival festivities were disappointing. Despite government decrees, there were a few firecrackers from midnight of the first day of the New Year, a fruitless show of hospitality for a deaf Buddha of Wealth. Like Father, the cadres from the Propaganda Team had gone home and didn't care what the peasants did. There were no feasts for anyone though, and for Liang Wei-ping and me, none of the traditional treats given by parents to their children, only a few kernels of popcorn tossed at us by an impatient Zhu Zhi-dao.

However, for me, the wonderful thing about Spring Festival was the chance to exchange experiences with Liang Wei-ping. The one trait that all of us Liang children seemed to have inherited from Father was a love of storytelling, and we listened to each other until late in the night, sitting in the kitchen by the embers so we wouldn't disturb anyone.

My second sister had been luckier than Liang Fang in that she had signed up to go to Yuanjiang County with a group of classmates, one of them her best friend, Peng Ming's sister. Expecting to be able to scoop fish out of the lake with a spoon, they were astounded to find themselves in what looked in cold December like the middle of nowhere. Since they were the only girls in the first group, the Grass Tail Commune had assigned them to the Production Team nearest town. The county government Educated Youth Office had given the local leaders 240 *yuan* for each of them so they could build them a house and 100 *yuan* for basic necessities. They were also to get 30 *liang* of rice per month while they earned their first work points, so at first it looked as if their situation was going to be all right. It was a kind of glorious adventure, their first time to set up house on their own.

What they hadn't counted on were the hard conditions, the differences in customs, and their own homesickness. What surprised Liang Wei-ping most was the peasants' stinginess; she had been told every peasant would treat her like his own daughter, but instead they begrudged even an egg. Still, they were honest, hardworking, and basically goodhearted, as Liang Wei-ping discovered when she plucked up valuable wheat thinking it was grass; the peasants merely laughed and didn't ask her to pay.

Liang Wei-ping told me a number of stories, such as about how one of the Educated Youths who went to the countryside with her ended up marrying a peasant boy. When they first arrived, the students were each assigned to live in a peasant home. This girl was given a bed in a room with the son of the family, and after she had been there less than a week, he raped her. Too humiliated to report the incident, she felt she had to bow to fate, and the family got themselves a bride—usually worth 1,000 *yuan* in that Team—free. My sister also told me how she had sneaked onto a boat to go back to Changsha during the first month, but was discovered by the Public Security Bureau and sent back again, and how she and her classmates had been robbed a number of times and finally caught a fellow Educated Youth. She told me how the peasants threw uncooked rice on their beds to keep away ghosts, and up on the roof in a strong wind so the grass wouldn't blow off. She described how they made poison by grinding up the dried bodies of insects and used it to revenge themselves on each other. But of all the stories she told me, the ones that made the deepest impression were the ones about the conflicts between the peasants and the Educated Youths, because they were closest to my own experience.

One night, when relations between the peasants and the Educated Youth contingent had deteriorated completely, five of the boys went to steal chickens in a nearby Production Team. They blundered in a dark kitchen and set the chickens to screeching, waking everyone in the house. The old peasants sent up a terrible cry and the neighbors came running. They beat the boys pretty severely, using sticks and fists and anything else they could lay their hands on. When they finally let them go, all five of the boys were bleeding.

It was their hotheaded lack of experience that led them to take revenge the same night—they were only fifteen, no older than I was. They waited until well after midnight, when everything was quiet, and then stole back and surrounded one of the old peasants where he lay in his bed. Who knows whether they had intended such violence, but they beat him around the head, and then pulled and twisted him until they had broken his leg. As a finishing touch, they overturned his furniture and broke dishes, pots, and anything else that would shatter. Then they ran, leaving him moaning in the ruins of his own home.

Liang Wei-ping and her girl classmates were asleep in their house some distance from the boys' quarters when they were awakened by the angry hum of a revengeful mob. They made out the peasants dimly, maybe thirty of them, with hoes and sticks in their hands and coils of rope across their chests. The women and children brought up the rear. "Give us the murderers or we'll wash your house with blood," they yelled.

It was the more terrifying because the girls had no idea what had happened. The crowd kicked at the boys' door as if to break it down. Liang Wei-ping was certain her friends would all be killed, for they were badly outnumbered, and even the Production Team leaders were in the mob. The girls made a desperate plan. With scissors, they cut their straw bedding and tied it onto the ends of some bamboo poles. Lighting their torches, they ran out at the peasants, shouting that if they didn't retreat, their straw roofs would burn and their houses be destroyed.

The boys took courage from the girls, and ran out into the flickering light brandishing sticks and shouting their vilest Changsha curses. They managed to surround some of the peasants in front while the girls swung their torches. The crowd began to draw back. Maybe that reckless band of lower middle-school graduates had succeeded in intimidating them, or maybe they feared the gods would be offended if more blood was spilled. In any case, what could have been a vicious battle was averted. By the light of the next day, more rational punishment was meted out: The whole group was forced to attend study class, and the five boys had to pay the medical expenses of the peasant they had victimized. The stealing went on as before, of course, but more cautiously, and not so close to home.

What I found most astonishing about all this was not the explosive scene Liang Wei-ping had described, for I had had many fights of my own with the peasant children. It was rather that my timid, conservative sister had engaged in such things, and bravely, and that she seemed to take her behavior for granted. She had her regrets, of course, as I did every time I fought or stole sweet potatoes; she told me never to tell Father or Liang Fang, who had written saying that her older group's relationship with the peasants was excellent. "How could Chairman Mao say that the countryside was a great land where we Educated Youths would have glorious successes?" Liang Wei-ping wondered. "I'm only afraid that when I go back I'll be sucked into that terrifying whirlpool once again."

CHAPTER SEVENTEEN

Interrogation

Soon after Liang Wei-ping left, Father returned to his work on the Propaganda Team and I went back to school to begin the new semester. My sister's stories had influenced me, and I resolved to improve my relationship with the peasant children. This was relatively easy to do, for I understood them very well. I knew they were more afraid of ghosts than of anything else, and I used to impress them by nonchalantly visiting places they believed haunted. My classmates were already a little afraid of me because of my height and toughness; now they began to see me as some sort of hero.

What really kept me out of fights was the discovery of the boarded-up storeroom. It was a flat-roofed building near the basketball court, and an idle moment's investigation through the cracks in the door revealed that it was full of books, probably from the pre–Cultural Revolution school library. I hadn't read a good book since the Red Guards' search raid more than four years earlier, and my heart pounded. I quickly organized my handful of best friends, now including two peasant boys, and swore them to secrecy. Late that night, we pried off a few boards and climbed in. The acrid dust and mildew irritated our throats, and spiderwebs were everywhere; the books lay in broken piles, and the yellow paper bindings were sticky to the touch. But I felt as though we had entered paradise!

Someone had a flashlight, and we passed it about with shaking hands as we made our selections. We rationed ourselves, as we did when we stole sweet potatoes, for fear of being discovered. I chose a history of Europe and translations of Hegel's *Dialectics* and Flaubert's *Madame Bovary*. We replaced the boards carefully when we left.

It seemed there would be no end to our secret new pleasures. My life changed completely. I read with a passion I had felt for nothing else, keeping a diary about everything. The world of the imagination opened to me; I had new dreams and ambitions. My fellow thieves and I held discussions on literature and even began to write poetry, meeting on the windy riverbank but never feeling cold. We were a small literary society of fifteen-year-olds.

One day a classmate—I never found out who—took one of my poems from my desk and turned it in to a political cadre. It was a pessimistic poem, about my road of life leading nowhere. I was publicly criticized, and "dissatisfied with reality" was written in my file. Even that didn't quell my literary fervor. I simply began to turn it outward, writing letters to faraway friends and family like Little Li, who was still in Changsha because his parents had not yet been "liberated" from the study class. I developed quite an active correspondence, receiving answers to all my letters except those to Peng Ming. I imagined he must be too busy making Revolution to write.

Then one Saturday morning, classes were canceled for a special schoolwide meeting. New slogans were up in the big classroom, all of them dealing with class struggle, so we knew something important was in the air.

The political work group was the section of the school Revolutionary Committee with the real power, and Liu Guo-rong, a graduate of the Hunan Teachers' College's Politics Department, was the head of it. This was his meeting, and he strode to the podium as if girding himself for a performance.

It was a short meeting, but an exciting one. Liu's gold fillings sparkled in his expressive mouth, and a fine spray of saliva rained into the first rows at emphatic moments. A new movement was on, he told us, to round up the counterrevolutionary "May Sixteenth" conspirators.

"This nationwide secret organization has tried to attack our beloved Premier Zhou En-lai by sabotaging diplomatic relations with foreign countries," he bellowed. "They have a manifesto and a plan. Their activities are vicious. They use our postal system to spread their pernicious conspiracy everywhere." Liu paused, and we held our breaths. Finally he hissed, "We have a May Sixteenth conspirator right here in this room!"

Pandemonium broke as we chattered excitedly and craned our heads about hoping to identify the culprit. My mind raced down the list of my simple country teachers, but it seemed impossible that any of them should be involved in something so terrifying, so dangerous. Liu continued, "After the meeting, the counterrevolutionary will come to my office and surrender. I will put up five locked boxes throughout the school so that those of you who think they have spotted other counter-revolutionary activities can put in their reports. Don't worry, I am the only person with the keys. No one will know about your suspicions but you and me." He flashed his golden smile. "Meeting dismissed."

In the classroom, I held a whispered consultation with the members of my literary group and we decided to disband and return the stolen books that evening. Other classmates were checking their desks to make sure nothing had been planted there. Then I felt a hand on my shoulder. It was Teacher Deng, a member of the school Revolutionary Committee. "Liang Heng," he said, "Liu Guo-rong wants to see you."

I hurried behind him past my classmates' stares, shame burning me. A direct confrontation with Liu Guo-rong was too terrible to con-template. I couldn't imagine what I had done.

The political work office held nothing but locked cabinets from floor to ceiling, the slogans on the walls, and some wooden chairs and a large desk. Liu sat behind this, smoking, a thick folder in front of him. He jerked his head toward an empty chair, and I sat down, trem-bling. Then he almost smiled.

"Did you forget to bring your ears with you this morning? You wanted a personal invitation?"

I flushed deeper in an agony of confusion.

"Well, you can still confess your activities as a May Sixteenth conspirator," said Liu, gesturing to a sheaf of blank papers on which I now noticed the heading "Confession" in big black characters.

My protests were useless. Liu shook his folder at me and claimed he knew everything, while I racked my brains for what the contents might be. Finally, he stood up and said, "You won't be leaving here until you've confessed, so you might as well begin now. Someone will bring you your lunch." I heard the key turn in the lock after him.

That morning the sounds of my classmates' voices rang in the corridors and I glued myself to the barred window hoping to catch a glimpse of a friend. I enumerated the possibilities over and over, rejecting them all: Could it be the books I had sent to Little Li in Changsha? Our literary group? The stolen sweet potatoes?

At noon, Teacher Deng came with food, and he whispered kindly to me, "You better confess, or heaven knows what will happen. The letter came from the Peking Public Security Bureau."

That explained it. Peng Ming must be in some kind of trouble. If I had come to the notice of Peking, things looked very bad for me indeed. But I recalled the content of my letters, and felt a bit calmer. I had done nothing but speak of our old friendship and ask Peng Ming if he could send me some materials on the arts; he was, after all, a composer.

Liu came back that afternoon to question me. His face was constantly changing, sometimes fierce, sometimes kind and smiling, until I felt numb and I wasn't really sure what was right anymore. On the one hand, he threatened me with jail; on the other, he promised me I could join the Communist Youth League if I only admitted my crime. "Your father came to the countryside with a black mark on his record, and before it's wiped clean you give him a counterrevolutionary son!" Liu said. "Think of the glory for your family if you tell the Party everything! Think how proud your father will be!"

At one point I mentioned Peng Ming's name. Liu lit up ecstatically. "Aha, you've confided the name of your counterrevolutionary contact to the Party! That's wonderful!" And he seized a piece of paper and, consulting his watch, noted down the exact moment of my "confession." Then he looked at me expectantly. "Go on."

I don't know how many times I explained the nature of my friendship with Peng Ming. I told Liu that we had been neighbors, that he had taken me with him on a New Long March. I explained that I had helped out in Peking, that his sister and my sister were classmates. But I insisted I knew nothing about any May Sixteenth conspiracy, nor that Peng Ming might have anything to do with counterrevolutionary activities. I didn't understand much of what was happening to me, but I thought I might as well die rather than confess something false that might be used against my friend.

In the late afternoon, Liu opened his folder and took out the letters

I had written to Peking. I broke out in sweat then: I had never dreamed the Public Security Bureau could be so thorough.

"These letters were written in your own hand, right?" asked Liu.

"Of course," I responded. I described again the nature of my friendship with Peng Ming and my reasons for writing the letters.

Liu wasn't happy. "You're only a fifteen-year-old boy, and you dare take me for a three-year-old child," he said, rising and approaching me threateningly. He seized me at the base of the neck and squeezed. "Confess your counterrevolutionary plot!" he commanded.

It hurt so much I couldn't control my tears. "I've never heard of any May Sixteenth conspiracy." I sobbed. "I've told you everything I know."

And so it went, on and on in circles. They made me sleep there on the desk that night, and the next, and the next. Liu came to question me every afternoon, sometimes hitting me, sometimes flattering me and trying to bribe me with political favors. Teacher Deng brought me my meals, and was kind to me with cigarettes and information. I think what hurt me most during that time was the way my friends betrayed me.

Every time Liu came in, he had new "evidence" in his hand, reports pushed into the locked boxes by the people I had trusted most. The people I had defended in fights turned me in, the people with whom I had stolen food. My literary friends told of our book thefts and our poetry meetings; my homeroom teacher wrote about my "bad thought." And when I called out the window to my round-headed friend Little Wu, he looked frightened and hurried away. Every day I traced out the history of my relationship with Peng on the papers marked "Confession"; every day Liu took them away, muttering, "Another crime."

It was Teacher Deng who gave me the strength not to "confess" a lie. He explained that the letter from the Peking Security Bureau had asked only that I be investigated, not that I be arrested. Still, I knew that Liu would have me arrested if he could. It would be great Revolutionary glory if he could ferret out a big counterrevolutionary in his little country school, a great boost for his career. So every night I cried, torn between the desire not to hurt Peng Ming and the desire to protect Father from yet another disgrace.

On the fifth day, Liu didn't come until late in the day, and he had a plainclothes Public Security officer with him. "This is your last chance," he announced with satisfaction. "If you don't confess today, tomorrow you'll go to jail." Before my eyes, he went to a cabinet, unlocked it, and handed my file over to the officer.

That night, as I lay on my desk, I had no tears left. I had lived fifteen years, but I had no desire to live even one more. I had been the victim of political movements since the age of three, first through my mother, then through my father, and now through an absurd coincidence in my own affairs. Society hated me. It had turned me into an outcast and a thief. My stepmother disliked me and my father was a broken man. I even hated him for what he had done to our family.

I imagined the next day I would be brought to jail as a criminal, paraded through the streets as the peasants shouted, "Down with the counterrevolutionary!" My friends would be among them, throwing rocks and sticks, laughing at my shame, glad that now the country would be that much more secure than it had been before the criminal's arrest. Perhaps first there would be a public criticism meeting, a beating, a humiliation. . . .

The dusty dark lightbulb hanging several yards above me was still visible in the night. Suddenly, I realized that I could die. I could unscrew that lightbulb and put my hand there where the current flowed and I would be dead. I should never again be tormented by memories of Mother's humiliated and accepting face as Father cursed her for betraying the Party's faith in her; of Nai Nai's swollen cheeks as she lay in her black coffin; of Father kneeling before his burning books, praising the Party; of Liang Fang's feces-covered shoes as she came home to write her Thought Reports. I should never again hear the words "stinking intellectual's son," or lie on my stomach in the sweet potato fields; my throat wouldn't hurt anymore where Liu had squeezed it. I was amazed at the simplicity of it all.

The thought came quickly and I acted quickly. Standing on the table, I reached the bulb easily and it unscrewed smoothly into my hand. It was a lonely action, and I felt suddenly angry that it should be so. There should have been someone to help me do it, or someone to urge me not to. I reflected bitterly that after my death the mob would stone my body just as it would if I were alive, the difference being that now they would say that the counterrevolutionary had killed himself because of his crime. I would never be able to explain to Father that I wasn't guilty, and I remembered his old, sad face, weeping, telling himself to be patient and tolerant, that someday his question would be made clear. Another thought struck me with equal force: If I died, Peng Ming's enemies could invent my confession, and use it against him just as if I had penned it with my own hand.

The desire to live came strong then, stronger than the desire to die. I remember Father excitedly recording the peasant boy's folk song by torchlight, still a man of letters even in the midst of greatest trouble. I thought of Mother and Waipo, waiting for me in Changsha, and Liang Wei-ping sharing her rice *baba* among the peasants. The hoodlums had cared for me so well on the streets, and Teacher Luo had forgiven me so graciously for the caricatures I had drawn of him. There was so much good in this crazy world, but so much more that was impossible to understand.

Why should two good people like my parents be forced to divorce each other? Why should Liang Fang raise a machine gun against her fellow teenagers? Why did the peasants fear the cadres so terribly if they were representatives of our great Communist Party? Why were people so determined to make me and Peng Ming look like counterrevolutionaries when we wanted only to make a contribution to our country? Why had the Revolution given us all so little when we had sacrificed everything for it?

That night, I resolved that I would seek the answers to these questions. If I was to live, it would no longer be numbly and aimlessly. I would live bravely. I would not be like Father, denying the facts and fooling himself, nor like Pockmark Liu, disillusioned and cynical. I would go to prison, but I would study so that I could understand why my country had produced such tragedies.

The next morning, Liu arrived, but he was alone. "You can go," he said dourly.

It was no wonder I believed in fate, my life was just that crazy. I thought I must be dreaming again, but I didn't want to question my luck. I stumbled out, blinking in the bright light.

Later, I learned that the Central Committee in Peking had issued a document saying that too many people were being arrested on May Sixteenth conspiracy charges, and that in fact the conspiracy was not so big. Liu had to let me go. Still, the incident was by no means easily forgotten. My classmates shunned me, and Liu had his ways of having his revenge. In my file he wrote, "Corresponded with person with serious political questions," and when my class finished lower middle school that spring, I was the only one not allowed to proceed to upper middle school. The reason: "Complicated Thought."

CHAPTER EIGHTEEN

Basketball

I had been back at the Production Team working in the fields for several months when Zhu Zhi-dao was cleared. In addition to the problem of her landlord background, she had been accused of being active in the KMT Youth League. A two-year investigation reaching as far as Heilongjiang Province in the extreme north had now revealed that the KMT sympathizer had been another woman named Zhu Zhi-dao, dead ten years. My stepmother could return to teaching school in Shuangfeng, this time in the county seat itself.

She and Father quarreled when she received the notice. He had been so ill that his colleagues on the Propaganda Team had helped him get sick leave, and he hoped Zhu Zhi-dao would stay and look after him. She said she couldn't bear the hardships any longer, that she had been a fool to follow Father to this place when the countryside near Shuangfeng would not have been nearly so poor. Father had little energy to plead with her, and she left the day after the letter of exoneration arrived.

The task of nursing Father thus fell to me, and we spent more time together than we had in years. I rubbed his numb legs for him and prepared his medicines. I learned how to cook, and tried in a hundred ways to stimulate his weak appetite. He took care of me, too, consoling me for my tragedy. "In our country, you must never write a letter lightly," he told me. "But I'm proud of you. You protected Peng Ming and kept your integrity." This seemed to be all he asked now of me and of himself. Gone were the days of ambition for the members of the Liang family to join the Party. Father now sought only peace, and his private judgment that he had done no wrong.

Week after week, he wearily submitted reports to the Chairman Mao Thought Study Class begging to be permitted to leave the countryside. "I have worked many years for the Revolution," he wrote. "Although I have made many errors, I have never lost confidence in the Party and in Socialism. Now I can make no more contribution because of my poor health. I humbly request that the Party take care of me. . . ." After half a year, an investigating group came from Changsha and determined that Father really was an invalid. They agreed to let him go. He was to be the first cadre in Hunan Province to leave the countryside.

Father had no family besides Zhu Zhi-dao since his brother and sister had gone to Taiwan with the KMT. The study class decided that our residence cards would be transferred to Shuangfeng with hers. Father would be given work at the Chairman Mao Thought Propaganda Station there. He had never dreamed of resuming his professional work at the newspaper, so he was overjoyed to have any work at all.

It seemed to me that the witchdoctor's prediction was right, I was finally leaving the sea of bitterness. I would be able to go back to school again, and Father's "second liberation" would restore our family's name. My only sorrow was leaving the peasants in our Team, especially Guo Lucky Wealth and his warm-hearted wife. She spent three days sewing Father a pair of cloth shoes, and we gave her our furniture and most of our belongings. When I visited ten years later, she was still using our cups and dishes. We arrived in Shuangfeng in February 1971, exactly two years after we had left Changsha. I was almost seventeen. Once again, a new life began.

Two rooms at different ends of a corridor on the second floor of the Propaganda Station served as Father's office and a home for him, me, Zhu Zhi-dao, and my old acquaintance, Cousin Bing. It was a bit crowded, but much more convenient; there was electricity, and the faucet was just down the hall so we no longer had to transport water great distances. The outhouse was still quite far away, but it was divided into sections for men and women, and there was a long string of holes so many people could use it at one time. I realized how much being in the countryside had changed the way I perceived things when I found myself looking down into the sea of night soil and thinking about how valuable it would have been to our Team.

Father worked like a crazy man. His co-workers were delighted to have him because, as they liked to say, he had "drunk more ink" than they. They were peasant Party members and retired actors, so they needed his expertise. He wrote speeches for the County Revolutionary Committee Party Secretary and plays for the local Propaganda Team. He edited the articles to be used in loudspeaker broadcasts, ran a magazine called *Arts for the Masses*, and administered the county library. He was so happy to work again that he was reluctant to remind his superior that he was a very sick man.

As for me, I discovered my own route to glory: basketball. Ever since the Cultural Revolution had begun to emphasize culture for the masses, sports, music, and dance had taken on an unprecedented importance all over the country. Nearly every work unit had established its own artistic troupes and basketball and ping-pong teams, and these competed with those of other work units within the same administrative system. Excellence often brought even greater recognition of Revolutionary achievement than high scholastic or production standards.

I had not been in upper middle school for a week when Coach Xie approached me. At 5'11" I was already the tallest in the whole school. It would be a real waste, he said, if I didn't learn to play ball. I had planned to focus on my studies, but after the coach visited our home to speak with Father, I began to understand the advantages of developing athletic skills.

Coach Xie had a sense of humor. "Is your father here a Party member?" he asked me.

"No."

"Any army men in your family?"

"No."

"Any Revolutionary cadres? No? Well, let me tell you something, my boy. During the past few years, nearly all of my athletes have found work. I have boys in the County Fertilizer Factory, in the County Construction Company. I have someone in the coal mines. What about other people? Your two older sisters, for example. They don't have work, do they?"

He was right, I knew. Every letter from Liang Fang and Liang Wei-ping spoke of the desperation of the Educated Youths trying to find work so they could leave the harsh countryside and return to their families. The rare openings were always taken by those who had gone "through the back door"—city relatives had bribed factory officials with wine, cigarettes, food ration tickets, and special products from other provinces; then, in return for agreeing to release those Educated Youths named by recruiters, the leaders of communes and brigades got to choose a few of their own favorites, the spies and flatterers, the givers of gifts and sexual favors. For an honest person with neither connections nor money, finding a job was a frustrating impossibility. In fact, Liang Wei-ping was soon to transfer to the countryside near Shuangfeng where proximity to Father and Zhu Zhi-dao might open a few back doors for her.

Coach Xie was still talking. "Let me tell you something else," he said, drawing his muscular body up to its full height and putting his hand on my shoulder. "In all my days as coach, I have never seen raw material like yours. You don't have to limit your ambitions to the county. If you work really hard, I swear I can send you all the way to Changsha!"

In one year, I went from bench-warmer to Team Captain, always playing center, towering over the other players by as much as a head. I trained from four every morning, using up so much energy that once I didn't shit for over a month. Nothing mattered to me except overcoming the limitations of my own body; I even stopped smoking and drinking. Then at last, I began to taste the sweetness of my efforts. Our middle school won the county championship, and we went to play in the in-tercounty districtwide meet. I had never had so much to eat in my life. For fifteen *fen* a day, there was meat, fish, soybean milk, porridge, dumplings. . . . One morning I ate fifteen *mantou* for breakfast.

We came in only fifth, but, more because of my height than my skill, I was chosen for the district team. During my vacations for the next year, I was sent to the Shaoyang City Amateur Athletic Training School. I played and ate as if nothing existed in the world except basketball courts and food, untroubled for the first time by political movements and pressures. I grew to a height of 6′1″, extraordinary in Southern China. As far as I was concerned, I had grown right up into heaven.

At last we were sent to play in the provincewide interdistrict meet, in Yueyang City north of Changsha. It was the fall of 1972 and I was eighteen. My teammates and I knew we had no possibility of winning, or even placing, but the enthusiasm of the fans was enough to make us play our best. Sports was the only area of life relatively free from politics, and despite the dampening effects of slogans like "Friendship First, Competition Second," the crowds were tremendous. Then, on the last day of the competition, the coach told me that a coach from the Provincial Sports Committee wanted to speak to me.

My heart pounded as the coach poured me tea. "Young man," he said, without further preliminaries, "your build is excellent and you've got great promise. Hunan Province wants to make you into a basketball player."

I could hardly control my hand to fill out the mountain of forms. I might have work, my own salary. Father would be proud; I could return to Changsha. When I was done, the coach shook my hand with the easy confidence of the professional athlete. "Just go home and continue with your studies," he said. "We'll have to discuss things and make arrangements, but you'll probably be hearing from us before too long."

My coach was so proud of me that on the way home he let me stop a few days in Changsha to see Mother and Waipo. It was a happy son who walked up the dirty alley, tall and strong, with weight on his bones and clean new government clothes. That visit was the greatest consolation I could have given them.

During my stay, I fell into conversation with a son of my stepfather's from his earlier marriage. The boy was a worker at the Changsha Shale Oil Factory, and he told me that his leaders happened to be passionate basketball enthusiasts. Factory work was much easier than full-time athletics, the boy pointed out. Since the position with the Provincial Sports Committee wasn't definite, why didn't he arrange to have me play for his factory during an upcoming Chemistry System Tournament so his leaders could get a look at me? I agreed, of course. The more opportunities I had, the better.

The match was held in the Workers' Palace, open to the late autumn stars with an audience of thousands. I felt unusually nervous as I went through my paces during the warmup; I knew my fate depended on how I played. Before I had a chance to really show my stuff, though, the judges disqualified me because I wasn't a Shale Oil Factory worker. The factory leaders were so angry that they were friendlier to me than ever. They had seen enough. "Go home," they said. "We'll have representatives out in Shuangfeng within two days."

Things were happening so fast I could hardly believe they were true, but I soon discovered that the obstacles were greater than I had expected. First I had to get Father's permission to be a worker, and to my surprise, he wouldn't give it. He wanted me to go to college so that I could have a literary career and continue for him the work that had been interrupted. He knew that I loved literature, and that I was quick in my studies. If I went down again to the countryside after my graduation from middle school, perhaps the peasants would recommend me as a worker-peasant-soldier candidate, one of the new students of the Cultural Revolution era.

Liang Wei-ping, who was now working as a cook in a nearby commune, did not hesitate to speak her mind. "Father, you're crazy," she said. "Do you realize how much of your salary has been spent on gifts to officials just to get me transferred this far? Do you realize how much it costs to build a good connection with somebody? If Liang Heng goes back to the countryside as an Educated Youth, he'll lose his residence card and who knows if he'll ever make it back, even as an outhouse cleaner! You think he could be a college student! Wake up, Father, times have changed. The only door to college is the back door."

Zhu Zhi-dao had her point of view, too. "It's terribly expensive for the family to live apart," she said. "Together, we can get along with only two dishes of fat pork and cabbage, but if Liang Heng goes back to the countryside, we can hardly afford to send him money every month."

We all sighed over the irony of the situation. Although I had just spent two years in the countryside, I was bound to return as soon as I graduated, unless I could get a medical exemption. Perhaps only a factory that wanted me badly could help bend the rules enough to save me.

The news that the Hunan Province Sports Committee had spoken to me spread fast, and the day after my arrival at home I received visits from representatives of no less than four Shuangfeng County factories, all offering me work. The Changsha Shale Oil Factory officials arrived too, and they all performed a delicate little play in our apartment, making small talk on various subjects so as to avoid stating the real purpose of their visits. At last only the oil factory representatives remained, and they spoke with Father long into the night, persuading him to let me become a worker. They would give me a "strenuous" job classification, they said, so that I could get generous rice rations. They would give me an extra-long bed so I would be comfortable. They would guarantee that I would be taken on as a regular worker after my three-year apprenticeship. Perhaps it was the thought that I would be able to settle in the city where he had worked for more than twenty years that finally melted Father; that evening, he gave his consent.

The transfer process was far from easy, even with the factory officials' support. First I needed to be declared ill, so as to have grounds for remaining in the city. Zhu Zhi-dao was rapidly becoming an expert in the art of going "through the back door," and she knew a doctor at the local clinic. She paid him a call, leaving a carton of expensive cigarettes discreetly on a side table as she left. Suddenly, I had high blood pressure and heart disease. Coach Xie assured school officials that my story was true, and I received permission to drop out of middle school.

The worst problem was yet to be solved. I needed the permission of the Public Security Bureau to have my residence card transferred to the city. Even in normal circumstances this was next to impossible, but the problem in my case was compounded because of the jealousy of the Shuangfeng factories that had failed to get me; they had threatened to complain to the County Sports Committee that a local talent was escaping "through the back door." If the County Sports Committee told the Bureau of Culture and Education that my medical excuse was a fraud, a word to the Public Security Bureau would close Changsha off to me forever. The two Shale Oil Factory officials rushed from place to place submitting reports like ants on a hot stove, but all their requests were turned down. Finally they asked my family if we didn't know someone on the County Revolutionary Committee. A telephone call from a really high official would solve the whole problem.

Father had been unusually withdrawn ever since I had returned with my news, and now he did not volunteer the information that the rest of us knew quite well: He was writing a speech for the County Party Secretary. After the officials left, Zhu Zhi-dao urged him to go see the man, and then Liang Wei-ping and I had our turns. Father adamantly refused. "I don't want to have anything to do with such practices," he said. "It's all I can do to write speeches about policies that have nothing to do with the practical situation. I won't go begging officials to do me favors as well."

It was clearly hopeless. Finally Zhu Zhi-dao stood up. "I'll go myself, then. Surely you can't object to that." She bent into the recesses of a wardrobe and drew out two dusty bottles of fine grape wine. She brushed them off with a cloth, put them into a plain black bag, and was gone.

Within an hour she was back, her bag empty. "It's settled," she announced. "It couldn't have been easier. I told him I was your wife, and he was very friendly. Then I told him about Liang Heng's chance to work—of course, I didn't mention that he's an athlete—and he was so sympathetic that he made a call to the Public Security Bureau on the spot."

That evening, the factory officials held a banquet for my family at their hostel and I had time to reflect on my good fortune. Others had to spend money to bribe factory officials, but factory officials were spending money on me, as if I were so precious that they were still afraid I might change my mind!

Father said good-bye to me that night. For a long time he lay on his bed without saying anything. Then he took out a yellowed collection of his poems and stories from the bottom of a wooden box. I had never known that anything had been saved the night of the search raid. Father gave these to me to keep, saying, "In our society you can't choose your occupation freely. As your father, I know you have a talent for literature. Even though the writing profession is a dangerous one, I still want you to follow that road." He swallowed. "I'm sure you'll find the factory a rich source of material."

These words saddened me even as they encouraged me. I saw that Father himself had given up. I looked one last time at the beloved face, the broad forehead lined with defeat, the sparkling eyes dulled behind thicker and thicker glasses. I said, "Father, no matter where I go and what I become, I will never find a better teacher than you. I won't disappoint you."

Before dawn the next morning, the factory officials roused me to catch the bus to Changsha. Weeks after, I learned that the County Party Secretary had rescinded his approval of my transfer at the request of the local Sports Committee, but it was already too late. Once again, I had a Changsha residence card. It was the most precious thing I owned.

CHAPTER NINETEEN

Eating Socialism

I had barely unpacked when my new leaders plunged me into interfactory competition. I played all week in units all over Changsha, barely even visiting my own gray oil factory grounds, forming only a vague impression of huge black oilcans, bad air, and a sticky mixture of oil and dust everywhere underfoot. True to my recruiters' promises, I was treated well: I had only one roommate, when normally the room should have slept four or five.

When my initial round of basketball duties was just completed and I was resting for the first time on my extra-long bed, I heard shouts from below saying that I had a telephone call. It was Coach Xie, come all the way to Changsha from Shuangfeng with important news for me. Within moments, I had pushed my way onto the bus that would take me from my factory in the northern suburbs to his hostel in the city.

He was pacing excitedly about when I arrived. "I knew it!" he cried, shaking a piece of paper in my face. "The Provincial Sports Committee wants you!" He explained that Father had shown him the notice when it arrived, but was of the opinion that they should do nothing about it, since I had already accepted the oil factory job. "But how could I do nothing!" my coach exclaimed, beaming. "My first professional athlete!"

I hesitated. I knew that professional athletes are often reassigned to factories when they pass their peaks; it was just a question of time when I became a worker anyway, and I was already playing a lot of basketball under the current arrangement. Still, I didn't want to disappoint my old coach, and I thought that if the province really believed in my potential, I shouldn't refuse the offer.

The Provincial Sports Committee facilities were impressive. Athletes were everywhere, tall women with long slender thighs, thick-built men with smooth swimmers' muscles. I could sense the sweat and comradeship there, and suddenly I wanted very much to belong.

I was introduced to a whirlwind of coaches and players, all of them welcoming me with the natural familiarity of fellow athletes. They put me through my paces in the gym, and even as I ran, jumped, passed, shot, I could feel how much they all liked me. Coach Xie, sitting there among the professionals, looked as proud and happy as I had ever seen him.

There was only one more step, they told me, a mere formality. I knew immediately from the tone of their voices that I had to pass a political test. But since my enthusiastic factory recruitment, this didn't worry me. I was full of confidence. When I showed up for my appointment the following day, I was on top of the world.

The political cadre in charge of the basketball team's thought and discipline was a hardened army man, so diminutive beneath his thick green overcoat that it was hard to imagine him controlling the lives of so many muscular giants. He asked the anxious coaches to leave so he could speak with me alone.

"Liang Heng," he said, breaking the silence, "you have a fine physique. The coaches like you very much. But you know, provincial-level players often have a chance to represent our great motherland in international competitions, and according to your father's file, you have an uncle and an aunt in Taiwan. We wouldn't want anything embarrassing to happen. If you thought of running away to your relatives, for example. And as for the question of your mother . . ." He smiled and shook his head.

Still the same old phrases! They burst in my brain like thunder. I had heard them too many times in my eighteen years. Everywhere I went, the same terrifying shadows followed me. All my suppressed rage exploded at once: I was on my feet, spitting onto the cement in front of the man's huge desk, slamming the door behind me with a crash that echoed through the building and reached other political offices and other arrogant army men deciding the fates of other miserable creatures with no court of appeal. I pushed rudely past the coaches huddled outside waiting for news, and ran out of the big main gate toward the Martyrs' Park. In the wildest part of the park near the north gate, I threw myself down by a dead thicket, protected from the gaze of the world.

I could have killed that army man, and all the rest of those "Revolutionaries" who had thrown my dreams back in my face in pieces. I also hated myself, though, for being so foolish as to think that I could pass a political test. I had forgotten too easily that I had long ago been branded an outsider forever.

I stayed there by the thicket until after dark, knowing that Coach Xie was waiting for my call. I made myself find a four-*fen* telephone in a shop, and, shouting at a floor attendant across the poor connection, finally got him to the phone. I couldn't bear to tell him the truth. I simply said I had decided to be a worker after all.

The autumn basketball season passed all too quickly, and I was assigned to the 100-man repair workshop as an apprentice in the riveters' group. On the first morning, I put on my stiff new denim workjacket, ate quickly, and arrived well before eight, full of eagerness to learn a trade and make myself useful. The shop was a high-ceilinged room full of greasy tools, broken valves, unnameable machine parts in various stages of disassembly, and some heavy iron chairs. Stamped notices of repairwork to be done were tacked on a bulletin board next to the dirtiest picture of Chairman Mao I had ever seen. At five of eight I was still the only person there.

Other riveters soon turned up, about twenty of them. Although they were strangers to me, I was quite familiar to them as the new basketball player. They engaged me enthusiastically in conversation about the recent basketball season, the men smoking and leaning against the walls, the handful of women sitting with their arms folded. They asked me solicitously if my new shoes fit me all right, if my workjacket felt small. None of them made a move toward their own jackets, hanging in an oily row on pegs along the wall.

By nine I could contain myself no longer. "Well, let's start," I suggested. "I have a lot to learn and I don't want to interrupt the normal schedule."

Everyone roared with laughter. "You sure have a lot to learn," they cried. "What's your hurry?"

The group leader, a wiry middle-aged man came to my rescue. "Never mind," he said. "He'll find out how we do things around here soon enough."

It was true. Before long I knew the routine. Every day we had to report exactly on time, but after that we were on our own. The first item on the agenda was what the workers liked to call "Socialist news"— tales of the neighborhoods where those who didn't live in the factory dormitories had homes. These stories of pickpockets and local scandals usually lasted an hour. After that, we "changed into work clothes," which took another half hour. Then, suddenly, the shop was empty. Some had gone to the clinic for minor medical complaints, some to the outhouse, some to the financial office to get expenses reimbursed. Others worked repairing their bicycles or making things for friends and relatives like locks, coal burners, and iron chairs. A third group gambled for cigarettes behind the big emergency water tanks.

Organization was near perfect. If any factory leaders came to check the shop or look for someone, there was always a sentry to say, "Oh, they were just here. Maybe they went to the stockroom to get some materials." If anyone wanted to know about a repair job that had been approved and stamped by the repair workshop, it was, "Sorry, we're understaffed today," or "Sorry, no materials." Sometimes the same jobs fluttered on the bulletin board for weeks.

By 11 a.m., everyone magically reappeared, and we sat and chatted until 11:30, when the group leader checked us out for lunch and a two-hour nap. In the afternoon the morning's performance was repeated. It added up to a full eight-hour day.

I was astounded at the workers' open indifference to the workshop and to the factory leaders' attempts to pull them into line. We had political study meetings on Tuesday and Friday afternoons, and spent at least one morning listening to reports on the general political situation. At school, the more rebellious of us had sometimes whispered to one another, but here the workers openly ignored whatever was going on at the podium, talking in groups about their own affairs, the women knitting long underwear and sweaters, the men smoking and spitting sunflower-seed hulls.

At first, I listened earnestly, but soon discovered that the meetings were unbearably dull. Every directive seemed to be about learning from Daqing, the model oilfield in the Northeast. Each worker was supposed to develop an "iron man spirit" so that even if a factory had poor conditions, it would progress through sheer self-sacrifice on the part of the workers.

Of course, the spirit of most people in those chaotic, anarchical late–Cultural Revolution years was just the opposite. Although the Chairman Mao worship activities had been drastically reduced since the exposure of his onetime successor Lin Biao, their architect, in 1971, there were still so many political movements that my co-workers used to pun and tell me, "You think you're the only *yundongyuan* (athlete) in our group, but actually we are all *yundongyuan* (movement men)." People were so tired of movements that nothing could get them excited. Even workers criticized in the meetings seemed unperturbed. They knew that no matter how inefficient they were and how many chairs they made for their friends, they would never lose their jobs; whether they worked hard or did nothing, they would still earn the same low salaries. Everyone saw the factory leaders give away truckloads of coal and steel to cadres in the countryside so they themselves could eat watermelon in summer and oranges in fall; the leaders' children were among the first to come back from their stints as Educated Youths, all with good jobs. No one criticized them, my fellow workers pointed out, so why shouldn't ordinary workers "eat Socialism" too? Compared with the feasts of the leaders, their share was only the barest nibble.

I decided to eat a little Socialism myself. My way was to study on the job. I started with technical books on welding, geometry, and other work-related subjects, but soon found that no one cared what I read, so I turned back to my real loves, literature and history. My penchant for books suited everybody, since I didn't mind standing guard while the other men gambled for cigarettes; the women didn't play cards, but they were eager to sneak home to prepare meals and take care of the housework.

Sometimes I didn't have time to hide my books when factory leaders checked up. Finally, my name was mentioned in a political study meeting. The factory leaders said I was going the "White Road"—the road of the intellect—and during working hours! Everyone laughed at this criticism, but I was a bit unnerved; I didn't want to become known as a troublemaker here as well.

I soon had the opportunity to make a better impression, for our factory was given a great honor. In the past, we had received only oil byproducts to turn into useable materials like grease for ballbearings and lubricating oil. Now we were to get small amounts of crude oil directly from the new Victory Oilfields in Shandong Province. The new operation was intended to illustrate our factory's dedication to the "learn from Daqing" movement. The leaders asked for volunteers to set up the workshop, and I signed up.

The older workers had heard too much grandiose talk to think that the project could succeed, despite the mobilizing meetings and meetings to "unify our thought." Nevertheless, most of us in the repair workshop were ultimately required to take part. A huge new building was erected to house the machinery, and our work began.

I gradually came to see that the problem in the factory was not unwillingness to work; the management and production system itself forced us to be lazy. There were vast stretches of time in which there was nothing to do even if we wanted to. We often waited days and days for a certain screw or a length of electrical wire. One day, for example, our group needed 8,000 feet of copper wire to install heat gauges. Our group leader asked me to come with him and make a requisition. First he wrote a brief report and got a stamp of approval from the repair workshop bosses. Suspicious that we might be ordering extra wire for our own use, they agreed to only 7,000 feet. Then we took our report to the factory leaders. They asked us to come back that afternoon after they had had a meeting and discussed it. We found they had approved only 6,000 feet. We took the report to the stockroom, and the staff there went to look and suddenly discovered that the type of wire we needed was out of stock. We would just have to wait, they told us, while they drew up a production plan and submitted it to the factory leaders. If the leaders agreed, the stockroom would give it to the purchasing department. As we walked back to our shop, my group leader guessed that it would be at least two weeks before we had our wire. The purchasing department would find it unavailable on the market. They would have to find a way of buying influence with the leaders of another factory so they could exchange their wire for some of our factory's materials. It was doubtful whether the purchasing department would even think it worth the effort; in the meantime, we could sit around and eat Socialism.

This kind of interfactory backdoorism was also the way things were done on a grand scale. If we needed certain machines, we had to wait weeks while the Yueyang Chemical Factory dickered with our factory for cement in exchange. After that it took more time to get bureaucratic clearance for our trucks to drive up and get them. Nothing seemed systematic, which was hardly surprising since the leaders were mostly old army men who knew nothing about running a factory. So we worked like this, more than a hundred of us, for nearly a year. There would be three sudden days of frenetic hammering and welding, dials would light up and steam would hiss, and then the new workshop would fall silent once again, waiting for some factory leader to return from a meeting in Peking so he could stamp a request for materials, or maybe just for the electricity to come back on again.

Still, even at this snail's pace, we finally finished our work. The factory held a celebration with red streamers and firecrackers, reported the happy news to the Provincial Chemistry Bureau, and prepared for final inspection by representatives from the Ministry in Peking. The whole factory got ready to make a good impression: One of Daqing's hallmarks was a "clean environment," and if we didn't pass on this count, it would be more than enough reason to deny us "Daqing-type factory" status.

We hated nothing more than these "hygiene" movements. They were always the same. For two or three days we would carry brooms about, sprinkle the sticky ground with lime, and lug heavy broken equipment onto the big dumping ground. Then a few weeks later there came the inevitable recycling movement, and we had to put everything back again, from the largest piece of junk to the tiniest screw. And so it went, back and forth several times a year, until we knew the steps as well as a Loyalty Dance.

When the Chemistry Ministry officials arrived in a fancy Shanghai-brand car, we were ready. But they went directly into conference with our leaders, stayed half an hour, and drove off, never even looking at the new workshop. The Victory Oilfields wouldn't be giving us any oil after all, since no one had considered the fact that there was no way to transport it from the railway to the factory.

In this relaxed but senseless way, I passed my months as a worker. But despite my generous study time, I still felt dissatisfied. Something was missing. When I crawled into bed at night, the nubbly summer terrycloth seemed to electrify my smooth skin and strong muscles. I found myself thinking back to the girls in the sports school. I remembered how they had sneaked thick chunks of meat from their bowls into mine, their chopsticks flashing out when they thought I wasn't looking, their cheeks flushing crimson when I caught them. I remembered how the water that they brought shyly to me after practice tasted unexpectedly sweet, as if they had secretly added spoonfuls of sugar. I dreamed strange, hard-to-remember dreams, and sometimes when I woke up I discovered my arms around my pillow or my leg flung over my thick quilt, pulling it toward me. I hardly dared to admit my longings even to myself.

Factory apprentices were not permitted to "talk love," even if they had reached eighteen, the normal minimum. This prohibition would not have stopped me in itself; the real trouble was that there were very few women workers at the factory, and I had no opportunity to meet anyone elsewhere. Then I suddenly thought of Sha An, the little Guangzhou girl who had been so kind to me and Liang Fang during our visit at the beginning of the Cultural Revolution, and remembered her sweet, tearful face as she promised me she would never forget me. So one night during a thunderstorm, when all the electricity had gone out, I lit a candle and composed a letter.

From a few days after I had sent it, I waited around in the mailroom every morning for Little Sha's reply. It came quicker than I had expected, written in clear, attractive characters. With warm words, she recalled our early friendship. She was a worker in a factory now too, but she was also Secretary of her Communist Youth League. This startled me a bit, for I was not usually on good terms with people with such outstanding political performances, but her friendliness overcame my hesitations.

Our correspondence began. At last I had an audience for my stories and poems, and she returned long letters of encouragement and criticism. After several months, she enclosed her photograph with a letter, and I saw a pretty girl with long, thick braids tied in ribbons, standing in Peking's Tian An Men Square and looking very much the same sweet child of six years earlier. In her letter, she invited me to come to Guangzhou to visit her; her mother was often away, so there was plenty of room.

That night, I tossed and turned, thinking of her. The next morning, I went to see the worker in charge of the informal "Workers' Bank" to which twelve of us contributed five *yuan* every month. According to the lot I had drawn, I was not to enjoy the sixty-*yuan* pot until November, more than two months away. But I negotiated a trade with the man who had drawn September. Then I asked, and was granted, the leaders' permission to take my twelve-day "visiting relatives leave." With a sense that something momentous had begun, I realized that I could count the days before leaving on the fingers of two hands.

The warm Guangzhou air was fragrant with the scent of flowers and ripe bananas. I stopped and bought myself a small branch of lichees, breaking open the tender red shells to the slippery white pearls beneath, the moist, oversweet fruit as extravagant as anything I had ever tasted. I remembered Little Sha's house easily enough, a cement-block structure behind a gate near the *Guangzhou Evening News,* the two-room apartment particularly luxurious in a Guangzhou starved for space and over-populated by its short, small-boned people.

Only Little Sha's father was at home when I arrived, and although he seemed astonished to see me, he welcomed me warmly. He was a robust-looking Hunanese whose desk had once faced Father's at the *Hunan Daily;* now he worked the night shift at the *Guangzhou Evening News.* I told him about my family's experiences and then I listened to his story. It gave me an odd feeling, because his family hadn't suffered at all. I thought anyone who had lived in such tranquility during the recent tumultuous years must be a rather slippery character. I felt even worse when Old Sha asked me for evidence that my unit had approved my trip.

I made awkward excuses, unable to admit that the factory authorities would never have given me permission to go off on a love quest. I had assumed that since I would be staying in a private home, it wouldn't matter; I had my work I.D.

Old Sha frowned. "This will be a bit embarrassing for me when I apply for your temporary residence permit," he said. "This family enjoys the confidence of the Party, but I don't like to jeopardize it by having guests whose papers aren't in order."

Fortunately, Little Sha came home just then, so I didn't need to continue this discussion. She looked lovely to me, with a suggestion of a full figure, and fair skin that looked even fairer in dark-faced Guangzhou. She turned pink when she saw me, exclaiming, "Oh! Look how tall you are!" and immediately took refuge in hostessing activities, her eyes lowered safely to her busy hands.

After dinner, her father went to work and we were alone. I told her all about myself, including my sorrows. I hoped that she would understand me and give me the love and comfort that I needed, but she seemed interested only in talking about our childhood games and her work as League Secretary. After a while, we had little left to say to one another. Deeply disappointed, I reluctantly decided that she was not the girl I had been looking for after all.

The following day, she went off to work and I got back into conversation with her father. He was clearly suspicious about why I had come, and cross-examined me, asking me if I often studied the newspapers, if I often reported my thoughts to the League, if I had written my application to join the Party. He was shocked when I said I wasn't even a League member. When I said I liked to read old novels, he narrowed his eyes and said, "The ideas in those novels are poisonous. You shouldn't be influenced by them. At your age, you should be learning to devote yourself to the Revolution, not thinking about 'talking love'!"

I argued with him. I said there were few new books available nowadays, and the movies were repetitious and predictable. Life was dull.

"What about Comrade Jiang Qing's Revolutionary operas?" he asked.

"Those are terrible, we've seen them hundreds of times!" I exclaimed. "None of us workers like them. Even if the factory invited us free, we wouldn't go!"

"What kind of attitude is that?" he said. "Your thought is dangerous! Why did your mother and father have trouble? Because they didn't watch their tongues. Why did I have no trouble? Because I went with the times, I followed the editorials in *Red Flag* and always did what they said. But you still haven't learned your parents' lesson. Just watch, someday you'll be a counterrevolutionary."

"The destruction of my family shouldn't deprive me of our ability to think," I protested.

This was the last straw. "You just listen to me, young man," he shouted. "You stay away from my daughter. I don't want you infecting her with your thought. I'm not going to let a misguided friendship for someone like you endanger her chances of joining the Party!" That afternoon, he went out to check the train schedule to Changsha. Then, when Little Sha came home, he ordered me into the other room.

To my complete surprise, she rushed to my defense. I could hear her shrill little voice crying, "He's my guest, I invited him here. It's none of your business." Then, half crying, she ran in and clung to my arm. In the next room, the front door slammed and I heard footsteps going down the stairs.

When he had not come back by six, we knew he must have gone to work. We sat in her room at the farthest possible distance from each other, she on the bed and I in a chair by the door, but still close enough to feel nervous. I was filled with gratitude and love for her, or at least yearning, and she was blushing as red as a painted slogan.

"What did your father say about me?" I asked.

She avoided my eyes and wouldn't answer. "He's crazy."

"It doesn't matter. I know he doesn't like me."

"He said you were a dangerous element, and I shouldn't listen to you," she said in a small voice, and then, half whispering, "He said you were 'after' me."

I was furious at her father, but also glad, since he had told her what I had been afraid to tell her myself. Our eyes met, and hers turned away, terrified.

"Do you believe what your father said?" I asked after a pause.

"I believe it," she answered, "but I don't dare to think about such things."

"What things?" I asked.

"You know perfectly well," she answered.

"Really," I burst out. "I like you very much! You don't know how many times I've read every single one of your letters!"

She looked absolutely charming, her fingers in her ears and her face screwed up so as not to hear. I wanted to embrace her and sat down on the bed a few feet away from her, but she squeezed away to the very end in terror. "Don't come over here!" she cried.

"I want to," I said, and regained my advantage.

She screamed and jumped up, running to the chair I had just vacated. "Now you stay right there," she ordered. Something beside my ardor seemed to be troubling her. Finally she spoke it out. "Why don't you join the Communist Youth League?"

Passion had driven away my reason. "I'll join it," I said, "if you'll only agree to be my friend."

Her face lit up, and then fell. "You don't really want to join the League," she said accusingly.

These words were cold water on my fires. My dear Little Sha, if you only knew. My sisters sacrificed everything but have never been allowed to join. My father and teachers all told me to work toward joining; in my factory, the leaders urge all the young workers to try to join. Do you really think I haven't tried? But with my background and political performance, do you think my applications were ever approved? I turned down the only chance I ever had, when I was locked up as a May Sixteenth conspirator. League membership was to be my reward for betraying my friend. If you were the Secretary of my League chapter at the factory, maybe it would be another story, you would help me. I looked at Little Sha and slowly shook my head. "No, you're right. I'm not interested in becoming a League member."

She was playing sadly with the end of one of her long braids. "Father taught me to be progressive," she said. "I don't understand you. Why don't you want to prepare for a good future . . . ?"

And so our brief romance ended, like Father's and Mother's, on the political battlefield. Little Sha's father came home from work the next morning with my return ticket, and walked between us all the way to the train station. We hardly had a chance to say a farewell word.

I left Changsha again within an hour of my return from Guangzhou, summoned to Shuangfeng by the urgent, three-day-old telegram that waited on my bed: "Father is ill." Cursing myself for the romantic notions that had delayed me, I ran to catch the five-hour bus, took the familiar stairs of the Propaganda Station three at a time, and flung open the door to Father's room. He was sitting in a chair, his head hanging limply toward his shoulder, his eyes staring dully into space. His mouth was slack and leaked spittle, while his left leg trembled violently. When he saw me he tried to get up, failed, and started to cry.

"Don't cry, Father," I begged, weeping myself. "Never mind, it will be all right." I seized his lifeless hand and stroked it frantically, hardly knowing what I did.

Zhu Zhi-dao came in from the corridor carrying a hot water thermos and told me what had happened. A week earlier, Father had been revising one of his plays along the lines suggested by the County Revolutionary Committee Propaganda Department when suddenly he fainted, knocking his teacup onto the floor. She had called a colleague and together they had carried him to the hospital, but it was too late. The doctor's diagnosis was partial paralysis due to stroke; the cause: protracted psychological stress and hypertension.

Thanking Fate that I still had most of my "visiting relatives leave," I quickly assumed the responsibility for caring for Father while my stepmother was away at work. I kneaded his deadened left side, hoping to bring back life to it, and administered acupuncture according to the doctor's instructions. I sat by his side holding his hand, listening to him mourn over and over again in his soft whisper, "I shouldn't have gotten sick. If I can't work, I'm a useless man."

Hiding the bitterness in my words, I consoled him. "Father, you've given your whole life to the Party. You've made contribution enough."

Father's mind no longer seemed entirely clear. He wasn't always connected to the present, but the past was as fresh as if it had happened the day before. He relived his pre-Liberation days with the Communist underground, his life as a newspaper reporter. When he was too tired to talk, he stared past the yellow newspaper-covered walls out the window at the sky. Sometimes he'd break suddenly into song, always the same graceful song that he'd written in his youth, tuneful and melancholy.

Why are you leaning on the temple door?
Why are you so silent?
What is the trouble
That locks the door of your heart?

On a fair day, I look at the white clouds in the blue sky,
On a foul day, I listen to the wind whistling around the points of the eaves.
Waiting and waiting for the dawn in the East,
Waiting and waiting for the light over the great land.

The cuckoo calls, the cuckoo calls,
The swallow returns,
Looking for the garden of his old home.
It is empty, it is barren,
The dream it ended long ago.

Father was saddest of all when he limped trembling to the window and looked out on the street where the purposeful working people passed. Then he wept, and I had to urge him gently back into his chair. "Never mind, Father, never mind." But when he was asleep in his bed, my heart bled and rage shook me. Not even the news that Liang Wei-ping had been recommended by the peasants in her Production Team to go to a small teachers' college in Shaoyang could soothe my pain.

Zhu Zhi-dao was of the opinion that Father should simply retire. Although he was only forty-nine, the doctor had said he would never be able to work again. If he retired, he could still draw eighty percent of his salary, and Liang Fang, still marooned in the countryside at the age of twenty-four without the slightest hope of finding work would, according to a new policy, be given a job. We knew the policy might change soon, so Father would have to act immediately if he wanted to save his oldest daughter. Still he adamantly refused, believing against all reason that he would soon return to work. For as long as I was there, I tried to stop Zhu Zhi-dao from forcing him to admit that he would be a cripple and an invalid for the rest of his days.

He finally gave in, several weeks after I left. The immediate consequences were unhappy. No sooner had he retired than the Propaganda Station demanded his two rooms, and he and Zhu Zhi-dao were required to move into a tiny room in her primary school, noisy with the shouts of little children. "Your father's colleagues never come to see him," wrote my stepmother. "When they pass the door they don't even stop. It's as if they've forgotten him completely. He's like a little child now, always standing by the schoolyard gate, looking out onto the busy street and weeping, singing some strange little song." Father's letters came in a quivering calligraphy I hardly recognized. "I never imagined life could be so empty. If they would only let me work in the mailroom it would be better than this. But I can do nothing more for the Party, so society has abandoned me. . . ."

For her part, Liang Fang was at last allowed to leave the countryside and take up a job as a language teacher in Zhu Zhi-dao's primary school. She was lucky; it wasn't until several months later that we realized just how lucky. Our cousin, her old classmate, had been in the countryside for nearly nine years, since her graduation from lower middle school in 1965. Now twenty-five, she was from a family entirely without access to back doors. Her fate was to marry a peasant whom she hardly knew, a young man who could barely read and write. There was no other way; at her age it was already late to settle her "personal question." But at least she would never have to face the scorn of her city acquaintances, for she would probably never see them again.

CHAPTER TWENTY

Searching for Peng Ming

I returned to my tedious factory life, but my father's tragedy gave a bitter, more urgent edge to my intellectual searchings. I read selections from Marx and Engels to find out more about the Socialism to which he had sacrificed his health, and the more I read, the more I compared the societies they described with the one in which I lived, and the more confused I became. Of course, I was not alone in this; my troubles were common enough and anyone could see there was a discrepancy between the glorious words of the newspapers and our painful reality. Together with a group of old friends from the *Hunan Daily*, I went evening after evening to parks and teahouses to discuss these questions.

Then one day I ran into Peng Ming's mother in the street near Waipo's house. She looked old and thin, and rather yellow, as if from some disease. As soon as she saw me, she began to weep and asked if I had had any news of her son. Perhaps it was the same whenever she saw anyone who had known him. "None of our letters to the Central Institute of Music have been answered. His younger brothers have been to Peking themselves looking for him—they even went to the Public Security Bureau—but they were both chased away and didn't find out a thing. I'm afraid he's dead."

I didn't want to tell her that I knew from my own unhappy experience that Peng Ming had been labeled a counterrevolutionary May Sixteenth conspirator, nor did I want to mention my own suffering because of his friendship for me. I comforted her as best I could, and returned to the factory preoccupied with memories of my friend.

Soon after, a co-worker whose family lived in Peking told me he was about to take his "visiting relatives leave." I decided to negotiate once again with my workers' bank for the pot (fortunately, it was already a new year, 1974), and within two weeks we were both on the train to Peking. Perhaps I could find out more than Peng Ming's brothers; after all, his old comrades had once been mine as well.

After getting settled in at my fellow worker's home, I went immediately to find the old members of the Red Cliff Struggle Red Guard organization. To my surprise, no one wanted to talk about their old leader. It was the same in all the troupes I visited. When I asked about Peng Ming, people avoided my questions. Of others they would say freely, "Oh, he's still in the countryside," but it was as if Peng Ming's name had not been mentioned there in years. Most of the people I talked to had already been through their re-educations and had been assigned work in various units accompanying Revolutionary operas or ballets, performing Revolutionary symphonies, or writing Revolutionary songs. I sensed that they were concerned with their own affairs and had no desire to jeopardize their "liberations" by talking about the past. In fact, all of Peking had apparently been so traumatized by the Cultural Revolution that no one dared to talk seriously or openly except to their immediate families. Even my friend was a disappointment. He seemed simply to want to stay at home. So I ended up spending my time wandering around Peking seeing the sights and trying to track down Peng Ming.

Finally, after nearly a week, I went back to the Central Institute of Music. This time, my inquiries bore fruit. Someone told me to go see an old repair worker at the institute named Chao Shui. I went to his poor-looking, flat-roofed hut, and when I knocked on the doorjamb beside the cloth hanging in the doorway, a thin old man with a wisp of beard came out.

"I'm a friend of Peng Ming's," I said. "I was here in nineteen sixty-seven and worked with him. I'm trying to find out where he is." Chao Shui looked me up and down, hesitating. "I used to be a neighbor of his family in Changsha," I went on. "His mother asked me to try to find him."

Finally the old worker asked me to come in, to sit down, to eat something. When I said I hadn't heard from Peng Ming since I had left Peking, he told me the story with no more prompting. It must have been a story everyone at the institute knew quite well, but only this lonely old worker had the good heart to tell it to me.

"He became a leader in the Rebel group of the entire artistic community," my host began. "He transferred from the Central Institute of Music to the Ministry of Culture. I guess he was way up there, because when Qi Ben-yu, Wang Li, and those other members of the Cultural Revolution Directorate lost power, Peng Ming fell with them. They were accused of opposing not just Liu Shao-qi, but Premier Zhou as well. It was what was called the May Sixteenth Conspiracy. Peng Ming was said to be a leader, and a mob came and arrested him."

For the first time I began to understand why that innocent letter of mine had caused me so much trouble. I had no idea that Peng Ming had risen so high, nor that he had become such a dangerous person. No wonder people had been unwilling to talk! Chao Shui continued, "I didn't hear anything about him for about a year, and then a mass meeting to criticize May Sixteenth conspirators was held in the Peking Workers' Stadium. Because most of the conspirators were from the art world, everyone from the troupes and institutes had to go. The Central Symphony was there, the National Ballet Troupe, the Central Institute of Music, the National Institute of Music, the Central Song and Dance Troupe, the Peking Opera Troupe. . . . There must have been several thousand people.

"All of the conspirators had confessed except Peng Ming, but they brought them all out together. His hair was long and he looked very thin. They had given him a black convict's uniform. The crowd cursed him and threw apple cores and rocks. Because he refused to admit his crimes, they wouldn't let him speak, and just made him stand with his head bowed and his hands behind his back as they criticized him."

I suddenly realized that Peng's two younger brothers must have heard this same account when they came to Peking. They couldn't bear to repeat it to their mother, so instead they told her they had failed. I knew that I would have to do the same.

Chao Shui went on, warming to his story. "Mostly they talked about how he had led a group of Red Guards to break into the Soviet embassy and shout slogans about Soviet Revisionism. They said he had deliberately tried to create chaos in foreign policy by making a bad international impression. They even implied that he wanted to have Premier Zhou assassinated. According to them, he was completely rotten, impossible to reform. I felt a little sorry for him, though, because the others who confessed were all his old friends and comrades. They put the blame on him and got off scot-free. If he hadn't been so obstinate and had gone ahead and confessed, things would probably have gone better for him." The old worker sighed. "That's really all I know about it. People don't much like to mention him. To them, all that's part of the past, and they're trying to save their own skins. But I'm an old man with no family to worry about, and I sometimes think about how dedicated he was, and how much people looked up to him. Sometimes I wonder whether they killed him." *

I had found out all I could, and it might even be dangerous for me to pursue my inquiries. It seemed that all Peking was infected by some sort of hidden disease, which weakened it and rotted it away gradually from within. I felt a terrible need to get away by myself, so I refused the old worker's repeated offers of hospitality, and made my way past the silent gray dormitories and out through the decaying imperial buildings and the heavy iron gate.

I walked along Changan Road, one of the busiest avenues in Peking. As I was buffeted by the crowds, I realized that I had been lonely during most of my visit. Even my fellow worker's family didn't really welcome outsiders, especially outsiders with a family history like mine. The basic relationships between people had become twisted. They had lost all warmth, and loyalty no longer counted for anything. People had turned against Peng Ming and forgotten him, so how could I expect my own friends to treat me any better? It seemed society no longer had any place for people of principle. With these black thoughts running through my mind I caught a bus to the train station and bought a ticket back to Changsha.

Peking had been a disappointment, but the journey back to Changsha redeemed things. I was sitting in the cheapest third-class "hard seat" section, since I didn't have ten *yuan* to spare for a "hard bed." The train was crowded and noisy, overloaded with purchases being taken from the capital back to the provinces where they were unavailable.

---

* Much later I learned what had happened to Peng Ming. He was thrown into jail and served five years in solitary confinement. When he was released, he was sent directly to the countryside for re-education. He is now composing music for a local television station.

Apples hung from the luggage racks, and the two men sitting across from me had bought four boxes of pressed duck, which they were probably going to sell in Guangzhou for double the original price. I was practically the only person who had bought nothing.

At about seven in the evening we arrived in Henan Province. Several people got on, including a group of three men and a girl. The girl looked very beautiful, healthy, with red cheeks. The seat next to me was empty and I moved my legs imperceptibly toward the window, praying she would sit down. When she asked if the seat was free, I was overjoyed.

We started to have an ordinary passengers' conversation. Her name was Bai Ying and she had been a middle-school student in Peking. She had been sent down to the countryside near Yanan as an Educated Youth in 1969. The men with her were fellow workers in the Medical Machine Parts Factory there, and they were going to the East Is Red Machine Factory in Guangzhou to learn how to use some new equipment.

She had taken out some bright green knitting. As she spoke, she knitted with great concentration, but when she learned I was using my vacation to travel because my home wasn't like a real home to me she stopped and looked up, sighing. Her quick response touched me, and I wondered more about her own story. There seemed to be unhappiness in her face.

I asked her what she was knitting. "Nothing," she said. "I knit because it gives me something to do. I've been trying to make a pair of gloves for a while now, but every time I finish one it doesn't seem quite right. So I unravel it and start again. Anyway," she smiled, "I don't have anyone to knit for."

As the evening continued, we went on talking. I never had much opportunity to talk with girls, and for some reason she seemed very eager to tell me her story. She was twenty like myself, and her fate had been very much like mine. She'd had a happy childhood, but her mother had died of heart trouble when she was eleven, and when the Cultural Revolution came her father was criticized for old KMT connections. In 1967 he lost his job as a film editor and was sent away to Guangzhou to be an ordinary worker in a collective lock factory, and her younger brother was now there with him. Because the boy was so young, her father had remarried, but the stepmother was greedy, and her son from a previous marriage cruel and bullying. There were constant fights in the house, and sometimes her stepbrother even beat her father and brother with a stick.

She was very worried about her family, but she was too far away to do anything. In Yanan she was lonely and unhappy. The peasants looked down on her because of her father, and she was the only one among the Educated Youth who lived too far from her family to go home on holidays. "I cry every day," she said, and then she used an old expression: "I am always 'looking through the mist but I can't see my home.' And now there is a terrible problem. My stepbrother has graduated from middle school and must go to the countryside as an Educated Youth, but he and my stepmother are trying to make my brother go in his place. My brother is only fourteen and still in school, but my stepbrother has a knife and threatens my father with it. My factory gave me this chance for study-practice so I could resolve my family problems at the same time, but I just don't know what to do when I get there."

She wept a little, and I sympathized with her. When she raised her head and saw that my eyes were wet too, she asked in gentle suprise, "Why?"

"Tongshi tianya lunluo ren," I said, using another old expression meaning "We have both been driven to extremities, and there is little difference between us." I explained my own family situation to her, but only briefly; we didn't need any more tears. The men sitting across from us had put their heads down on the table and were trying to doze off, and I felt very much alone with her in the dark night. The rhythm of the train enveloped us in silence. "Life is both good and bad." I tried to comfort her. "When you are unhappy you should see that there is still some hope, and try to live bravely. You say that you have no friends, but I want to be your friend, if you are willing."

I felt very close to her as the night passed. Sometimes she leaned her head back against the seat and slept for a little while, and I squeezed against the window so I could look at her. I had never talked for such a long time with a girl. I felt that if she wanted me to, I would do anything in the world for her. My experiences in Peking had made me determined to reaffirm some kind of basic kindness and concern toward people. If I could help this girl, that might help fill the emptiness inside me.

In the morning at eight, the train pulled into Changsha and I had to get off. It was raining hard. Bai Ying looked at me almost as if it hurt her to do so. Finally I asked her if she had a pen, and we exchanged addresses. She didn't get up to see me off, and I suspected she turned her face away so soon because she was crying. When I got back to the factory, I noticed that beneath her address she had written the words *"Tongshi tianya lunluo ren."*

In less than a week I got a letter, the whole thing smeared with tears. She wrote, "When I got home, everything made me wish that I had never come. It's even worse than before. My stepmother and stepbrother insist that my brother go to the countryside. My stepbrother curses my father and hits him with the back of a chopping-knife. I have told my father that I hope he will get a divorce, but it seems he needs a home. He doesn't want to talk about family matters with me, so aside from what my brother has told me, I've seen the rest with my own eyes. The only comfort I have is the things you said to me on the train, but all that seems too far away, almost unreal. Now 'as long as I am a monk, I go on beating the gong'—doing what is required of me and living from one day to the next."

I felt like a fire had burned my heart and decided to go immediately to see her. In order to be able to get a bed at a hotel, I asked for a letter of introduction from my factory so that I could "learn from" a factory in Changsha, and altered it so that it said I was visiting a factory in Guangzhou. Then I took a bus to Shuangfeng and borrowed eighty *yuan* from Liang Fang. Within three days, I was in Guangzhou.

I called Bai Ying at her factory as soon as I had secured a dormitory bed and visited the bathhouse. She sounded very surprised, but very happy. We made an appointment to meet at the Zhu River bridge at 5:30.

She flew up to me like a bird. "I never dreamed you would come."

I said, "I've come to try to help."

"But what can you do?"

"Don't worry, I have a plan. Just tell your father I'm a friend from the basketball team here in Guangzhou and that you've told me about the situation. I'll come to your house tonight. But don't be surprised if I look a little different than usual."

That evening, I disguised myself as a high-ranking cadre's son. I put on black corduroy shoes, wide blue pants, and a huge imitation army-style coat that my mother had made for me. I topped this off with a white face mask and a pair of gloves, and I was ready.

Bai Ying lived down a cobblestone lane in a two-story wooden house. There were winter flowers in a small garden behind a bamboo fence, and when I knocked at the gate she came out immediately. She saw at once that I had a performance ready.

Her father stood up when we came in, a short man with a small face and white hair. He laughed nervously as we shook hands. "I want to speak with your stepson," I said.

Just then the boy himself came down the stairs. Cantonese are very small, and he looked like a miniature hoodlum, with his tight little pants and long hair. I walked up to him, nearly two heads taller than he, buried in my enormous overcoat. I said, "I know all about what's been going on here. About what you've done. My friends are very upset about it. They want me to talk to you." I narrowed my eyes and enunciated carefully, "Only cowards beat up old men. And only cowards try to make others do their duty for them."

He postured defiantly. "So who are you?" he demanded, clearing his throat to spit. I slapped him across the face before the wad hit the floor and he fell back against the rickety stairs. I leaned down and grabbed his collar with one hand, and I could feel his hard breath in my face.

"So you want to fight, do you?" I asked. "You can call your friends and I'll call mine, and we can go fight in the street. Do you know who I am? I'm the son of the Vice-Secretary of the Public Security Bureau of Guangdong Province." I knew this would terrify him. Whenever there was a public fight, people with connections were released and their opponents locked up. My words had much more impact than my gentle blow.

The boy's skinny mother hurried down the stairs then, cursing me for hitting her son. He was afraid of me, though, and sniveled, "He didn't hit me, Mama, I fell down."

I resumed my lecture. "If you don't go to the countryside willingly, my friends and I will see to it that you go on your ear. And if you treat your father badly, we won't be polite." Then I relaxed my expression, pulled out a pack of expensive cigarettes, and tossed it to him. "We'll be friends, all right?"

Bai Ying showed me out. As soon as we had rounded a corner she grabbed my arm excitedly and said, "That was wonderful!"

"It should work," I said. "He's only just entered street society and doesn't really know how to handle himself."

We met the following evening after her study-practice at the factory and walked by the bank of the river. The lights on the masts of the junks shimmered on the water like fish scales. For a long time we didn't speak.

Finally Bai Ying broke the silence. "You're a real magician. If I could live with someone like you, that would be real happiness."

Her words frightened and excited me. I knew that what she needed was to leave the Northwest, to come back to Guangzhou to live, not to have a love affair with someone like me, but she looked beautiful there by the water, half-hiding her face from me, the light from the water in her hair. With great reluctance, I removed her hand from my arm and said gently, "What you really need to do is find a husband here so you have some chance of transferring back to be with your family again."

She listened without moving, thinking hard. Although my rejection was obviously a blow, she must have known that I was right.

I felt badly for her; even with all my ill luck, I had more ways to protect myself than she. "If you want to come back here, it won't be easy," I said, taking out my sister's fifty *yuan*. "You'll have to buy a lot of gifts for the people who control residence card transfers and job assignments. You'll need a lot of money. Please take this." I thrust the crisp bills toward her.

"How could I possibly accept that?" she asked, pushing my hand away. "After all you've done!"

There was only one way. "I'll throw it in the river if you don't take it, really I will. I don't want it, and if *you* don't want it, let the fish get rich!" I started to climb down the bank as if to toss the money in. The current was flowing dark and fast, and it would have been gone in a moment.

"Don't do that!" came her panicked voice. She believed me. I climbed back up and put the money into her shaky hands, and she folded it awkwardly and tucked it deep into an inner jacket.

I saw her back to her home, but then she insisted on accompanying me to the bus stop. Then I saw her home again, and she took me again to the street. I think we knew we would never see each other again.

I finally returned to my hotel and lay down on the bed. I needed to pay for my stay and now I didn't have a *fen* over what I needed for my train fare home. I passed the night worrying, and then before dawn, when the other travelers were still snoring beneath their mosquito netting, I crawled out the second-story window, climbed down a drainpipe, and ran. Fortunately, my introduction letter had been a fake, so I couldn't be traced. After I was a few blocks away I breathed easy. I took out my metal bed identification tag and put it on my keychain as a souvenir.

My train wasn't due until evening and I wandered the streets, very hungry. The food stands with their steaming pork buns and bananas obsessed me. Finally I couldn't bear it any longer. I picked out one of the busiest ones, and walked in.

In Guangzhou, you eat first and pay later. I helped myself to two bowls of rice porridge with thick chunks of fish, two plates of egg cakes, a glass of milk, and a dish of ice cream. Then just as the sharp pain of hunger was giving way to the fear of being caught, I noticed that the waitress figured out what the customers owed by counting the plates in front of them. Some customers who had paid still sat resting at tables that had been cleared. So when the waitress wasn't looking, I slipped over to an empty table, sat there for several seconds, and walked out the door. I had eaten more than two *yuan*'s worth of breakfast for nothing.

By noon my stomach was growling again. I wandered toward Sha An's house thinking to borrow money, but when I came to the gate I remembered her father's fierce expression and just passed by without going in. I didn't dare try anything else at the restaurants; my body ached as if I were running a fever, and I knew I might not have my wits about me a second time. It was all I could do to hold my place at the ticket window without collapsing.

When I finally got home to my factory room in Changsha, I stayed in bed for a week. No one came to see me. I thought for a long time about how helpless I was to change anything, and wondered again what kind of a society it was that produced such unfortunates as Peng Ming, Bai Ying, and myself.

CHAPTER TWENTY-ONE

Little Gao

During 1975, production gradually became more orderly, because the much-maligned Deng Xiao-ping had been reinstated as Vice-Premier. Everyone I knew welcomed his emphasis on Socialism as a means of improving the living standard of the people, for we were tired of being told that zealous self-sacrifice should fill our lives and bellies when we had only half a pound of meat a month, and even toothpaste was rationed. In the factory, we were supervised more strictly than before, but I didn't mind because the crude oil workshop plan was dusted off and steel allotted for an auxiliary rail line from the main track. The oil would be delivered after all; our work would not be wasted. Best of all, those of us who had been assigned to the shop were to have the chance to visit oil refineries in Shanghai.

Shanghai! That symbol of quality and abundance, sophistication and industry! Shanghai bicycles, basketballs, shoes, silk, and hand creams—to us Changshanese they revealed either pull and status, or back doors and waiting lists. My co-workers quarreled with each other over who was to be in the first groups to go, afraid that the travel policy would change before they had their chances at the shops. The first waves went off with nothing in their canvas traveling bags but a toothbrush, hand towel, tin cup, lists of things to buy for their family and friends, gifts to open up back doors, and dozens of net bags for their purchases. They returned with glowing tales and bundles of treasures; even the brown paper in which their things were wrapped seemed finer and smoother than Changsha's. Only one unfortunate worker was dissatisfied.

He had bought three pairs of black cloth shoes for his family, only to discover when he arrived at the factory that the characters on the plastic soles read "Yuelu Mountain Brand, Changsha." He scraped the offensive words away with a pocketknife as we looked on and teased him. How his wife would scold when she noticed that the soles were glued and not sewn to the cloth!

My turn came at last, in October 1975. Although I had no savings to spend, I was as excited as the rest. I had always chosen to spend my money on travel, and now I could do my adventuring free of charge. My train tickets and hotel bed would be paid for by the factory, and I would have one *yuan* fifty per day for expenses. I would even have a bed on the train, in the "hard sleeper" section. Only the highest cadres of rank thirteen and above were given beds in the "soft sleeper" section at about double the price. They had only four to a compartment, lacy curtains, and a separate meal with better food, but the three-tiered bunks in the noisy "hard sleeper" car seemed luxurious to me after my exhausting experiences with the rowdy and uncomfortable "hard seat" cars. I immediately hung my hand towel neatly on the car-length rack to reserve its place, and settled by a window to watch the whirring scenery. My companions were already deep into their usual card game, and I knew I could count on them for little conversation for the duration of the twenty-three hours to Shanghai.

Some time later I was trying—and failing—to latch the toilet door when a young conductress noticed me. She looked up from her mopping and watched in amusement. Finally she commented sardonically, "Such a big man can't close such a little door!"

I was insulted. Without thinking, I blurted out, "What's the matter with your train anyway? Everything's broken!"

She looked me up and down. "What do you do for a living?" she asked, in the same ironic tone. "You don't look like a cadre!" When I said that I was a worker, she broke into a delighted smile. "That's wonderful! Then you can repair the door for us!" Then she marched up and shut the thing with a smart little snap.

Maybe it was her humor that rooted me there. She looked older than I, and she wasn't particularly pretty with her thick skin and chopped-off braids. Her uniform hung wrinkled on her thin frame, and the small red conductress sign lay flat on her chest. But she had flashing straight teeth and a light in her eyes, and I was tired of memorizing English words while my companions played their interminable cards. So we stood there chatting, and at last her sharp tongue softened and she offered me some hot water from a thermos in the tiny conductress's room just opposite the toilet. A thin sheaf of handwritten papers lay on the metal table there, and when I asked what they were she answered indifferently, "It's a report written by someone who was victimized. You can read it if you like."

The fifteen-page report was disorganized and a bit incoherent, but I was very moved by it. The writer was a woman chemistry teacher from Hunan who had gone to visit relatives in Shanghai. A neighbor with whom her family and several others shared a kitchen had been sent thirty *yuan* by a son working in Xinjiang Province, but she was out when the postal messenger arrived. Another neighbor, an old lady, had taken the mother's seal out of the kitchen drawer where it was kept, affixed it to the notice, gone to the post office to get the money, and spent it as if it were her own. When the son's letter came several weeks later, the mother made inquiries. Frightened, the old thief accused the visiting chemistry teacher of stealing the money, saying she had seen her with her own eyes taking the seal out of the kitchen drawer. To defend herself, the teacher had gone to the post office and spoken to the messenger, who said he remembered that an old lady had stamped the notice. He agreed to testify.

With this kind of evidence there should have been no further problem for the chemistry teacher, except that the old lady's son was a Party leader in a Shanghai District Revolutionary Committee. When the postal messenger was summoned to testify before the investigators, he suddenly couldn't remember anything about the incident. Whether the Party leader had dealt with the man through threats or favors wasn't clear, but to me this was an obvious case of a leader misusing his power for his own interests. I was furious.

Encouraged by my anger, the conductress explained how she had become involved. She had noticed a woman passenger weeping on the train back to Changsha, and as she was comforting her, had listened to the whole story. She had promised the woman to help her if she would put it all down on paper, and just a few hours earlier, in the Changsha railroad station, the manuscript had been delivered.

I was deeply impressed by the girl's willingness to help a stranger, and just as deeply astonished that she thought anything could be done.

She told me that a comrade-in-arms of her father during the Liberation war was now a leader in the Shanghai Municipal Revolutionary Committee, and she planned to ask him for help. I suggested that she also submit a copy to the Shanghai newspaper, and she thought that a wonderful idea. But the report could never be submitted in its current messy state. I offered to revise it.

The girl left to pour hot water, issue metal bed tickets, sell meal coupons and packets of tea leaves, sweep up apple peels, open doors, and perform all the other tasks that keep conductors constantly busy. She shut me into her compartment. It was peaceful there, the loudspeaker only a muffled wail. I cut and corrected all afternoon, and at last I heard the key turn in the lock. The conductress entered with a huge bowl of steaming noodles, colorful with yellow eggs, green scallions, and lean pork.

I was shocked to think that she had spent so much money on me; the food looked much better than anything I ate at the factory. Then she explained that it was free to the train staff. We talked about our jobs, and I learned that although we were both No. 2 grade workers, her salary was forty-two *yuan* while mine was only thirty-five. Train work was of course much coveted, and most new workers on the line originating in Changsha were the children of army officers. I hesitated to ask the girl much about herself, but when she told me her name was Gao Wei-jun ("Gao Protect the Army"), my suspicions were strong that she must be very well connected indeed.

Just before our arrival in Shanghai at noon the following day, the girl called me back to her little room. She had two neat piles of paper on the table to show me, and from her reddened eyes I saw that she must have been up all night copying the report. I was more impressed than ever at her selflessness. Still, I never thought of further acquaintance, and was astonished when she looked at me with complete seriousness and said, "I noticed you were studying English. I want to learn too. Give me your dormitory number, and when you return to Changsha, you can help me."

This was laughable, as I had just begun to study myself. I didn't want to embarrass her though, so I jotted down the number on a scrap of paper. After the train pulled into Shanghai, I didn't think about her again.

·   ·   ·

We quickly dispensed with our factory "study" (our Shanghai counterparts worked in pretty much the same surroundings we did, but were less free to play cards on the job), and we were free to do what we had come for. We wandered up and down the long and famous Nanjing Road, looking into every shop and marveling at the variety of products and the way there were separate stores for everything from musical instruments to paper fans. (Shopping was not so easy; you had to get hold of precious Shanghai ration coupons, all of which had their price.) We visited the waterfront to stare at the boats and the big Western buildings. We spent a day at the zoo. But I didn't feel I could really relax and enjoy myself until I had done what my stepfather, Uncle Lei, had requested and called on the family of his scientist sister.

I already knew that she had committed suicide. Her husband, my Uncle Song, had written to Uncle Lei about it in 1970, two years after the event. He gave no details, and my prudent stepfather had never dared to inquire further, lest his letter be opened. Both she and her husband were dangerously prominent, for she had been a famous botanist at the Shanghai Science Institute and he was once the chairman of the biology department at the Shanghai Medical Institute, a geneticist. Now I could go in person, and find out exactly what had happened.

Perhaps it was the construction of the underground air-raid shelters that gave the Shanghai Science Institute its look of demolition. Dirt, junk, and concrete lay everywhere, and the single-story barracks seemed barren and cold. My aunt's home had been divided up soon after the beginning of the Cultural Revolution and her family squeezed into two of the smaller rooms. So I was not surprised that the man who answered the door said he was not my uncle. "In there," he gestured with his head.

The white-haired, round-bellied man who came to the door to greet me spoke in a half-whisper. He pulled me inside and shut the door quickly, as if he were guilty of something. The rooms seemed even smaller because they held the furniture of a huge apartment. There were school-style bunk beds in one, while the double bed in the other had a Western-style mattress that was so soft it sank deep beneath me when I sat down.

Uncle Song invited me to have coffee, and as I had never tasted that drink of Western novels, I eagerly accepted. The black liquid was bitter and sweet like Chinese medicine, and immediately made my stomach and bowels so active that I thought I would be ill. I wondered at my uncle's persistence in this habit, obviously acquired in America; he finished his cup with a relish that showed through his nervous manner.

The elder of his two daughters came home while we talked. She was a pretty girl, dark and vivacious and about twenty-five, four years older than I. Her arrival relieved the tense atmosphere, although she too spoke softly and glanced frequently at the door. I recognized her as the child playing the piano in a small photo under the glass on the desk, and learned she had been good enough to win a place at the Central Institute of Music in Peking (where I had been with Peng Ming), but the Cultural Revolution had intervened and she never went. She had been at home; when it came time for Educated Youths to go to the countryside, she and her younger sister had to decide which of them would go, since only one could get a permit to remain in the city and take care of their father. Normally, the elder was to go, but in this case the younger one, the violinist, had insisted, because she said that her youth would make it easier for her to find a place in a factory and come back again. But now she had been away in Anhui Province for six years, while her sister worked in a weaving factory and dreamed of the day they could be together again.

I had a lot of stories to exchange for this one, and soon we were talking quite comfortably together. My uncle's habit of tiptoeing to the door to listen was an unnerving one, but it was nearly always followed by an interesting piece of information. It was after such an excursion that he urged me to stay with them for the duration of my visit. "The barefoot doctors have taken over, and your uncle who studied medicine for more than forty years has almost nothing to do," he whispered. "Stay with an old man and keep him company."

It was easy to decide to stay, but more difficult to bring the conversation around to the subject of my aunt. I now wanted more than ever to know what had happened to her, but was embarrassed to ask. Then one night when his daughter had gone to work her night shift, he told me everything without being prompted. I had been confiding some of my own bitterness. Suddenly he fumbled deep under his mattress and came out with a small packet of photographs. All of them were of his wife, a tall, graceful woman with an air of Shanghai elegance. In one picture she was in a laboratory pouring something from one test tube into another. In another, she stood with her two girls. There was even one that had been saved miraculously, of her wedding to Uncle Song while they were graduate students in America at the University of Pennsylvania. She wore a white wedding gown, and he was in a dark suit with a flower pinned to the lapel.

"We came back when China entered the Korean War," my uncle said. "We didn't feel right staying in a country that was fighting against our motherland, and we had learned enough in our studies to be able to make a contribution. For nearly a decade we dedicated ourselves to our work at the institutes here."

My uncle lowered his voice even more, so that I had to bend my head to hear him. "Then the Cultural Revolution broke. They attacked us both, but she was the major target because she had relatives in Taiwan. They said we worked for the CIA, and proved it by pointing to what they called our 'bourgeois lifestyle.' I was criticized in posters and the Red Guards came to the house and insulted me, but she was taken away and locked up in a basement. They wouldn't let me see her for months. Then they told me I could go if I would persuade her to co-operate. She had bruises all over her. She said they wanted her to name the 'other' scientists who were CIA agents, and they would let her go."

His voice shook, but he didn't weep. "They had been injecting her with drugs that confused her so much that she didn't know what was true anymore. She told me at the time she couldn't take much more. Then they called me a second time, a week later. It was to get her corpse. She was all swollen with water. I hardly knew her for my wife. Like a huge pustule. They told me she had killed herself, a class enemy because she had rejected the Party's investigation. Then they took her away and burned her." My uncle's own face looked lifeless: "Later a worker told me that they had immersed her up to her neck in stinking slime. For three days he heard her screams, and then they stopped. I suppose she ripped her own clothing into strips to make the rope that hanged her."

My eyes were wet for the two of us. The photographs had made this woman alive for me, especially when I saw how much she looked like my stepfather. I tried to control myself so that I would not sadden Uncle Song any more, but I need not have done so; he had lived so long with his grief that he could now comfort others. "Tell your Uncle Lei that his sister found her rest earlier than the rest of us," he said gently.

I left Shanghai with my group a few days later. Their enjoyment of the scenic West Lake in Hangzhou where we stopped to visit our next factory was unsurpassed, and the boat ride up the Yangtze River from Nanjing to Wuhan was the biggest meal they had ever had on Socialism. But I kept remembering the serious-looking scientist who died before I had even known she was my aunt. I had heard about the suicides of many other intellectuals, including the father of Liang Fang's best friend, but never before had this aspect of my country's tragedy seemed so real to me.

It was a Saturday afternoon a few weeks after my return. I was studying, of course; Deng Xiao-ping's recent suggestion that university entrance examinations ought to be held again had fanned my hopes of continuing my education. A *History of Modern China* had so engrossed me that I didn't hear my roommate, Masterworker Tang, come into the room. Suddenly his dinner spoon clanged against his metal bowl not three inches from my left ear while he whispered hoarsely into the right, "Wake up, bookworm, your girlfriend's here to see you!"

I was startled, confused, and embarrassed all at once, and my heart pounded even faster when I saw that a thin little figure actually stood in the shadowy doorway. Her braids were stiff and neat, and she wore a clean army-green jacket and baggy blue pants. Her white teeth flashed. "Hello, am I welcome?" she asked in that knowing, ironic voice. It was Gao Wei-jun.

My first reaction was panic that she should see my room. It was big enough, but my long-unwashed quilt lay in a crumpled mess on the warped wooden bed, and the sharp smell of oil had permeated my clothing and seeped through the leaky gray window. Masterworker Tang's things looked even more tattered than mine, for he had four children and a wife to support in the countryside.

I was right to worry. As my roommate made an excuse and courteously disappeared, Little Gao took in the situation. Under the pretense of examining my disordered books, she knelt down, shook the dust off, and arranged them in neat piles. I looked on helplessly as she stood up and, scolding gently, folded my quilt into an attractive diamond. At last she brushed her dusty hands on her thighs and her eyes met mine. They softened with the same abruptness with which she had offered me tea on the train. "Shall we study English?" she proposed.

She had done what mothers and sisters always seemed to do automatically, but it had been so long since anyone had taken care of me like that that I was overwhelmed. The invasion of tenderness left me spinning. Still, how could I teach her English? I smiled awkwardly. "The monk is knocking at the door of the wrong temple," I said.

"Don't be modest," she said. "I saw all your books."

In fact, I had been studying for the past few months with an engineer who had once lived in England. At first, he had denied that he could remember anything at all—I suppose he was remembering the trouble his knowledge had brought him—but after I had visited him three times, my persistence moved him and he agreed to help. The condition was that I keep our lessons a secret. In Little Gao I saw a determination to match my own, and knew that further protests were useless. With a sigh, I opened a book to the first lesson. She perched on the edge of the bed armed with a sharp pencil and a new notebook. "A," I read aloud, suddenly uncertain of my own pronunciation. "A."

After that, she came to see me whenever she could. Between each train run she had three days in Changsha, but two of them were taken up in political study. On her free day she came to the factory, sometimes tidying my room while she waited for me to get off work, leaving precious rice tickets in my drawer for me to find after she had gone. She always insisted on carrying away my dirty clothing, and she returned it clean and folded, the holes neatly patched. Knowing the gossip her visits were sure to cause, she pretended she was my older sister and signed the name "Liang Wei-jun" at the register by the gate. But it was soon all over the factory that I had a girlfriend.

At the same time, I had learned enough about her to be concerned about our relationship. Her military name was the first warning, and as I came to know more about her, I felt more than ever that we were from two different worlds. Her father was no ordinary officer, but the Assistant Commander of the Xiangtan Military District to the southwest of Changsha. During the period of martial law imposed in late 1967, he had been in charge of public security work for the whole of Hunan Province. Her mother was an army doctor, her older brother and sister were in the air force, and her younger brother was a worker in a secret military factory. Little Gao herself had been in that group of high-ranking cadres' children who had become unusually young soldiers when the order came for Educated Youths to go to the countryside. While I was descending to peasanthood, she was rising to the greatest possible Revolutionary glory, a career in the army. How could there fail to be a great distance between us?

Still, as I got to know her, I discovered that our ideas were quite similar, and I enjoyed our conversations more and more. The fact that she had not joined the Party, for example, as did almost all high-ranking cadres' children with military careers, was revealing. In her opinion, most young people who had joined in her army unit did so to gain personal advantage, and she had no interest in such hypocrisy. She also told me that she hated the way her father had been pretending he was sick for the past two years, living at home but still drawing his astronomical salary of 240 *yuan* a month. But what drew us together most of all was our indignation over our failure to help the chemistry teacher, who had finally paid the thirty *yuan* she was accused of stealing, fearful that rumors would spread in Changsha about her if she delayed any longer. Little Gao told me angrily that her connection in Shanghai had said such "misunderstandings" were too common for him to bother with, and the newspaper had refused even to read the report. Our discussion of the sad state of our society led us to trust each other and make more and more daring statements. And her continuing kindness to me convinced me of her indifference to the conventional values that dictated a separation between people of "good" and "bad" background. Even as I wrestled with the feeling that such a friendship was as dangerous as it was sweet, she sought to dispel my fears and break down the barriers between us.

Then one night she stayed past nine and missed the last bus. The electricity had failed and I was worried that she might be attacked by hoodlums if she walked home alone, so I offered to accompany her. It was a cold, pretty night with only a gentle edge to it, and the darkness in the city made us notice the late-winter stars. The silence felt comfortable, and as we crossed the railroad tracks and made our way into the maze of alleyways that was the shortest route to her unit, I could sense the warmth of her body and hear the soft rush of her breath. I felt happy, but purposeless, and wondered as I had so many times why she seemed to care so much about a friendship that could have no future. Instinctively, I tried to maintain the distance between us as we walked, at first unaware that there was something deliberate in the way her arm brushed mine and her hand swung freely by my thigh. Then suddenly, as we came abreast of a dark tree, her hand took mine. It felt tiny, cool, and a little rough at the base. My own went lifeless in terror.

My lack of response annoyed her. She threw down my hand and walked quickly ahead as I stood by the tree stupefied. All of my hesitations over our five months of friendship welled up one last time, and then my anger at my stupid fears overcame them. I caught up with her and reached for her; her thin body quivered against my chest and her hair brushed my chin. I trembled violently.

"I've loved you for such a long time," I whispered.

"I know," she nodded.

"I was afraid," I said. "Your family won't agree."

"What makes you so sure?"

"Reality. Life. My fate."

"Nonsense."

"Everyone at the factory says you're my girlfriend. They tease me." She laughed. "They're right."

"But if they knew your background they'd never believe it. What's the advantage in your being with me?"

"Advantage?" she asked. "I love you and you love me, isn't that enough?"

A bicycle bell split the night and something dark swished past. We reeled apart, certain that we had been discovered. My blood was racing, and I still trembled, but I didn't dare to touch her again; I felt as guilty as if I had been caught stealing something. Now it seemed that the glowing cigarette ends that passed us in the blackness noticed us, and every shadow belonged to a spy who would bring our immoral case to the harsh court of gossip for sentencing.

We walked slowly, enjoying the beauty of the world around us. The big wooden doorways were shut against the cold, and the ancient eaves curved above us, sheltering us. I wanted to walk like this with her forever, not speaking, just knowing that somebody loved me, that to somebody in this world who I was mattered more than where I had come from.

We approached her unit all too soon, but lingered in the shadows on the other side of the street. It seemed we were both waiting for something. Little Gao shivered. "Can I kiss you?" I asked finally.

Of course, I had never seen anyone perform this mysterious action, so I didn't know how to go about it. I put my mouth on her hair but somehow that didn't seem right, so I put it on her upturned forehead. Perhaps her instincts were better than mine, or perhaps the angle from which she was approaching the matter gave her an advantage. She found my chin and cheek, and then the corner of my mouth. Her lips were hot against my face and her nose was so soft that I didn't know where her face began and mine ended.

Our love became sweeter and sweeter, because now that we were a real couple we could go beyond the walls of my room into the parks and streets. I saw Little Gao off every time she left the city (now she worked a Changsha-Peking route, called No. 1 to honor the birthplace of Chairman Mao), and met her on her return to help her carry the heavy Peking goods she had bought as favors for friends. Only the political atmosphere clouded our happiness, for the year 1976 was turbulent, and struggle in Peking was acute.

It began with the movement to criticize Lin Biao and Confucius. Political study was stepped up to the point where nearly every afternoon had to be spent listening to documents which were a confusing amalgam of classical lore and modern policy. Most absurd of all was to hear our barely educated political cadres giving us history lessons about how two thousand years ago, Confucius was supposed to have tried to restore a slave society, even as certain unnamed leaders were trying to do now. They also warned us that the Cultural Revolution was far from over; it was our duty to attack the new Capitalist Roaders who had infiltrated the Party at the highest level.

It wasn't until April, when Deng Xiao-ping fell from power for the second time, that we finally understood the real meaning of the movement. It had been leveled against him. His policies were now openly criticized as attacks on the Cultural Revolution, and in every unit public security personnel tracked down the sources of rumors about Jiang Qing and her associates. It was a frightening time of betrayals and arrests. Husbands and wives reported on each other's private thoughts; best friends turned out to be spies. My roommate, Masterworker Tang, was among the unlucky ones, for someone had reported he had heard from him that Jiang Qing and her Shanghai clique were trying to seize power. He took it all in stride, though, and said he had merely overheard some women gossiping on their side of the public toilet. He knew no more about it than that. I was comparatively lucky, I suppose, as it was the first political movement that did not affect me or my family in some way. But Deng's fall had been a serious blow to me, for with him and his ideas for rebuilding the country went my hopes of being able to take a college entrance examination.

I was despondent for a long time. Then one early summer afternoon when Little Gao and I were preparing to go to the Martyrs' Park, I picked up a book for my pocket out of habit. Suddenly recollecting its uselessness, I threw it angrily back down on the table. My friend looked at me thoughtfully and commented, "You know, the more you read, the stupider you get. Aren't two workers from your factory chosen to go to college every year? Why couldn't you go in 1977?"

The workers she was talking about were "worker-peasant-soldier" students, pretty much the only students who had been allowed to go to the universities since they had reopened in 1970. They took no entrance examinations, but were supposed to be chosen by their peers. In reality, the people who controlled the decision were the leaders, for they had to choose among the candidates and approve them. The grounds were, as usual, the old ones—background, political status (most successful candidates were at least Communist Youth League members), and, of course, relationship with the leaders. With my background and open indifference to political study, I had never even considered this route to higher education. But I suddenly realized that with Little Gao's access to hard-to-buy consumer goods, I was in at least as good a position as anyone else to try to open that back door. I already enjoyed the respect and friendship of the workers in my group, so the initial step would be easy. The tough part would be to convince the five leaders of the factory Revolutionary Committee to choose me. The actual recommendations would not be made for more than a year, but I would have to begin my work now. Grasping Little Gao by the hand, I pushed her to a sitting position on the bed and excitedly found a piece of paper on which to draw up a strategy.

We decided on watermelons as our first gift. They were very sweet and thirst-quenching in Henan Province, and Little Gao could buy them on the platforms when the train made its five-minute stops. The heavy heat that gave Changsha the nickname "half-furnace" was already settling in, but here we hadn't yet seen a single melon. The gift of such a delicacy would be a favor hard not to repay. I pressed my savings on

Little Gao, all ten *yuan* of it, determined to conquer by any means necessary the five officials who were the obstacles to my happiness.

Little Gao returned from her next trip with two fine small melons and a carton of expensive Peking cigarettes. These were available on the train to high-ranking cadres in the "soft sleeper" section, but of course train workers had access as well. For the first time, I was grateful for Little Gao's "good" background.

I had decided to work first on Vice-Secretary Tian, famous for his early participation in the Revolution and his way of meddling in anything that promised him some kind of advantage. I worried for days about how to present my offering, because he lived far from the factory in his wife's unit. Finally I thought of going to see him in his office during the two-hour post-lunch siesta. Wrapping a melon in newspaper so no one would notice it, I put it carefully into my net bag and walked through the stifling heat to the offices of the Revolutionary Committee.

Vice-Secretary Tian was lying on a bamboo couch, fanning himself while he read a newspaper. My heart pounding, I hesitated several moments outside the door before saying, "Vice-Secretary Tian. Sorry to disturb you. May I trouble you for a minute?"

Noticing my bashful manner and the bag in my hand, Vice-Secretary Tian grasped the situation in a moment. He sat up and motioned me to a seat with a smile that was almost a giggle. I soon discovered that he laughed nervously no matter what the subject under discussion.

My face burned and I couldn't control my words. My desire to study poured out as I begged him to help me. I would come back to the factory afterward, I said, to help in production and planning. I wanted only to make a greater contribution to my Socialist country. I would thank him for a lifetime.

Vice-Secretary Tian listened abstractedly, laughing whenever he mopped his dripping face with a handkerchief. "I'm not the only person making the decision," he said when I stopped for breath. "Our Party leadership is collective."

"I know," I said, and remembered to flatter him. "But Vice-Secretary Tian's long experience makes him a man to be listened to above all others. Only Vice-Secretary Tian has such a deep grasp of the great cause of our country." I pulled my bag up into my lap and fumbled inside for the watermelon. "Vice-Secretary Tian, please accept this small gift as a token of my great respect. The thing may be insignificant, but its meaning is great."

Vice-Secretary Tian had been laughing and waving his hand in deprecation during this little speech, and now his eyes widened at the sight of the hard green rind. For a full five minutes he refused to accept as I urged it on him, but both of us knew he would give in in the end. He rose to see me out, grinning broadly. "You're welcome to come see me anytime," he said.

My heart was heavy as I related this inconclusive interview to Little Gao. She was delighted, however, and rebuked me for thinking things would be settled on the first meeting. "Follow it up next week with the cigarettes," she said. "Then we'll see what he says."

Vice-Secretary Tian ate my watermelons three more times and accepted two cartons of cigarettes. At last, at the end of one of our midday conversations he clapped his hand on my shoulder and said as if he had forgotten something unimportant, "Oh, about that little matter of your studying. If the question comes up, I've nothing against it."

In this same painful way, I won over three other leaders. Two of them were just as expensive as the first and consumed everything from apples and wine to theater tickets and cloth shoes. Only one, an old cadre who had just returned from his re-education in the countryside, insisted on paying me for his melons. "Studies are one thing, melons another," he said forcing the money into my hand. I finally accepted it with happiness, seeing that something good lay where I had least expected to find it. The last and easiest leader remained, one of the men who had first recruited me because of his love of basketball. Surely he wouldn't deny me my ambitions, not after I had played for him nearly five years.

But this Vice-Secretary proved the worst stumbling block of all. He flatly rejected my gifts, and informed me that the factory needed me to play basketball, and that no worker had any use for education. A good pair of hands was enough. My fourth visit was my last. "It's out of the question," he said, his friendliness having long ago yielded to impatience and his impatience now yielding to anger. "We trained you for three years, and now that you're a real worker, we can't just let you walk away. I don't want to hear anything more about your crazy ideas."

I wept tears of defeat as I left his apartment that night, but Little

Gao, waiting for me in my room, comforted me with the thought of yet another tactic—"walking the high road." This consisted of using a superior leader to overturn the decision of a subordinate one, and if anyone was in a position to try this, it was she. One of her father's former military friends was a director of Industry and Transportation in the Changsha Municipal Revolutionary Committee. My oil factory fell within his sphere of control.

The thought of asking anyone so high to become involved terrified me, but Little Gao said she would take care of everything. She wasn't going to speak to the man, anyway, she explained, but to his son, a boy our age, whom she had known since she was a little girl. "He'll settle everything," she said and, smiling mysteriously, went off to fetch him. We would meet in a cold-drink shop in the city.

The boy was short and thickly built, with about twenty long dark hairs on his chin. He had a talkative and boastful personality, and before we had finished even half our glasses of cold milk, I knew all about how he had gotten one person a Changsha residence card, solved the housing problem of another. He didn't volunteer to tell us how he had been paid, but from his robust air I guessed that he wanted for little in life. While he listened to my tale he squinted in a practiced way and then said, "Easily done, my friend. Your problem is solved."

I had always thought of myself as imaginative, but I couldn't keep pace with him here. The following afternoon, he and Little Gao paid a visit to my recalcitrant leader, and she returned glowing triumphantly. What they had done was so bold that only the children of high-ranking cadres would have attempted it.

The boy had introduced himself and Little Gao as his father's son and daughter, and the Vice-Secretary had fallen all over himself to pour tea and find fans for them. Then the boy explained that I was his "sister's" boyfriend. We were soon to be married, and his father was greatly concerned about his future son-in-law's career. He hoped, in fact, that I would have the chance to attend college. He had asked his children to convey his message because, regrettably, he was tied up all week in meetings. He asked the Vice-Secretary to forgive him.

It never occurred to this Vice-Secretary to doubt the veracity of this message, for the resemblance between his superior and the boy was striking. (The boy's "sister," he probably wondered, must take after her mother?) His resistance evaporated. "My level of political understanding is too low," he said humbly. "Our leader considers the larger picture and the advantage of the whole country, where I thought only of our poor little factory. Please tell your father that I support Liang Heng's application with all my heart."

I felt that the best cigarettes and all the watermelons we could carry would have been far from enough to repay Little Gao's new brother, but apparently he was satisfied merely to demonstrate his power and cleverness. Although it was still a year before I could enter college, Little Gao and I went out and, in a delirium of happiness, purchased a stack of school supplies that would have lasted an ordinary person ten years.

CHAPTER TWENTY-TWO

An Egg Strikes a Stone

Perhaps Little Gao had an additional motive for helping me to conquer those leaders: She wanted to make me more attractive when she finally unveiled me to her parents. Every time I had voiced doubts about my reception, she had quelled them with her supreme assurance, but there may have been some significance in the fact that only a week after our last victory, she announced that we were going to Xiangtan to meet her family. My own mother and grandmother had long ago welcomed Little Gao into their home and I had written to Father about her, so the visit was long overdue.

The day before we left, Little Gao presented me with a light blue shirt, a pair of pants made from good-quality fabric, and new Peking cloth shoes. She also cut my longish hair with her own skilled hands to make me look "fresh and young." All this should have made me feel more confident, but it didn't. I wondered again how I could satisfy her powerful Revolutionary father.

These anxieties dissolved as soon as we arrived; the spacious apartment was full of preparations for a feast. My girlfriend's older brother was killing a chicken in the kitchen, her older sister and younger brother were wrapping dumplings, and her mother was chopping mountains of meat and vegetables. Her father, the man I had been dreading so long, welcomed me effusively with a powerful, double-handed handshake. He seemed much more informal than I had dreamed the former head of public security for the province could be, with his shirt unbuttoned at the top to reveal plenty of wine-darkened skin, his baggy military pants bunched at his waist with a length of rope, and plastic military sandals on his gnarled feet. "When she was small, she listened to us," he said smiling and gesturing toward his daughter. "Now she's grown wings and flown away. Such an important thing, and she tells her family last of all!"

Little Gao's mother was the one to cross-examine me. "And what do you do for a living?" she asked in her beautiful Peking accent, bringing me a steaming basin and towel. "A worker? What's your salary?"

Little Gao eagerly stretched the truth before I had a chance to answer. "Forty-five *yuan* a month, including overtime and heat compensation."

"What about your family?" she asked, and once again Little Gao answered. When she came to the word "stepmother," her mother frowned a bit, but just then the assistant commander came to the rescue, urging everyone to come to the table and eat.

It was a true banquet, high-ranking cadre style. There was beer, grape wine, and burning white liquor, and dish after dish of delicacies from frog's legs to snake meat. Little Gao's older brother and sister hardly had a moment to sit down, so busy were they in the kitchen frying and arranging the food. Little Gao and her mother drank only politely, touching their lips to the grape wine, but Litte Gao's father was a white liquor drinker, and he proposed so many toasts that my cheeks were soon flushed and my head was spinning.

My relief at having passed the test made me loquacious and generous, and soon I was offering toasts of my own. We drank to the Chinese army and to Assistant Commander Gao and his wife; to the Chinese air force and to "big brother and big sister Gao"; and to the friendship between industry and the military. Nothing in anyone's manner indicated that I was anything less than a future son-in-law.

My belly had been stuffed well beyond capacity and I was being force-fed candies and apples when the time came for us to catch our train back to Changsha. I was disappointed to hear the assistant commander suggest that his daughter stay until the next day, as it had been many months since she had been home, but then it occurred to me that it would give my new family a chance to make final arrangements. Little Gao's father loaded me down with choice leftovers and several pounds of apples and led the whole family to the train station to see me off.

The whole way home, I thought of Little Gao's face as she waved me off. Someday in the near future, I was certain, that girl made pretty with happiness would be my wife.

Life continued its cruel pattern of painful surprises. When Little Gao came to my room the following night, her eyes were red and her hair was disheveled. She fell into my arms and burst into tears.

It took me a long time to make out what had happened, for she was incoherent with grief. Her father had tricked us both. He was a "smiling tiger." Even before I left, he had made up his mind to oppose the marriage, but he didn't want to make a scene with a stranger. As soon as the family returned home, he had begun to rave, pointing at the framed family photo and saying, "The man who will stand beside my daughter will wear a green uniform and have a red star on his cap like everyone else, not a greasy worker's uniform or, even worse, the eyeglasses of a complicated intellectual!" When Little Gao had defied him, he had rolled up the bottoms of her pants and beat her about the legs with a length of steel wire until she agreed to break off with me. Little Gao showed me her legs. They were bruised from the knee to the ankle, with deep red welts where the skin was broken.

I sobbed too, with rage and pity. What an irony it was, that a man who had killed to establish an "equal" society had such feudal ideas! "The type of seed you plant will be the type of fruit you pick," he had said to his daughter. Was that any different from the early Red Guards' notion that only the "five red types" had the right to rebel? Or any different from the feudal notion that you were born to a certain place in a hierarchy and kept it all of your days? Sometimes I felt that our society couldn't have strayed farther from Socialist ideals if it had tried to do so deliberately. And now it was doing so at my beloved's expense! I fell to my knees in front of her and caressed her poor legs as I had never dared to do in moments of more peaceful tenderness.

She was still sobbing. "If we don't obey him, he'll go to your leaders, and mine. We'll never be able to get our units' permission to get a license. He's even threatened to have me transferred to another city, but I begged him not to. I said I'd been here long enough to be able to join the Party." She laughed bitterly, and then wept again. "Maybe he'll try to do something to your mother. . . ."

It was really over, then. I had fallen into the old trap, and there were still knives at the bottom. I could brave anything directed at me, but I didn't want to cause my mother pain. I wept in earnest now, big soundless sobs that shook my body like whips. I could hardly believe it when Little Gao said, "We'll have to stop going out in public. No one will know we still love each other. But I won't give you up. You're a human being, not an animal. You have the right to be loved."

Most young couples in our society would never have dreamed of staying together in opposition to their parents' wishes. The Confucian tradition of obedience and filiality had been instilled over thousands of years, and even after marriage it was unclear whether your main loyalty was to your spouse or your parents. On the other hand, love suicides in the face of parental disapproval were not uncommon, for most of us believed that love comes only once in a lifetime. Holding the trembling Little Gao in my arms, I felt the strength of her determination and was flooded with love for her. Then I despaired again; we did not, after all, live in a vacuum, but in a world where power could accomplish anything and parental support was an economic necessity for nearly every new couple.

The next day, deeply depressed, I went to tell my mother what had happened. She shook with anger, but this time, instead of blaming herself for the troubles she had caused me, she blamed me for not breaking off with Little Gao at once. "When an egg strikes a stone it will break," she said. "Don't bring any more unhappiness to your family, we've had enough as it is." She pleaded and argued with me until I felt like a very bad son indeed, and left feeling even worse than I had when I came.

I was never aware of a conscious decision to end it. The troubles wearied me, and the fear of being spotted and betrayed spoiled my feeling. Perhaps my mother's fears played a role, too. At the time, it just seemed that Little Gao and I stopped getting along. My temper became uncontrollably bad. Every time I got angry I hated myself for my cruelty, but the next day there it was again. Little Gao's love seemed to close in on me, and I became evasive and critical. My fellow workers thought I treated her badly and told me so; their attitude was that if she was good to me, I should love her. To me, the matter seemed far more complicated, and the longer our quarrelsome meetings dragged on, the less I felt that Little Gao and I were suited to one another. At last, with regrets on both sides, we decided to give each other up. I was left with nothing but a reputation—completely undeserved, I thought—for immoral behavior.

There were far greater losses than mine that year. On September 9, Chairman Mao died. It had been no secret that he was ill, and everyone was extremely worried about the future of our country. What would happen when our Red Sun vanished, when our Great Saving Star set, when there was no Great Helmsman to steer our ship? The country was unstable, for the Cultural Revolution had been a game of flipflops, an ironic joke. The leaders had been reshuffled, a few fresh ideologues added, and the bodies buried, but the old disputes over Leftist principle, as well as the tensions between masses and leaders, had continued. As always, struggles on unimaginably high levels would determine the fates of all of us.

The public funeral ceremonies seemed oddly to be almost routine. A lot of old leaders had died that year and we workers already knew all about making paper flowers for wreaths and assembling for a memorial meeting. At three in the afternoon the sirens went off all over China, and everyone stood and lowered their heads in respect, whether they were out on the streets or in an assembly hall like me. The main ceremony in Tian An Men Square came to us on television. Our own program was held simultaneously so we could share Peking's funeral music, the rows of half-raised flags, and the somber processions of officials carrying wreaths as tall as themselves.

The older workers who had lived in old China were perhaps the saddest of all of us. The door to the outside world had been closed so long that no one could compare conditions in China with those in other countries, but the older people could compare the present with the past, with its illnesses and famines, its crowds of beggars, its lack of work. Despite the shortages, the corruption, and the political troubles, most of the older people felt that Chairman Mao's Socialism had brought them a better life. It didn't matter that for many the improvement could be measured in pennies; they were deeply grateful, and wept as if they had lost one of their own parents.

Despite the pomp and the plentiful tears, I just couldn't seem to make myself cry. "Chairman Mao" had been one of the first names I had uttered, and "The East Is Red" had been the first song I sung: I had not grown into my love of Chairman Mao like the older people, it had been handed to me. What he brought me was not a better life, but one political movement after another until the very word "Revolution" had become tedious and meaningless. As I looked around the assembly hall at the other mourners, I thought about how for thousands of years our ancestors' reverence for their emperor had made it easy for him to control them. If they had grievances, they assumed that the emperor didn't know, that the evil ministers around him were keeping him from the truth. And so it was even now. No one blamed Chairman Mao. "An old man sometimes becomes confused" was the harshest thing I had heard against him even during those days of violence.

A frenzy of national joy followed the national sorrows by less than a month. On October 8, every radio broadcast the electrifying news: "The Central Committee, under the leadership of First Party Vice-Chairman Hua Guo-feng, has completely smashed the counterrevolutionary group, the Gang of Four!!!!" Then we heard statements made by Chairman Mao before his death criticizing Jiang Qing and her three influential henchmen for their desire for power. No one questioned the authenticity of these hitherto unpublished remarks, despite the fact that the "Gang of Four" had been major figures in carrying out Chairman Mao's own beloved Cultural Revolution. Then came reiterations of Chairman Mao's pleas to the people to trust Hua Guo-feng as himself, and the famous deathbed words, "With you in charge, I am at ease." We knew now that there were no more obstacles between Hua and the Party Chairmanship.

At last we had someone to blame for our miseries. Cadres, workers, soldiers, intellectuals, and peasants, people of all different degrees of political awareness, we were once again swept up in a political movement. All our hate was directed toward four miserable creatures. It rose into delirium. We bought liquor, bottle after bottle until the shops were empty, and paraded on the streets setting off firecrackers until the shells were a crackling red carpet underfoot. The workers in my group organized a banquet. We held it in our workshop, each of us contributing two *yuan* and carrying in coal burners so we could cook the whole thing right there beside our oily machines. I got drunk that night, drunk so that I couldn't remember who took me home or, in the morning, what had happened to make me feel so incredibly ill.

Never, since I came to the factory, had we workers participated in any movement so enthusiastically. In the name of criticizing extreme Leftist thought, we could give vent to any and all grievances—the way the leaders always snapped up the bicycle tickets and gave them to their friends, making it all but impossible for an ordinary person to obtain one; the way the back door had destroyed normal relationships between people; the way the Gang of Four had kept salaries low for ten long years.

The newspapers talked on and on about how the Gang of Four had brought our country to the edge of economic collapse and social anarchy. We were urged to develop a new spirit of self-sacrifice, since the new government could not bring the country back to health immediately, nor redress everyone's grievances at once. The articles I read most avidly, of course, were those about the "educational front"; certain people in the "two schools," Peking University and Qinghua University, were under heavy attack for forming a "theory team" and writing propaganda for the Gang of Four. I worried that the hunt for other Gang supporters might close down the universities entirely and I would lose my chance to study. By April 1977, I was going to the factory Revolutionary Committee office every day after work to ask if there was any news. Every day the leaders assured me that their promise to recommend me was still good; as soon as the school notices arrived, they would act. But in September, to my dismay, I was told that enrollment had been postponed pending the establishment of new educational policies.

Then in October came the startling news that entrance examinations were to be held once again! All for nothing had been my worry and exhaustion, my 200-*yuan* expenditure, my scheming and flattery. The back door to college was closed to everyone. Still, I was overjoyed. I much preferred to have the chance to enter the university in a dignified fashion, by doing well on an examination.

There were only two months between the announcement and the examination. I buckled down, sleeping as little as five hours a night on occasion just to give myself a few extra hours of review time. My fellow workers found ways to let me study on the job. They helped me in another important way too, with favorable comments about my political showing; such approval was the first step in the political screening for the examination. The forms then went to the leaders of the workshop, to the factory office, and finally to the Municipal Enrollment Committee, where they would be attached to my examination scores and a final political report. This time, I wasn't worried about the political check, because the newspapers had said those to be screened out were hoodlums and candidates with extreme Leftist thought.

When the day at last arrived, I went with the thousands of other workers from Changsha's Northern District to our assigned examination center, the No. 14 Middle School. It had been so long since I had set foot in a classroom that I felt a thrill of excitement in entering even this place, only to notice with sadness that most of the windows were broken and the walls were thick with many layers of criticisms and slogans, records of the revolution in education.

It was extremely cold, but my hands were sweating. I had only to look about me at the tense faces of those who shared my examination room to feel the significance of this, the first entrance examination in over ten years. There were all kinds of people, aged eighteen to thirty-five. This was our only chance to lift ourselves out of our dreary labors and reach toward something higher: precious but dangerous knowledge.

The two-and-a-half-hour morning Chinese examination was, for me, the most important, as I was applying to the Chinese Language and Literature Department of the Hunan Teachers' College. I had never even considered other fields, for literature was the love my father gave me and hoped I would carry on for him. Even as the proctors read out the rules of discipline and passed out the examination booklets, I thought of the joy it would bring him if I passed and went to college.

Then the proctor announced we could begin. I turned the front page in the gray booklet to read, "Question One, Composition: The Words I Have in My Heart to Tell the Party."

I trembled and pitied myself. How could I possibly answer? I was no longer a primary-school child tracing out the characters, "Long Live Our Great Communist Party." Nor was I an eager Rebel at the start of the Cultural Revolution, responding to Chairman Mao's call with passionate purity. What I had in my heart was bitterness, my life's accumulated bitterness, the accumulated bitterness of the lives of the people around me. Time raced away as I struggled with the horrible thought that I would have to turn in a blank piece of paper.

At last I shook myself loose and went on to the latter half of the test, forty points' worth of questions on basic knowledge. This was simple for me, but I had already lost many minutes. Finally, with only half an hour remaining, my determination to get into college cleared my mind and I wrote without stopping:

> Dear Party, the picture of Chairman Hua now stands beside the picture of Chairman Mao in every corner of the land. If the Party, under Chairman Hua's leadership, had not smashed the Gang of Four, there would have been no entrance examinations and I would have had no hope of serving the country with knowledge. The Party raised me as a true son of the Revolution. A thousand languages, ten thousand sentences, cannot express my love for the Party. A thousand songs, ten thousand poems, cannot express my loyalty to the Party. . . .

None of the other examinations caused me such terrible suffering. The politics examination dealt with straightforward Party history and current events, and in the history and geography examinations the only traces of politics were questions about the county of Chairman Mao's birth and about the exact location of the model commune Dazhai. In the mathematics examination, only the word problems were political. At the end of the two days, I felt I had done the best I could. All I could do now was wait.

Within a week I was notified that I had achieved at least the minimum necessary score and could go to the No. 3 Hospital for a physical examination. The final political check took half a month more. Then a letter arrived from the Hunan Teachers' College saying that the "1977 grade" would begin their studies in February 1978; I should report to the Chinese Language and Literature Department, where I would be trained for four years to be a middle-school or college Chinese teacher.

I was the only person in my factory to be enrolled in college. Suddenly, I was the glory of my unit. My name appeared in red on announcement boards hitherto reserved for Party and League members, and a celebration assembly was held in my honor, attended by everyone in the factory. I received at least ten invitations to meals, and my workshop had a party and hired a photographer to record it. The leaders who had once publicly criticized me for "going the road of the intellect" now smiled and shook my hand. As a final gesture, they arranged for a car to take me the short distance across the river to the college, just like a high-ranking cadre. It was the first time I had ever seen the inside of an automobile.

CHAPTER TWENTY-THREE

Teacher Xia, the American Expert

I hadn't been to the West Bank since those terrible days of armed struggle more than ten years earlier. It seemed peaceful now, the Yuelu Mountain protective and the air fresh and clean, although cold because of the winds blowing off the river. The broad new bridge built as part of the late–Cultural Revolution effort to honor Chairman Mao's home province had brought new activity to Rongwan Town. In the Teachers' College, bright multicolored posters glorifying study now covered over the red ones criticizing Confucius and Lin Biao, and the old painted slogans had begun to chip and fade away.

I registered in the dark crowded gymnasium with more than fifteen hundred other new students. Some had been teachers, others workers like myself, and others Educated Youths coming directly from the countryside. These were easy to recognize because their bedrolls were covered in plastic to protect them during the long rainy walks from Production Team to bus station. Rooms had all been preassigned. The two hundred students in my "1977 grade" of the Chinese Language and Literature Department had been divided into four classes of fifty each, and the fifty students divided again into six groups of about eight each. These groups were to be roommates and mealtime tablemates; each of them had a group leader and group vice-leader chosen (as I later discovered) on the basis of political status and performance. Even at registration I had an uneasy feeling about this elaborate organization; it would make it very easy for the leaders to keep track of everyone.

I had been put in a narrow room in one of the four four-story dormitories. There was little space for anything but the eight old wooden bunk beds and the eight desks placed face to face down the center. The walls had been covered with slogans by the worker-peasant-soldier students, and the two lightbulbs hanging from the ceiling were bare, dim, and covered with dust. A washroom a few doors away stank and leaked water into the dark hallway, making everything dank and musty. But none of my roommates complained. We felt proud and hardy, the first to enjoy higher education on the basis of merit since before the Cultural Revolution.

The next morning, the loudspeaker sounded at 5:30. As we had been instructed in our discipline meeting of the previous evening, we pulled on our clothing and jogged out to the sportsground with thousands of others to do "broadcast exercises." I had lingered in bed until the last possible moment, so I had to wait until later to relieve myself, wash my face, and brush my teeth. It was fortunate that I hurried, because my group leader, a League member and ex-cadre in a commune school, took careful note that we had all arrived. A history of latenesses and absences would be construed as a sign of insufficient "Revolutionary discipline."

During the first week, we were subjected to one of the most detailed and complex political indoctrinations I had ever undergone. Big and small report sessions, discussion meetings, thought education meetings, all of these had only one message: the purpose of our education was for the Revolution. Of course, all of us knew the usual ways of turning this off. We chattered, read novels; the bold, myself among them, sometimes even skipped the meetings entirely. But this first experience of college left me with a stifled feeling; my chaotic factory life had been much freer than this.

I hoped that classes would be better, but in fact only a small number proved to be of much interest. Most of the time was wasted in memorizing dogma. In philosophy class, for example, I learned that "philosophy is Marxism." Art theory taught simply, "The purpose of art is to serve the politics of the proletariat," and "Literature is the life of the society reflected in the mind of the writer." My modern Chinese literature textbook told me, "China's modern literature is the literature of the proletarian leaders, the masses of the people, the anti-imperialists and anti-feudalists." In contemporary Chinese literature class, we read copies of newspaper articles about cultural meetings; as for Party history, I had learned it all in middle school.

Like my classmates, I quickly learned that only three classes deserved attention—ancient Chinese literature, ancient Chinese, and modern Chinese. Where other classes were often only two-thirds full, these were so crowded that you often had to carry in a chair from another classroom or stand at the back. The professor of ancient Chinese literature was a real scholar, so immersed in his books that he was oblivious to his own popularity. He would have taught the same class to an audience of two or a hundred. His glasses perched on his nose, he would pace slowly back and forth holding some collection of poetry in front of him, and, waving his head slowly from side to side, chant in a high-pitched voice some ancient line like, "At dawn purple smoke rises from the censer-mountain."

I was starved for more stimulation of this sort, and it occurred to me to visit the professors at home. I wanted especially to study the history of European literature, so I sought out the art theory professor. His classes were notoriously dogmatic and dull, but I thought that he, of all the teachers, must know a lot about European culture.

His red brick dormitory was about halfway between the Teachers' College and Hunan University, a bit up onto the hill with the other teachers' homes. I explained my ambition to him, and he seemed flattered and pleased that I had come. "It's not easy to be a teacher," he said apologetically. "You have to try to satisfy the students but avoid making political mistakes. Who can guarantee that the Cultural Revolution won't come back again?" He shook his head. "A bad dream. A terrible, terrible dream." Only then did I realize I had misjudged him and many other teachers. Their first concern was to protect themselves. If they had their own opinions, they masked them in a welter of political jargon.

To my joy, the art theory professor agreed to coach me, and from then on I went nearly every evening to his house. We began with Plato and Aristotle. I found them so interesting that I was soon spending hours in the library, checking off book after book on the professor's reading list and openly cutting almost all of my classes. I was not the only one to develop my own plan of study; eventually the empty classrooms came

to the notice of the Department Party Branch. The leaders threatened
and exhorted us in political study meetings, and managed to bring back
most of the students (many with novels in their hands). But even then,
I remained absent. In this way by my second year of study I became
known as one of the students with the poorest "discipline" in the entire
Chinese Department. Perhaps only one student was more criticized than
I. He was a successful writer who lived on the other side of the river
and rarely bothered to set foot on campus at all.

Of course, students like us were rare. Most were worried about
their political performances because they were trying to join the League
or Party, or because they dared not lose the financial supplements
awarded on the basis of need, political showing, and grades. I no longer
had even the vaguest hint of political ambition, and, as one of the
students enrolled from a work unit, I had my salary of thirty-five *yuan*
a month and was financially independent. Another difference was that
although most others were at least as cynical about life as I, only a few
were as rebellious. I had developed a kind of pride and confidence
despite my many disappointments, and would no longer allow myself to
be controlled without a fight.

I had another advantage, too: I had a good memory. With a classmate's notes and a textbook, I could cram for a week for a course I had
never attended and get an examination grade in the nineties. We were
never required to formulate an original opinion, so doing well was a
simple matter of repeating selections from the books and lectures.

Still, the examinations were a considerable strain. As part of the
new educational policy, our future job assignments were supposed to
be based in large measure on our academic performance. This was, of
course, preferable to the old, purely political, system, but sometimes
we felt as if examinations would determine where we would be for the
rest of our lives. We worried most that we would be sent to the countryside far from family and friends. Those who came up from the country
were particularly anxious; there were rumors that unless their grades
were exceptional, they would be the first to go back, despite the fact
that many had originally been Educated Youths "sent down" from the
cities. So, because of the enormous importance of the examinations, in
this area I could not be my own master. I had little courage to choose
a path which might prove harmful to my destiny. My only choice was

272 SON OF THE REVOLUTION

to memorize the insipid course material and write it down on the examination papers, knowing that I had sold the chance to express my own thoughts for my high marks.

The question of future job assignments was the reason most students became increasingly intimidated by the leaders. No matter how highly the professors praised a student, everyone feared that the final arbiters would be the members of the Department Party Branch. The students were so cowed that a hated portion even became "ankle-rubbing" flatterers and filers of "small reports"—repetitions, for the leaders' private ears, of what some other student had said or done. The most commonly chosen confidant was the cadre directly in charge of students, a worker-peasant-soldier student who had come by his job by gaining the leaders' trust with similar slimy tactics.

The college abounded with rumors about job assignments. Every night, after the central electricity was cut at ten, we groped our way to bed and told each other the latest gossip. This or that student had been promised a position at the college by this or that leader. Hunan University would be taking a lot of new teachers. The entire 1977 grade would be sent to middle schools in the countryside after graduation. . . .

It was only after the announcement came that certain schools would be enrolling graduate students that I became less worried. With my art theory professor's encouragement, I began to prepare for the aesthetics examination for the Peking Social Science Institute. If I succeeded, I could leave all these questions of job assignment behind, like a bird leaving wingless creatures rooted to the earth.

Of course, study alone didn't satisfy my needs. I longed for a lively social and cultural life. Although movies were shown twice a week at the college sportsground, they tended to be predictable, moralistic, and disappointing. Occasionally, the Student Committee organized a dance, but the policy on whether or not dances were politically sound was constantly changing. One week our student officers said the national Communist Youth League allowed dances, the next, that the Hunan Communist Youth League condemned them. So if a dance was not suddenly canceled, it was held with a tentativeness that kept most of the girls away and the rest on the sidelines, while we boys pushed each other in ungainly fox-trots across the cement classroom floors. About the most exciting thing that could happen in those days was the arrival of a foreign film in Changsha. Then the eight of us in my bedroom would take turns going across the river to hold a place in line from before dawn, hoping that eight of the precious tickets would be left when our man's turn came at the ticket window.

Then one spring day in 1979, I heard that the new American teacher in the Foreign Languages Department was scheduled to perform some dances at the Art Department in the college's southern campus. Her name was Xia Zhu-li ("Summer Bamboo Beauty") after her American name, Judy Shapiro, and she had arrived only a month before, as a result of the normalization of relations between China and the United States. I went, of course, enormously curious. This was the first chance I had ever had to see one of those high-nosed, big-eyed creatures in person. It seemed strange to me that an English teacher could also be a dancer, for few in China had the opportunity to pursue an interest in anything beyond their own professions.

At last the curtain parted on something called "Insect Dance." A contorted green figure was crouched in the center of the stage, looking completely unlike a human being. It gradually awakened and began to pursue and consume invisible, smaller creatures. Then, moving infinitesimally slowly, it rose to one leg with its foot in its mouth, collapsed, rolled, and rose again. Having repeated this several times, it seemed to have exhausted itself, and it returned to its original position as if to sleep. I applauded wildly. I had never seen any "dance" without music before, and this was abstract, humorous, and eerie all at the same time. I felt as if a new and fresh world had opened up.

The next dance was called "Dance to U.S.–Chinese Friendship." Suddenly the green insect had become a lovely young girl, moving with large, free movements to a tape of a familiar Chinese folk song. She seemed so relaxed and yet so skilled, very different from the Chinese women dancers, who controlled their bodies tightly and locked their knees together while tiny movements of their hands and eyes suggested delicate subtleties. This Western dance was so pleasant to watch in its immeasurable freedom! I couldn't grasp what was at the heart of it or feel I really understood it, I only knew I wanted to see more.

The following fall, the fall of 1979, my application to graduate school unexpectedly reduced the distance between myself and the exotic fairy I had seen on stage. I was required to submit an essay in English, and after I had made a primitive translation of a paper I called "Natural Beauty," I went to the Foreign Languages Department for help. The professors there suggested that I go see Teacher Xia, the American expert. She was kind and scholarly, and wouldn't refuse to correct my paper.

When I had gotten over my initial hesitation, the idea seemed more and more attractive. There was another reason to go see her, too, an even more compelling one: I had heard she had an extensive library, which she was willing to share with teachers and students. Perhaps I could find some materials on Western literature there, or perhaps she had magazines with pictures of the outside world.

I asked my best friend to go to her home with me, and he was shocked. People might suspect us of all kinds of things if we sought out a foreigner! But when I said I would go without him, he insisted on coming along, for my sake. If I were questioned, he could bear witness to the innocence of what had been said and done.

That morning we skipped the between-class "broadcast exercises" and made our way up the steep hill past the college offices to the new cement-block building for high-ranking cadres and professors. The red gladioli in front had grown strong under the pleasant autumn sun, and a toothless old lady was spreading hot peppers out to dry on a broad low wall. We asked her timidly where the American teacher lived, and she raised her chin toward the second-floor balcony without asking us who we were. Apparently she was not a lookout to keep people away from the foreigner, as I had first feared.

There was nothing on Teacher Xia's door to distinguish her apartment from anyone else's. I peeked through the cracks in the already warping yellow door, and the inside looked ordinary enough as well, with cement floors and institutional wooden furniture. As my friend hung back on the stairs below the landing, I screwed up my courage and knocked.

Close up, Teacher Xia looked much less foreign than she had on stage. She was of average height, short, I supposed, for a foreigner, and her hair was dark. She wore baggy blue pants and a short-sleeved Chinese blouse, and her hair was pulled back in a single braid; from a distance she might have been Chinese except for one thing: She was barefoot. Controlling my surprise at this eccentricity, I introduced myself and my reluctant friend politely, explaining as a first step that we wanted to borrow some books from her library.

Teacher Xia was apparently very busy, for she didn't ask us in. She was warm and friendly, though, and told us to meet her at her office after lunch. To my surprise, her Chinese was quite pleasant to the ear, if not entirely idiomatic.

At noon, she loaded me down with books. The American embassy had given her some volumes written in Chinese, and the students in her own department showed little interest in borrowing anything that was not in English. She also found me several copies of the famous *New York Times Book Review* and a number of colorful news magazines. I was overwhelmed by her generosity with these treasures, and felt encouraged to ask if she could find some time in which to discuss literature with me. She was very happy to agree because, as she explained, she wanted to work on her Chinese but she felt a strong responsibility to speak only English with her students. "In any case," she said laughing, "they're all from Hunan and have indecipherable accents!" I explained that I too was a Hunanese, but had learned standard Chinese when I was young. "Lucky for me," she said.

My friend refused to come with me to her home the following Thursday night, but I had already been so attracted by her comfortable warmth that I went alone. She must have been about the same age as my girl classmates, but how different she was! Instead of sitting there tongue-tied and blushing, she engaged me in a conversation that ranged over literature, education, and aesthetics. I thought it astonishing that a girl of only twenty-five should be so well educated. She had two master's degrees and there seemed to be nothing that she did not know; I felt more bitter than ever that the Cultural Revolution had interrupted my education. I was also deeply impressed by the fact that she never asked me about my political background, and she seemed admiring instead of concerned when I said I was from an intellectual family. For the first time in my life, I felt I was being accepted for who I really was.

I asked Teacher Xia about herself. She said she had studied anthropology and Chinese for many years, but had always felt she didn't know what it was really like to be Chinese. That was why, when the Chinese government had invited her to come to teach, she had accepted so eagerly. That was also the reason she wore Chinese clothes, to diminish the distance between herself and the people here, to make them trust her. She had fought against being given special privileges, too, such as a car and driver. "I'm just an ordinary person," she said. "If my country had been closed to the East for thirty years and you were invited to be a teacher there, you would be a Foreign Expert too."

I was moved by this simple explanation, and felt the gap between us narrow. Suddenly, although it was late, I felt an overwhelming desire to talk about the subjects I avoided with my classmates: my mother, my father, the Cultural Revolution. . . . Teacher Xia had offered me some wine, and the building seemed so tranquil compared with the noisy dormitory. I suppose my love for her began then. She listened to me with such sympathy, such horror, and such tenderness. . . . Even on that first evening I knew that this was the girl from whom I wanted to hold nothing back.

She had strong feelings about me, too. I was helping her to understand aspects of China that everyone else had passed over out of caution in dealings with foreigners and reluctance to speak of those years of privation and pain. She told me gratefully as I left that she had learned more about China from me in one evening than in her previous six months there. She hoped I would come again.

As I walked out into the dark night, so late, I thought with a rush of fear that I must be crazy to stay so long with a foreigner, and a female one at that. I had been in some other world just now, a world of equality and respect, and it had made me forget the harsh world of political judgments that was my reality. Fortunately, the dormitory door was unlocked, and I found my way up the dark wet stairs to my room. My heart still pounding, I mumbled an excuse to the group leader and climbed up onto my bed. But when the mosquito net was safely closed and I was deep beneath my quilt, I thought back on the evening with enormous pleasure. I hoped fervently that Xia Zhu-li would remember what I had said about keeping our meeting absolutely secret. The trial of Wei Jing-sheng, the dissident accused of revealing state secrets to a foreigner, was being discussed everywhere, and I knew that I could be sent to a distant province for even a minor transgression. Still, I wanted desperately to see her again.

Our friendship grew quickly, and soon occupied most of my thoughts. It was difficult for me to tear myself away from her apartment, and I found myself making excuses to go there. She always welcomed me with pleasure, and I began to understand that she, too, was lonely, for although the teachers and students treated her warmly and spoke of the great contribution she was making to the Foreign Languages Department, no one dared to be her real friend. Over time, our relationship became so precious to me that I no longer thought what might happen if we were discovered. One night, as I stood at the door saying good-bye to her, it seemed the most natural thing in the world to take her in my arms and kiss her.

I had kissed Little Gao, but never like this. I was usually a most realistic person, but my long education in self-protection dissolved in the flow of emotions.

I wanted to give this woman everything. Our language, race, and culture were entirely different, but they seemed far less significant barriers between us than had questions of salary, occupation, and political status between me and the Chinese girls. As I looked down at Xia Zhu-li, I resolved that this time I would stake everything on this love, even if it meant going to prison.

Still, as I left that night, my heart was in conflict. My action had been both courageous and blind, for I had no idea what obstacles lay ahead or how to struggle against them. I felt angry, too, that these worries should intrude upon my happiness, when I had finally found a love that was worth so much.

The first obstacle I knew how to deal with. I had to make "Judy," as I learned to call Xia Zhu-li, love me. Chinese girls had always admired me for my height and athlete's build, but physical attraction would not be enough: In the West, people said, a kiss was taken as lightly as a handshake. Instinctively, I knew that if I could make her understand me, I would win her. So I shared my past with her in great detail, omitting nothing. She was so moved by my story that she wrote it all down, evening after evening, until she had two notebooks full. As she listened and wept with me, I felt her feelings and respect growing, and at the same time my wounds seemed gradually to dry up and heal, my self-hatred and self-pity decreasing and my burden becoming light. I discovered a playful, happy part of myself that had been buried since the Cultural Revolution, when I had first learned to be tough and reticent. It was then, too, that I saw the enormous difference between my love for Judy and my love for Little Gao, for where my love for the commander's daughter had become more and more painful until I no longer had the strength to pursue it, my love for the American expert gave me such confidence that I felt I could take on the world. For the first time, the words Little Gao had said to me seemed true: I was a human being, and I had the right to be loved.

I had learned something else from my later months with Little Gao: Love doesn't flourish if it is confined always within the same four walls. Not that it was easy to get out without being recognized; Judy's responsibilities in the Foreign Languages Department involved 600 students and 100 teachers, so she was the most well known of the six foreigners in Changsha at the time. We developed a habit of meeting in the city parks after nightfall, Judy in a white face cloth to hide her straight nose, and a pair of glasses to cover her round eyes. We looked just like other romantic couples. Our other haunt was the countryside, where the peasants minded their own business. We would take our bicycles (Judy had bought me one with her high salary and exemption from the bicycle ticket system) and, with me at a safe distance in the lead, ride out until we were well beyond the city limits. We could picnic and "talk love" on the dry hills above the rice fields, incurring, at worst, only the startled glance of a boy on a water buffalo.

Inside Judy's apartment, we had many ways of deflecting suspicion, the first step being to fill in the cracks in the door with toothpaste. When Judy's housekeeper came, we told her that I was from the Provincial Drama Troupe, and had come to use Judy's typewriter. She assumed I was married and accepted the situation. We could also use an inner room with a convenient lock on it. I remained there for hours at a time, studying, while Judy dealt with her many visitors. A cement ledge in the bathroom just big enough for a man to lie on was essential in emergencies.

But you cannot use paper to conceal a fire. One winter evening at around 9:30, I was standing stark naked in the bathroom pouring a kettle of warm water over myself when a knock came at the door. My clothes were in the outer room, so all I could do was pull the door tight shut and hope. I could hear the voice of the cadre responsible for Judy's daily affairs. He was apparently dropping off her monthly salary (an astronomical 560 *yuan*) and she was nervously telling him about a dancer friend who had stopped by to exercise with her and was washing up. After the man had left, I came out and saw to my horror that scatterbrained Judy had neglected to hide my pants and shoes, unmistakably those of a large man.

We were very frightened. Although Judy insisted that the old cadre had given no sign of noticing anything unusual, we decided it would be safer to make our relationship public, at least to the man who had come so close to discovering us. She went out to find him the next day, and returned half an hour later, glowing with excitement. "He said it's wonderful that I have a boyfriend," she reported happily. "And he said Chinese-foreign marriages are permitted now!" Relief flooded my heart, but I knew too well how extraordinary was the step we had taken to think that everything would work out so smoothly. Sure enough, a few days later the leaders of my department called me in for a talk.

There were three of them, all political cadres, and they had no interest in international diplomacy. "Remember that you are Chinese," they said sternly. "You must love your motherland. There is a difference between insiders and outsiders."

It was easy enough for me to answer that my love was strong. But I was unprepared for their next move: They would go into town, they said, and ask my mother for her opinion.

This could be disastrous, as I had not yet taken Judy to meet my mother. Since I had entered college, I went rarely to her home, for she and Uncle Lei were living in a distant suburb in a room borrowed from a relative of his. According to custom, I should have introduced Judy to them, but I had been reluctant to frighten Mother with the news that I was involved with a foreigner. If a daughter of an army commander had seemed too high, how much further out of reach must a foreigner be! The only solution was to race into town ahead of the cadres to explain the situation and obtain Mother's support. Without her approval, we would never get permission to love each other.

Mother and Uncle Lei were always at home now, for they had both retired, and their poor health limited their activities. They were horrified by my news. I spent nearly three hours there talking them around, beginning by assuring them that such a relationship was now legal, despite so many years of anti-American propaganda. Then I had to allay their fears about her character.

With confidence, I explained that what Judy needed was exactly what I could give her most easily—a permanent, loyal relationship. In America, she had told me, contrary to what Chinese propaganda said, the young people *are* raised with the desire to make deep commitments.

I also told my mother that Judy loved China deeply, that she had spent eight years learning Chinese, and that her work would be connected with China for her whole life. We would be able to help each other.

"She really loves me, Mother," I said proudly. "I can swear to you that she will be a good wife."

"But where will you live?" asked Uncle Lei, a new fear emerging. In fact, Judy and I had not discussed this question. How could we, when I had never seen America? But she seemed happy in China, loving her teaching work and the sense that she was making an important contribution. "We don't know yet," I said gently. "If we are together we will be happy. But we would never leave China forever."

The following day, Uncle Lei came to my dormitory. He was furious. The cadres had indeed followed me to my mother's. They had said the friendship would never work because Judy was from a Capitalist country and I was from a Socialist one. Also, my salary was one sixth of hers, so we were obviously unequally matched. Judy would just leave me behind when she returned to America, or, if she took me with her, abandon me there without family or friends. "Westerners marry and divorce just for the fun of it," they had said. "We're just trying to protect your son."

Uncle Lei and my mother had told the cadres they approved of our relationship and that they regarded such statements as insults to the American expert. "But your mother is a very careful woman," he said. "They asked her to take responsibility if the higher leaders criticized you, and she just couldn't do it. I think they may be planning to go out to Shuangfeng to talk to your father."

My father! What if officials from Changsha turned up unexpectedly on his doorstep, announcing that his son was carrying on with a foreigner! He would think that the nightmares of the Cultural Revolution had returned! I could imagine him hearing the news, sitting in his chair with his left hand trembling more violently than ever. I dared not think what the shock might do to him.

That night, I could hardly sleep, and the next afternoon, I learned I had been right to worry. Liang Fang arrived, so frantic that she practically ignored Judy, launching immediately into a torrent of accusations about my selfishness and lack of concern for Father's health. It seemed the cadres had made it sound as if I were practically in jail already, and then demanded to know if Father approved my actions. It was all he could do to appoint Liang Fang family deputy before collapsing, shaking, onto the bed.

Gradually, my older sister began to realize that I had done nothing wrong. Judy entered in too, and I could see that her simple clothing and unpretentious manner pleased my sister. I felt sorry that this had to be their first meeting, for in her furious and near-hysterical state Liang Fang did not much resemble the brilliant and independent-minded rebel I had described to my future wife. Only after Judy's cadre returned from the Foreign Affairs Office with a copy of the document permitting Chinese-foreign marriages did Liang Fang relax a little and smile. Father would believe a Party document, she said; since we said Mother supported the relationship, she would tell the leaders that Father did too. She left the college only hours after she had arrived, going across the river to spend the night at Mother's so she could catch the first bus back to Shuangfeng in the morning.

On the evening of the following day, Judy and I bicycled from the West Bank across the Xiang River bridge. We turned north along the dark road by the river, and within a half hour we had arrived at the suburb where Mother and Uncle Lei lived. Their room was so small that when I stood in the middle of it, people had to crane their necks to see each other's faces. Only when I was seated could Mother get her first good look at Judy. I suppose she had imagined that all foreign women had painted lips and fingernails, and here was one in army sneakers so simple that only peasants would wear them! Suddenly Mother seemed completely at ease. She began to fuss over Judy as if she were her own daughter.

During dinner, Mother and Uncle Lei shared their experience in the art of self-protection with us. We must offer to hold an engagement party, they said, and invite all the appropriate cadres. In this way, as a family, we would show a united front, making unpleasant incidents less likely. Although the ceremony of engagement had gradually fallen out of disuse in the cities since the beginning of the Cultural Revolution, I was deeply moved by Mother's warmth and determination to help. "My life is nearly over," she said. "I no longer have any great desires for myself. I only want to see my children happy."

We conveyed Mother's suggestion to the leaders, but it proved unnecessary to hold a ceremony to announce our engagement. The news announced itself. Every time I returned to my dormitory, my roommates told me the latest gossip. The whole city was speculating about me. I was said to be a man of mystery, the son of a high-ranking cadre, a man of extraordinary good looks, an immoral bastard who had had many girlfriends. Some said I wanted to get rich and go to America, others that Judy and I had signed a contract for a temporary alliance that would end when she left the country. And when we went out walking together, openly now, people no longer stared at the foreigner, but at the unfathomable Chinese who had dared to court her. If I waited at a bus stop, a circle gathered around me; if I bought cigarettes at the school shop, the salesgirls hurried to wait on me so they could get a closer look. I even began to dread going to class, where I would have to deal with my classmates' incredulous questions. The general reaction was a shock to Judy, who came from a country in which marriages between people of different cultures were not uncommon. I soon found myself protecting her by keeping most of the gossip to myself. She clung to our friends' explanation: *shao jian duo guai,* "What is seldom encountered is found to seem strange," and hoped that the wave of talk would pass quickly over.

I was more worried about whether we really would be able to marry than about the rumors. My experience told me policies were constantly changing; it was hard to predict what would happen in a few months, let alone in a year or two. At first, Judy didn't fully understand my concerns and felt that since we had official approval there was no need for haste. Eventually she too was convinced that the safest thing to do was get married as soon as possible.

Judy's parents offered their long-distance congratulations. Her mother, a professor, was immediately enthusiastic about the idea. Her father, a doctor, was more cautious, for he feared she would settle in China, far from home. However, after a number of intercontinental telephone conversations, he too agreed warmly, talking about learning Chinese and insisting that I come with Judy to the United States during the summer vacation. So with both families already celebrating, we asked for permission to be married.

The local Foreign Affairs Office, which had authority over Judy, presented no objections; the document permitting Chinese-foreign marriages came from the ministry in Peking. The problem was the authorities over me, the college officials. We went to visit Vice-Dean Yin.

She gave us a cool reception in her dark apartment, not even pouring us tea. Apparently she had heard all about our request, and her mind was made up. When she spoke, she addressed Judy alone. "You are a foreigner. Perhaps you don't understand our Socialist country. Ours is a collective leadership, carrying out policies according to documents transmitted from higher levels. Several months ago, we received a notice from the Ministry of Higher Education via Hunan's Department of Education forbidding student marriages. Liang Heng is a Chinese student. He must obey the decision of the leadership."

No matter how we explained our thoughts and pleaded with her, she repeated the same words. When I spoke she avoided my eyes, as if a mere student had done wrong in daring to speak with a college administrator. I should have remained in my place and spoken only to the people in the rung above me in the ladder, my department leaders. When I expressed my fears of not being able to marry if we waited until after I had graduated, she said, "Your suspicions of Party instability show that you lack faith in the Party. This is an incorrect viewpoint." Then she rose to see us out, shaking hands warmly with Judy, but waving my outstretched hand away.

Judy and I were both furious at her arrogance. It was the first time Judy had had the chance to see the way certain high leaders treat ordinary people. Now she could understand better how helpless I had felt over much of my life, and how absolute and demeaning was our system of ranks. Of course, you could accept your fate as it was handed to you as my father and mother had, and there would be no conflict. Or you could struggle to change your fate. In that case you had to be prepared for agonizing difficulties.

For nearly two months, Judy and I spent every moment of our free time writing reports and making telephone calls, crossing the river to urge the Foreign Affairs officials to use their influence with the college, trying in every way possible to convince some group of leaders to dare to make a positive decision. Every day we suffered and wept, but we were very strong, too. If anything, our love became even more powerful in the face of all of our troubles.

Many teachers told Judy, "This is a bad place. In another province, it would be easier." In fact, Hunan *was* very backward. Since Deng Xiao-ping's reappearance in the summer of 1977, the newspapers had been full of attractive new slogans about reform and "thought liberation," but in our province the influence of the Gang of Four was unusually pernicious, and the new policies were resisted at every turn. We were kicked back and forth like footballs between the Foreign Affairs Office, the College Office, and the Provincial Education Department, each group of leaders claiming it had no power to act. They did have the power to say no, though. When Judy applied for a week's leave to go to Peking and see if she could get things straightened out at the higher levels, the college leaders told her, "We do not approve your request. It is unnecessary to bring this matter to Peking. If you insist on going, we will dock your pay and terminate your position here when your contract expires."

At last we decided that there was only one solution: I would drop out of school. The loss of my hard-won chance at education seemed a small price to pay to ensure that we wouldn't lose each other. But as one last desperate gesture, Judy wrote an impassioned letter to the highest leaders in Peking, including those at the Ministry of Higher Education and the Peking Foreign Experts' Bureau. As an afterthought, we also addressed a copy of her letter to Deng Xiao-ping, Central Committee of the Chinese Communist Party.

It seemed incredible then—and still seems so now—but Deng, the most powerful man in the country, read Judy's appeal. An official later told me privately that he frowned impatiently, said, "Of course they should be allowed to marry," and scrawled instructions that approval should be sent down via Premier Zhao Zi-yang. The First Party Secretary of Hunan Province would relay it to the college.

We had won. At first, I could feel nothing, I was so exhausted. But then came the joy. We went up the Yuelu Mountain that sunny spring afternoon, and climbed past what remained of the ancient temples all the way to the top, where we hugged and laughed and wept together, vindicated. The day before we had been racked with frustration and despair; today we could discuss wedding plans. Such reversals had been the pattern of my life, but I would never grow accustomed to them.

My mother and girl cousins willingly offered to prepare the marriage bed, since the bride's mother was absent. I hadn't seen Mother so youthful in years. She went all over the city looking for the best silk for two new quilt covers, selected hand-embroidered pillowcases with a shrimp pattern in the style of the famous painter Qi Bai-shi, bought fresh towels, sheets, and a mosquito net. All these things were laid carefully aside, not to be touched until the wedding, now planned for a Saturday two weeks later. Every day, teachers and students called with gifts and wedding decorations cut painstakingly from red paper. Soon butterflies of happiness fluttered on every windowpane and a large paper "double happiness" lantern hung on our door. A table was heaped with everything from ancient-style paintings to inflatable plastic giraffes, gifts for the child that people assumed would follow within a year of the marriage. At last all the preparations had been completed and only one thing remained: to take Judy to Shuangfeng to meet Father. He was too ill to make the long trip into Changsha for the wedding, and in any case it would have been intolerably embarrassing for my parents to meet again.

It had been a long time since I had been to see him, not because I didn't miss him, but because he lived in an extremely painful place in my heart. I loved him too much. If I spoke or thought of him in his pitiful state, the distress I felt lasted for a very long time. So it was with conflicting emotions that I asked the Foreign Affairs Office to permit Judy to travel with me to the "closed-to-foreigners" area where Father lived. In the midst of my life's greatest happiness, I was forced to think of its greatest sorrow.

To make the situation worse, when we got there the whole town turned out to see the foreigner. Judy and I had been to many out-of-the-way places before and found that people rarely gave her more than a curious glance, so much did she look like a Uighur or one of the other national minorities from the Sino-Soviet border. However, the Foreign Affairs Office's well-meaning notification of the Shuangfeng Public Security Bureau, and Zhu Zhi-dao's excitedly wagging tongue, had ensured that the swarm in the busy free market in the center of town would notice Judy and crowd around her as if she were some sort of rare animal. We had to run to the school where Father and Zhu Zhi-dao lived, most of Shuangfeng at our heels. Fortunately, there were two policemen standing beneath the cracked red star at the gate, waiting to protect us. For the first time, I really felt I was getting married to a foreigner.

It was touching to see how Father and Zhu Zhi-dao had covered the cracked walls of their room from ceiling to floor with copies of the *Hunan Daily*. They hadn't wanted the foreigner to see their poverty, but somehow their pitiful effort to spruce things up seemed to emphasize it even more. I wept inside to see once again the wretched conditions in which it seemed Father was destined to end his days. "The room looks beautiful," I told Father gently, kneeling beside him and taking him by the hand, but he didn't seem to have heard me, for he was weeping with happiness.

After we had been there a short time, the Public Security Bureau, tired of pulling children from the windows, arranged for the whole family to stay at the town reception station, where we could be undisturbed. I met my sisters' husbands for the first time; Liang Fang's was a student in a workers' university, and Liang Wei-ping's was a hydroelectric engineer from Shanghai. I liked both of them very much. Liang Wei-ping had other good news, too: She had been asked to stay at her college in Shaoyang to manage the chemistry laboratory. So all three of Father's children had found peace. That, at least, should be some consolation to him.

Judy was shocked when she heard Father was taking no medicine and hadn't seen a doctor in five years. Poor Father! Only when he got a foreign daughter-in-law were his most basic needs attended to. Within hours, the best doctor to be had in Shuangfeng appeared at the hotel, a young Shanghainese "sent down" during the Cultural Revolution with his wife. I think it mattered even more to Father that he was being treated with courtesy than that at last there was some chance of an improvement in his condition.

On the evening before we were to go, Father asked to speak with me alone. "Little Xia is a fine girl, very intelligent," he said to me. "I am very satisfied that she will be your wife. You must grow old together, be loyal to each other. Don't make the mistake I did." This was the first time I had ever heard Father speak this way about his divorce, and I looked at him with surprise. "Your mother is a good woman," he said abruptly, and changed the subject. "When I think that someday you'll go to America . . . you'll learn a lot of things you cannot learn here. . . . Everyone has forgotten your old father, but I know you won't forget me. . . ." He was sobbing now, and I rushed to embrace his knees. The bones were sharp beneath the thick rough cloth, and the left leg trembled. "I'll come back, Father. And I'll write to you often, every week if you like," I said. But even as I spoke I felt I was lying. Every time I said farewell to my father it seemed as if it was for the last time.

CHAPTER TWENTY-FOUR

Questions

One sunny afternoon soon after our return from Shuangfeng, Judy and I bicycled down to the Western District Revolutionary Committee to pay eight *jiao* for our marriage license. With a minimum of fuss, the official there gave us a lovely document decorated with pictures of flags, the Daqing Oilfields, and the model commune Dazhai. The whole process took only fifteen minutes.

Until the very end, our wedding was subject to the demands of politics. Originally scheduled for a Saturday, it had first to be postponed because of a projected weekend of mourning for the now-rehabilitated Liu Shao-qi. Then, when the mourning was itself rescheduled, the wedding was held on Saturday after all.

The Foreign Affairs Office had arranged everything, reserving a huge room in the exclusive Xiang River Hotel. They also graciously offered to help out with expenses, which mostly involved the purchase of nearly one hundred pounds of candy for the four hundred guests (at least two pieces per person were necessary to ensure good luck). We might have been happier with something simpler, of course, but the overtones of international diplomacy were overwhelming.

All my relatives from Mother's household were on hand: Waipo, Mother herself, Uncle Lei, Mother's brother Uncle Yan, his wife, and my three cousins. None of them had ever dreamed of entering the hotel compound, and they stared in awe at the marble floors and lofty ceilings. It was a moment of great joy for me when I took Waipo, now nearly seventy-five and almost toothless, into the elevator and up to the top floor, the ninth, to see the whole city. Waipo had never even been across the river to the West Bank to see the Lovely Evening Pavilion, and she had tears of excitement in her eyes. Then we rode down again, Waipo pushing the button herself, and we walked into the meeting room where everything was ready for the ceremony to begin.

It was a real "Revolutionary comrades" wedding. The chairs had been set up in a square pattern facing toward the center, and Judy and I were placed in one of the front rows, with the head of the Foreign Affairs Office next to me and a college leader next to her. Beyond them were my mother and Uncle Lei, and the handful of other foreign teachers working in Changsha. The head of the Foreign Affairs Office, as the highest-ranking leader present, opened the meeting. "I represent the Hunan Provincial Party Committee in congratulating the Foreign Expert Xia Zhu-li and Comrade Liang Heng," he said, standing and reading from a slip of paper. "Since the smashing of the Gang of Four, the United States of America has become one of China's closest friends. The marriage of Xia Zhu-li and Liang Heng symbolizes this friendship. We hope that your love will grow stronger and stronger just as the friendship between the two countries grows deeper and deeper. . . ."

Nearly all the speeches used this language of international relations. Even Mother read something in the same spirit, her voice so timid that the crowd could barely hear her. "I hope my son, Liang Heng, and his wife, Xia Zhu-li, will make a great contribution to the understanding between the United States and China. I would like to thank the many leaders for their great concern, and for making this joyful occasion possible. . . ."

Judy and I followed through. How could we fail to rise to the great occasion? The fact is that both of us really were moved a little by the political overtones; it gave us a peculiar sensation to find that our marriage had such significance.

At last the meeting was over. Someone turned on a cassette player and asked Judy to dance. It was the first time she had ever worn her native costume in China, and I thought that in her white Western dress she looked absolutely beautiful. She looked beautiful on the way home, too. As we washed ourselves thoroughly three times as Waipo had instructed, despite the icy water and the absence of heat, and climbed between the bright new pink and green silk sheets, I thought how very worthwhile all our struggles had been.

After our marriage I moved the last of my things to Judy's room and we got a gas burner so we could cook for ourselves. My passport application, as thick and complicated as an application to join the Party, was approved at last, and in late June we set out on a tour of the United States that for me was a dizzying series of firsts: first terrifying airplane trip, first superhighway travel, first sight of women in bikinis, first taste of a hundred new foods, both delicious (hamburger) and strange (cheese). I used my fifty days to the utmost, overwhelming Judy's family and friends with questions about America—to them, the questions must have seemed peculiar indeed, but they knew I was from a world that had been cut off for more than thirty years, and they answered them all with patience and warmth. The visit was fascinating, too fast, a dream, and before we knew it we were back in China again, Judy teaching as before, I with one more year of study before graduation from college.

There is much worth telling of my experiences during that final year at the Hunan Teachers' College, but I find myself thinking back on one experience in particular, the month I spent practice-teaching in a middle school. It was that experience that made me want to write this memoir.

I was assigned to a middle school attached to a machinery factory in Zhuzhou, three hours south of Changsha. It was said to be the best school in the city because of its excellent facilities, and I expected to see great differences between the education these post-Cultural-Revolution-era young people were receiving and my own "Revolutionary" education, which had been so narrow and so burdened with slogans. But to my surprise, little had changed. The blind obedience that had made the Cultural Revolution possible was being fostered still. No one was being taught how to think. On the contrary, the same old empty banalities were everyday fare. A politics examination, for example, read as follows:

I. Short Answers   10 points each, 40%
   1. What is morality? What is the standard for Communist morality?

2. We must uphold the Four Principles of the Socialist Road, Marxism-Leninism-Chairman Mao Thought, the Party Leaders, and the Dictatorship of the Proletariat. Which of these Principles is the kernel of the four?

3. What is the glorious responsibility of our nation's young people?

4. What are the major characteristics of Communist society?

II. Answer the Following Questions   10 points each, 30%

1. Why do we say Communism will inevitably be realized and Capitalism wiped out?

2. To obey the Party and be the Party's good sons and daughters, what do we have to do?

3. Discuss the dialectical relationship between thought, study, and physical health.

III. Analysis   30%

In our nation, some people say "Without the leaders of the Party, we can still realize the Four Modernizations." Please criticize this incorrect viewpoint.

I became most discouraged when I was asked to supervise a political study class. The students were supposed to read an editorial from the *People's Daily* calling on all Chinese people to learn from the selfless soldier Lei Feng, who for longer than I could remember had been held up as a model for public emulation. I called for a discussion. First I asked, "Why do people say that Lei Feng has come back?" No one volunteered, so I called on a Communist Youth League member. His political awareness was supposed to be higher than that of the other students.

"Because of the Gang of Four's destruction," he answered smoothly, "and the disaster of the Cultural Revolution, the relationship between people has become distorted. Now the Gang of Four has been smashed, and we must restore Lei Feng's spirit of helping each other and self-sacrifice."

I recognized the words; he might have been reading them from a newspaper. "Yes," I said, "ten years ago the young people also learned from Lei Feng. Can anyone tell me more about what happened since then? Between ten years ago and now?"

The students looked at each other, repeating vaguely what they had heard and read in propaganda organs. "The workers didn't go to work." "The students weren't in school."

"Who can give me a specific example of what happened?" I asked.

They looked at each other again, but this time they were silent, and then all forty-two pairs of eyes turned to me.

As I looked back at them I reflected that in 1966 they hadn't even been born yet. But could it be that they apparently knew *nothing* about the Cultural Revolution? "Do you know what your mothers' and fathers' and older sisters' and brothers' lives were like at that time?" I asked. "Do you realize that in this factory compound where you live, people used guns to kill each other?"

They looked at me in disbelief. Finally, the other Communist Youth League member in the class, a girl in glasses, said, "We are a Socialist country. How could it be that people killed each other?"

How could I dare to answer such a question? I turned instead to another girl, who said, "My mother said she went to a Chairman Mao Thought Study Class. Could you please explain what that is?"

After I had told her, the room was filled with questions. Why were the cadres and intellectuals forced to do manual labor? Why were some old cadres put in jail? Why did the Red Guards fight among themselves?

That evening I returned to the dormitory worried and depressed. These children who knew so little about the Cultural Revolution could easily go the way my sisters and I had gone fifteen years earlier. Their political indoctrination was the same as ours had been before the great upheaval; they were certainly not being taught to evaluate things for themselves, and movies and books about China's past were still above all else political documents, criticized and censored. There seemed to be no way to ensure that the same tragedy would not be replayed.

As Judy and I made our final preparations to go to America so that I could enter graduate school, I thought less of the world that awaited me than of the world I was about to leave behind. Although my memories were full of sorrows, they returned to me uncontrollably now, and I realized how deeply I loved my motherland and her people. My fortunes had changed so radically, so often, yet in the end fate had been extraordinarily kind to me. I knew that I was lucky to have the chance to go abroad to gain experience and knowledge. So many young people of my generation were passionately thirsty for truth, but they had no way of analyzing anything but their own circumscribed plots of earth. Still, I reflected, by experiencing disaster my generation did learn one terribly important thing—the danger that lies in blind obedience. We have regained the ability to see the world critically when my father's generation no longer has the strength to do so. I fervently hope that this lesson—paid for with the suffering of our fathers and mothers, and of ourselves—will not be wasted. It can do more than any amount of propaganda to make China a better and happier place.

Appendix

ROMANIZATION AND PRONUNCIATION

We have generally used the Chinese *Pinyin* system of Romanization but have put hyphens between syllables of given names as a pronunciation aid. Some proper names, such as Chiang Kai-shek, Peking, and Kuomintang, have been written in the way most familiar to Western readers. Most letters in *Pinyin* represent sounds more or less similar to English sounds, with the exception of the following:

Chinese letter		English sound
c	=	ts
q	=	ch
x	=	sh
z	=	dz
zh	=	j

WEIGHTS AND MEASURES

A *liang* equals 50 grams or approximately 1.76 ounces.

A *jin* equals approximately 1.1 pounds. (One *jin* equals ten *liang*.)

A *li* equals approximately .3 miles.

A *mu* equals approximately .16 acres.

CURRENCY

The *fen* is the smallest unit of Chinese money;

a *fen* is a Chinese cent.

Ten *fen* equal one *jiao*.

Ten *jiao* equal one *yuan*.

It is nearly impossible to provide an accurate comparison of the purchasing power of Chinese money and sterling, because major expenses in the two countries take such different percentages of people's budgets. At the time of writing the official pound-*yuan* exchange rate is £1 = ¥2·98. As for purchasing power, where one egg may cost five to ten *fen*, a family's rent may be as little as five *yuan* a month.

POLITICAL DIVISIONS

A commune is divided into brigades and brigades are divided into Production Teams. As commonly used, the term *Production Team* can refer either to the geographical division or to the group of people living within that area.

NAMES

All names have been changed except those of famous people and those of the members of Liang Heng's immediate family. Chinese family names come first, then given names.

Index

rise in, 17-18; meningitis, 110; New Long March epidemic, 109–10

divorce, 11–16, 19, 238

dress, 150; factory, 219; New Long March team, 102–3; peasant, 92; Red Guard, 68, 150

dropsy, 17–18

"East Is Red, The" (song), 61, 114, 124

economy, 187; early 1960s hardships, 17–18; Liu Shao-qi's policy on, 179, 182

Educated Youth movement, 142–7, 163, 198–200, 211–12, 237, 247

education, 189; cadre/peasant rural re-education, 161–210, 230–1; college entrance examinations, 249, 254, 265–7; Communist youth group, 14, 15–16, 35, 37–9, 228, 272; early, 6–8; Educated Youth movement, 142–7, 163, 198–200, 211–12, 237, 247; English study, 249–50, 273–5; and Gang of Four criticism movement, 265, 290; Hunan Teach-ers' College, 130–1, 266, 267, 268–84, 289; and job assignments, 271–2; middle school cadre re-education, 189–91, 198–210; politi-cal study, 40–1, 46–8, 51–2, 253, 290–1; post-Cultural Revolution, 289–91; Red Guard student, 66–70, 76, 142–7. *See also* child-care cen-ter; college; middle school; youth

Engels, Friedrich, 232

English study, 249–50, 273–5

examinations, college entrance, 249, 254, 265–7

exchange of experiences movement, 101–10, 111

factories: athletes assigned to, 213–16, 217; hygiene movements in, 223; interfactory backdoorism, 222–3; late-Cultural Revolution laziness in, 220–2; learn from Daqing movement in, 222–3; oil, 213–16, 217, 219–22, 242; work routine, 219–21, 222

family, 4; Confucian tradition in, 9, 262; background, effect on young love, 251, 255–63; in-law relations, 5; Rightist background, 10–16, 22, 29, 34, 35, 37–8, 56, 218–19

family-planning campaigns, 193–4

famine, 188, 191–2; early 1960s, 17–18

farming: early 1960s difficulties, 17–18; fertilizer, 173, 176–7, 197; gov-·rnment quotas, 187–8; peasant, 24, 25, 170, 172–3, 176–7, 180, 185, 188, 197; rice, 180

fertilizer, 173, 176–7, 197

firewood, 23–4, 188

Five Black Types, 66–8

Five Red Types, 66, 68

food, 155, 260; early 1960s shortages, 17–18; New Long March, 109–10; peasant, 21, 24, 92, 96, 170, 171, 172–3, 177–8, 182–8, 190–1; res-taurant, 241; rice coupons, 34, 172; stolen, 191–2, 199–200; train, 243, 245

"Foolish Old Man Who Moved the Mountain, The" (Mao Ze-dong), 78, 175

foreign-Chinese marriage, 279–91

Four Olds criticism campaign, 68–71

funeral: customs, 18, 26–7; of Mao Ze-dong, 263

Gang of Four, 264–5, 283–4, 290

gang wars, 151–3

garbage collection, 87–9

Get Rid of the Four Evils hygiene movement, 12

Goose Court commune, 168–87

Great Alliance, 138

Great Hall of the People, Peking, 115, 124

Great Leap Forward, 23, 40, 157, 179; Changsha deforestation of, 162

Great Proletarian Cultural Revolution. *See* Cultural Revolution

Great Wall, 26

Green Tree Town, 91–2, 97

Guangdong Province, 103